Business and State
in Contemporary Russia

The John M. Olin Critical Issues Series

Published in cooperation with
The Harvard University Russian Research Center

Books in This Series

Business and State in Contemporary Russia,
Peter Rutland

Building the Russian State,
edited by Valerie Sperling

The Rule of Law and Economic Reform in Russia,
edited by Jeffrey D. Sachs and Katharina Pistor

The Sources of Russian Foreign Policy After the Cold War,
edited by Celeste A. Wallander

Central Asia in Historical Perspective,
edited by Beatrice F. Manz

Forthcoming

The Collapse of the Soviet Union,
Mark Kramer

Business and State in Contemporary Russia

EDITED BY

Peter Rutland

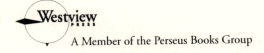

A Member of the Perseus Books Group

The John M. Olin Critical Issues Series

Copyright © 2001 by Westview Press, A Member of the Perseus Books Group

Published in 2001 in the United States of America by Westview Press, 5500 Central Avenue, Boulder, Colorado 80301-2877, and in the United Kingdom by Westview Press, 12 Hid's Copse Road, Cumnor Hill, Oxford OX2 9JJ

Find us on the World Wide Web at www.westviewpress.com

Library of Congress Cataloging-in-Publication Data
Business and state in contemporary Russia / edited by Peter Rutland.
    p.   cm.—(John M. Olin critical issues series)
  Includes bibliographical references and index.
  ISBN 0-8133-3656-2 (pbk.)
  1. Industrial policy—Russia (Federation).   2. Business and politics—Russia (Federation).
I. Rutland, Peter. II. Series.

HD3616.R92 B87   2000
330.974—dc21
                                                         00-043987

10   9   8   7   6   5   4   3   2   1

Contents

Illustrations

Acronyms

APK	the Russian agroindustrial complex *(agro-promyshlennyi kompleks)*
CIS	Commonwealth of Independent States
COMECON	Council for Mutual Economic Assistance
EBRD	European Bank for Reconstruction and Development
ECU	European Currency Unit (forerunner of the euro)
EES	Unified Energy System, the Russian electricity monopoly
FAPSI	Federal Agency for Government Liaison and Information
FBIS	Foreign Broadcast Information Service
FIG	financial-industrial group
FNK	Petroleum Finance Corporation (*Finansovaya neftyanaya korporatsiya*)
FNPR	Federation of Independent Trade Unions of Russia
Gazprom	a privatized corporation with a monopoly in production and distribution of natural gas
GDP	gross domestic product
GKAP	the State Antimonopoly Committee *(Gosudarstvennyi komitet po antimonopol'noi politike)*
GKO	short-term government treasury bond
GNP	gross national product
GKI	State Committee for the Management of State Property (*Goskomimushchestvo*)
IMEMO	Institute of World Economy and International Relations
IMF	International Monetary Fund
ITAR-TASS	Independent Telegraph Agency of Russia–Telegraph Agency of the Soviet Union
JSC	joint-stock company
KGB	the Soviet state security/intelligence agency (*Komitet gosudarstvennoi bezopasnosti*)
KPRF	Communist Party of the Russian Federation
KTR	Labor Confederation of Russia
MFK	Moscow Finance Corporation, part of the Oneksimbank group
Mingazprom	Ministry of the Natural Gas Industry
Minnefteprom	Ministry of the Petroleum Industry
Minneftekhimprom	Ministry of the Petrochemical Industry

Mintopenergo	Ministry of Fuel and Power of the Russian Federation
Moskomimushchestvo	Moscow Privatization Committee
MVD	Russia's interior ministry *(Ministerstvo vnutrennikh del)*
MVES	Russian Ministry of Foreign Economic Relations
NATO	North Atlantic Treaty Organization
NDR	Our Home Is Russia political movement *(Nash dom— Rossiya)*
NPG	Independent Miners' Union
NTV	Russia's most influential private television network
OECD	Organization for Economic Cooperation and Development
ORT	Russian Public Television
RF	Russian Federation
RIA-Novosti	state-owned Russian news agency
ROPP	Russian Unified Industrialists' Party
Rosugol	the Russian government's coal monopoly
RTR	Russian Television Network
RSPP	Russian Union of Industrialists and Entrepreneurs
RTS	Russian stock exchange
SIF	social insurance funds
SISTEK	Union of Information and Collaboration in the Fuel and Power Complex
SNGP	Union of Oil and Gas Industrialists
Sonek	Union of Oil Exporters
TACIS	Technical Assistance to the CIS (a program of the European Union)
TEK	fuel/energy sector *(toplivo-energeticheskii kompleks)*
TNK	Tyumen Oil Company
TsTK	Central Fuel Company
VGTRK	All-Russian State Television and Radio Company
VPK	military-industrial complex *(voenno-promyshlennyi kompleks)*
VTsIOM	All-Russian Center for the Study of Public Opinion

Preface

In 1991, Russia broke with its communist past and started to construct a market economy and liberal democracy. Today it is apparent that neither the capitalism nor the democracy that have emerged in Russia operate in the traditional Anglo-American manner. The Soviet legacy, and other cultural and geographical features, have produced a political and economic model with distinctively Russian characteristics.

Much of the research on Russia has assumed that we know the end-point toward which Russia is headed: the market and democracy. Less attention has been paid to the possibility that Russia may develop a hybrid form of political economy that does not correspond to preexisting models. The premise behind the market reform program launched in 1992 and applauded by the West was that economic decision making would be separated from the state through liberalization and privatization, while the political process would be democratized. This has not happened to the extent the reformers initially hoped. Rather, what we see is a fusion of political and economic power, the rise of a new ruling elite, and the emergence of new and complex patterns of political and economic authority. Unpacking the hybrid model of Russian capitalism cannot be accomplished simply through examining macro-economic performance data or studying the results of periodic elections. There is a need to dig deeper and look at the actual processes of bargaining over resource allocation in specific sectors of economic life.

Even after a decade of wrenching social change, the Russian political economy is still at a critical juncture. The August 1998 financial crisis deflated many optimists who had argued that Russia was or would soon be a stable, Western-style market economy. Rising awareness of the entrenched nature of crime and corruption led to growing doubts about the real nature of political and economic power behind the façade of market and democratic institutions. There was a realization that Russia was not necessarily in transition to a more efficient and transparent political economy: that it might remain trapped in its current semi-market, semi-democratic system for years, if not decades. Still, hopes that Russia was in transition to a different, brighter future were revived by the departure of President Boris Yeltsin in December 1999. Many believed that the new president, Vladimir Putin, would put Russia back on the reform track—still assuming that they knew where Russia was headed.

What exactly were the forces keeping that system in place and preventing more full-blooded reform? Russian institutions were weak: Real power was usually exercised through personal networks, forming and re-forming according to the ebb and flow of events but hidden from public view. As a result, outside analysts were reluctant to rush to judgment about the character of the Russian system. Confident predictions about a decisive breakthrough toward economic stability or political accountability were likely to be disproved by the next morning's headlines.

The chapters in this volume do not aspire to offer a definitive account of this painful process of political and economic rebirth. Rather, they are snapshots of the embryonic formations that are emerging from the ruins of Soviet central planning and one-party rule. In the absence of rule of law and open market competition, the interplay between political power and economic transactions is key. Chapter 1 provides an overview of how the political system works and the key role therein of the new business oligarchs. The following chapters examine new sources of political power, such as the media business, vital to electoral success in Russia's formless democracy (Chapter 2), and regional power elites, represented here by a study of Yurii Luzhkov's Moscow (Chapter 3). They include case studies of the oil industry (Chapter 4), which has a seemingly bright future, and of coal (Chapter 5), which has seen a massive fall in employment over the past decade. Chapter 6 examines the curious fate of Russia's trade unions, whose 60 million members were unable to utilize the power of the vote to forestall a massive erosion in their income, social benefits, and life chances. The book concludes with a study of the causes and consequences of the August 1998 financial crisis. Once the dust had settled, it became apparent that the crisis had brought about major structural changes in Russia's political and economic system and in its operation.

*   *   *

The chapters in this volume were originally delivered as papers in the John Olin Critical Issues seminar series at the Davis Center for Russian Studies, Harvard University, in the academic year 1997–1998. Thanks are due to Timothy Colton for selecting this topic; to the Davis Center staff members who helped run the seminars and the Center associates who took part in them; and to the scholars who gave talks in the series but who are not represented in this volume: Julian Cooper, Thane Gustafson, Barry Ickes, Anne Nivat, Don Van Atta, and David Woodruff.

Introduction:
Business and the State in Russia

Peter Rutland

Until 1991, comparative economics knew two alternative models of economic organization: the market economy and central planning. The collapse of the Soviet Union and economic liberalization in China have shattered the latter model. Now there is only one game in town: the market economy, in which private ownership is the dominant framework for wealth-creation. But there are many different ways to organize a market economy, particularly with respect to the relationship between private business and the state. What is the balance between the pursuit of private interest and public good? How can a liberal democracy insulate public decisionmaking from the influence of powerful business elites? This is a particular problem for new democracies, where public interest groups are weakly organized but business groups inherit institutional resources and wealth-generating capacity from the old regime.

Today, the outlines of an answer to how these dilemmas are being resolved in Russia is slowly emerging. Russia has developed its own hybrid political economy with many contradictory and unstable features. Some elements of the Soviet past have been jettisoned surprisingly quickly (for example, rigid protectionism was replaced by a rapid opening to privately run foreign trade). Other elements have stubbornly persisted, reinventing themselves in new forms (e.g., political clientelism).

Contemporary Russia conforms neither to the model of pluralism, in which a variety of organized interests compete for influence over the state, nor to the model of corporatism, in which interests are brought into more or less permanent institutional relationships with the state. Rather, it represents a type of oligarchic capitalism in which a few powerful structures—some state, some private, and most a mixture of the two—collude and compete for influence over public decisionmaking.

The Rise of the Dual Economy

The development of post-Soviet Russia presents observers with a fascinating puzzle. On the one hand, Russia has introduced the basic institutions of a market economy and pluralist democracy. It is hard to recall that just a short time ago the country was still reliant on state ownership, central planning, and the rationing of most consumer goods. Now 70 percent of industry is privately owned, there are few legal barriers to entrepreneurs wishing to start their own businesses, and 90 percent of foreign trade is in private hands. The ruble is now a convertible currency; and after several years of high inflation, the money supply was brought under control and annual inflation came down to single digits. True, the August 1998 financial crash punctured this image of macroeconomic stabilization. The Russian government suspended payments on its debts, and the ruble lost 75 percent of its value against the dollar. However, to the surprise of many, the August crash did not trigger an inflationary spiral, and the correction in the ruble's value even stimulated a domestic manufacturing boom.

On the other hand, behind the attractive façade of a functioning market economy lies the chaotic, messy reality of daily life in Russian farms and factories: a reality in which the traces of the Soviet-era economy are still visible. Fully half of industrial transactions take place through the medium of physical barter, the accumulation of arrears, and the exchange of various types of paper securities (bills of exchange, tax arrears scrip, and many other varieties). Informal networks of political and economic elites somehow maintain a balance between the monetized and nonmonetized sectors of the economy—an arrangement in which organized crime and corrupt public officials play an important role.

This situation of a half-barter, half-market economy may not fit the neoclassical textbooks that recently have been translated into Russian, but it seems to be fairly stable. This form of economy has produced a small number of winners and a large number of losers, as measured by living standards and access to political power. But social protests have been surprisingly muted, and the main opposition force, the Communist Party of the Russian Federation, is unable to draw more than 30 percent of the vote—enough to maintain a powerful presence in the parliament but not to capture the all-important presidency. One of the major flaws of the hybrid economy is that it seems to discourage investment (both domestic and foreign). As a result, the post-transition recession lasted seven long years, and it is not clear whether the growth spurt the country experienced in 1999 will be sustained.

Another puzzle: Russia has undergone revolutionary socioeconomic changes over the past decade without a revolutionary change in leadership. Institutional collapse and systemic change have been accompanied by relative stability in the political and economic elite. The Soviet Union broke apart as a result of the fragmentation of the ruling elite and the collapse of its ruling institutions (central planning, the Communist Party, and Soviet federalism), and not as a result of a popular revolution. Powerful groups within the Soviet *nomenklatura* abandoned the centrally planned economy (and the one-party system that went with it) and embraced private property and market forces. Boris Yeltsin, a career Communist Party official, forged an alliance with the fledgling democratic opposition—and at the same time an alliance with his fellow ex-communist presidents in the non-Russian republics.[1] The state bureaucrats of the Russian Federation followed Yeltsin, as did the *nomenklatura* capitalists, who in growing numbers since 1987 had been cutting themselves loose from central planning.

From Socialism to Capitalism in One Stride

The failed August 1991 coup undermined the leadership of Soviet President Mikhail Gorbachev and shifted power into the hands of Yeltsin, who had been elected president of the Russian Federation in June. Yeltsin was faced with the daunting task of introducing a market economy in Russia. The basic ideas about what a market economy entails came from outside the Russian system, but Russian elites sought to adapt them to suit Russian conditions—or more exactly, to suit their own interests. The process went through three overlapping phases: systemic collapse, "wild capitalism," and the emergence of a system of oligarchic capitalism.

Systemic Collapse

The first phase unfolded between 1987 and 1990. By 1990, five years of abortive reform under Gorbachev's leadership had wrecked the control systems of the Soviet economy without creating any effective new mechanism in their place. Gorbachev shied away from full-blown market reform—in part because he knew such policies were bitterly opposed by the Communist Party and state bureaucracies, who were in a position to delay and dilute the adoption of such reforms and to sabotage their implementation. In response to his half-hearted reforms, the economy spun out of control. The planning system broke down: government spending and wage payments soared, triggering inflationary forces. The maintenance of price controls prevented open inflation, and so the growing imbalances showed up in the disappearance of goods from store shelves. Production slumped as plan targets were abandoned and control over enterprises devolved to plant level, a process facilitated by the 1987 Law on the State Enterprise, which freed factory directors from many central planning controls. In the summer of 1989 Russia saw open worker unrest for the first time in 80 years, as coal miners struck for better pay and improved food supplies—and were *not* met with state repression. Nationalist unrest in the Baltic and Caucasus was another headache for Gorbachev, diverting attention from the question of economic management. For two or three heady years, the country was held together by massive foreign loans (which accumulated to US$80 billion), while Gorbachev pleased Western lenders by allowing the dissolution of the Soviet empire in Central and Eastern Europe. In 1991 the Soviet federal budget collapsed as republic governments followed Yeltsin's lead and refused to pay taxes to the federal center (the "war of laws"). The scarcity of goods increased, and open inflation took hold.

"Wild" Capitalism

As central planning controls disintegrated and private enterprise was legalized, two waves of business formation took place. From above, there was a process of spontaneous privatization from 1989 on, as various state enterprises (e.g., the giant Kama Truck Factory) or even entire ministries (e.g., the natural gas ministry) turned themselves into independent legal entities (variously titled "state concerns," "holding companies," and the like). At the same time there was a wave of private small business start-ups from below, initially registered as cooperatives (under a new 1988 law) or leasehold enterprises *(arendy)*. These new businesses were usually registered and operated under the auspices of a Communist Party or Komsomol (Communist youth league) organization. These two waves of business formation, from above and below, were closely intertwined. The people setting up the new small businesses usually had close connections to the people running the state enterprises (sometimes they were the same people; other times, they were related by family ties).

Oligarchic Capitalism

The Soviet collapse opened up a legal vacuum in which the *nomenklatura* capitalists moved to advance their own interests. Irrespective of the legal ownership status of the enterprise, the period from 1990 to 1992 brought the effective privatization of the revenue stream of many plants, as directors channeled sales and purchases through privately owned trading firms that acted as middlemen. Most of Russia's 2,000 commercial banks were created at this time. They originated in the accounting departments of individual state firms, which were then spun off as independent legal entities. Apart from handling firm accounts (and skimming off a lucrative percentage), they grew fat through currency speculation, handling government accounts, and trading in treasury bills.

Into this chaotic environment stepped the International Monetary Fund (IMF) and sundry Western advisers with a strategy for rebuilding Russia. They offered the same recipe for rapid market liberalization that had been introduced in Poland in 1990, which had succeeded in halting runaway inflation there and restarting economic growth by 1992. The IMF approach to the market transition focused heavily on macroeconomic policies. Questions of market regulation and institution-building were to be postponed to a later date. It was argued that premature moves to increase state control over the new agents of the market economy—before liberalization was completed—would merely provide a cover for communist reactionaries to reimpose a state-controlled economy. It was assumed that the institutional infrastructure necessary for a market economy (laws, courts, regulatory agencies, and so on) was either in place already or could be built quickly—either imported wholesale from the West or speedily created by the enlightened self-interest of the new Russian elites.

In the event, both the model of rapid, technocrat-led liberalization and the resulting economic system proved flawed in the Russian case. It turned out that the main threat to the Russian transition came not from communist reactionaries or social unrest but from some of the very elites who were leading the charge toward the market economy. These elites fell prey to the temptations of corruption, and only tolerated liberalization to the extent that it lined their own pockets. They adopted a very short-term frame of reference and made little attempt to build a framework of public accountability and respect for rule of law, since such institutions would only constrain their wealth-gathering activities.[2]

At the end of 1991 the new government headed by Prime Minister Yegor Gaidar had little choice but to opt for price liberalization, since the state had lost its ability to plan the economy. Events in 1992 seemed to be following a script provided by the IMF, as the Russian government struggled to introduce the holy trinity of policies deemed necessary to effect the transition to a market economy: liberalization, stabilization, and privatization. (This policy package came to be known as the "Washington consensus."[3])

Liberalization meant lifting restrictions on business activity, domestic and international. Those who subscribed to this approach believed that price controls should be removed and subsidies ended. Restrictions on new business formation should be scrapped, and private businesses should be given free access to foreign trade. Quotas and duties on exports should be eliminated and import tariffs lowered. Liberalization of foreign trade was important because import competition would force the monopoly suppliers inherited from the Soviet economy either to become competitive or to go out of business. Free trade would reveal Russia's comparative economic advantage and would draw resources into the sectors with growth potential. Trade liberalization was also a prerequisite for the influx of foreign investment and technology that Russia urgently needed.

Most price controls were lifted on January 2, 1992, and the rudiments of a market economy quickly surfaced. With entrepreneurs free to charge market-clearing prices, the store shelves quickly filled up, and thriving street markets emerged. Energy prices, in contrast, remained under state control. Domestic oil prices eventually were freed in 1996 (under pressure from the IMF) and rose to proximity with world market levels; but prices for gas, electricity, and housing remained under state regulation and were heavily subsidized. Foreign trade liberalization led to a flood of imports, which soon accounted for about half of all consumer spending (including food). After a year's hiatus there was also an export boom, as producers switched their sales of oil, gas, metals, and chemicals from the cash-starved former Soviet republics to hard-currency markets in the West.[4]

Stabilization proved more difficult to achieve than liberalization. It involved the introduction of a convertible currency and the conquest of inflation, the argument being that without stable money the price system cannot work effectively and investment is severely constrained. Establishing a freely convertible ruble capable of maintaining its nominal value against the U.S. dollar became the centerpiece of the Russian government's economic strategy and a litmus test of the success of its reforms.

Why emphasize the convertibility of the ruble as the key to stabilization? In light of the August 1998 crash, this approach seems rather ill advised. Given the problems with measuring changes in consumer prices and the money supply, an easy way to check whether a country is succeeding in price stabilization is to use the exchange rate as the "nominal anchor" of the stabilization program. This method has the virtues of transparency and simplicity: Everyone from the Wall Street banker to the street-corner *babushka* knows the ruble/dollar exchange rate on any particular day. In addition, due to the resource constraints under which even the IMF must operate (lacking the personnel to monitor the Russian economy directly), the adoption of the exchange rate as a barometer for measuring the success of Russian economic reform was attractive.

However, it took three years of political infighting before the government was able to bring the money supply and budget deficit under control.[5] Only in mid-1995, after two earlier efforts had failed, was the government able to stop excessive growth in the money supply. The year 1992 saw heavy lobbying for the release of subsidies from the state budget and soft credits from state-sponsored banks. These pressures spilled over into an inflationary surge in the money supply after the appointment of Viktor Gerashchenko to head the Russian Central Bank in June 1992. In addition to direct subsidies and credits, firms were given a broad variety of privileges in the form of tax waivers, import and export licenses, and the like.[6]

The high inflation of 1992—when prices leaped upward by more than 2,600 percent—brought rich profits to the Central Bank and to the new commercial banks, who together may have captured some 10 percent of Russia's gross domestic product (GDP) as profits in 1992.[7] Foreign banks were prohibited from entering the Russian retail banking sector by a November 1993 presidential decree, much to their chagrin. The Russian banks were the major group to benefit from the partial reforms of 1992; and their success was due not so much to political influence as to simple luck—being in the right place at the right time. The Soviet economy had largely functioned on a non-cash basis, and the government did not even have a treasury system for collecting and distributing state funds. Hence these functions were contracted out to a select list of commercial, "authorized" banks.

The government's halting efforts to tighten the money supply were accompanied by the dollarization and demonetization of much of the economy.[8] With rubles being in such short supply (the ruble money supply shrank below 20 percent of GDP) and so unreliable a store of value, most people converted all their cash holdings to U.S. dollars, and many companies transacted business in dollars. The resultant shortage of dollars led many firms to resort to barter of physical goods or of scrip of various types (bills of exchange, tax receipts, and the like). By 1997 the value of U.S. dollars in circulation exceeded the stock of rubles, and barter accounted for half or more of all transactions in some industrial sectors (especially energy).[9] Arrears also became a substitute for money: arrears owed to suppliers, to tax authorities, and to workers.

A key factor behind the difficulties in controlling the money supply was the yawning federal budget deficit, which was running at 5–6 percent of GDP. Tax revenues had collapsed following the dismantling of plan controls and the precipitate fall in GDP. In 1995, on the advice of the IMF, it was decided to finance the budget deficit in a "noninflationary" way—by issuing short-term treasury bonds

(GKOs) rather than by printing money.[10] This came at a price—punitively high interest rates and a mounting pyramid of debt. The theory was that stabilization would bring economic recovery and foreign investment, which would allow the government to pay off the debts.

On the surface, everything looked fine. Inflation came down from an annual rate of 204 percent in 1994 to 129 percent in 1995 and 22 percent in 1996.[11] The ruble held its value against the dollar within the corridor announced by the Central Bank in July 1995—and even appreciated in real terms. The remaining capital controls were steadily dismantled, and in 1996 the ruble established full convertibility under Article 8 of the IMF charter. Despite these apparent successes in monetary stabilization, however, a dual economy had emerged in Russia: one that was monetized, taxed, and recorded for the international community; and another that was hidden from view, demonetized, and at best paying taxes in kind, in goods and services, at the local level.[12] The rise of this hidden economy—a phenomenon not seen in East-Central Europe—was not tracked in official statistics, and its presence was largely ignored by the international community until 1998.

There were some disturbing trends even in the macroeconomic data being monitored by the IMF. GDP plunged alarmingly in 1992 and continued to fall through 1997, with a cumulative loss of 40–50 percent—greater than that experienced by the United States during the Great Depression. Living standards also fell, but to a lesser extent. (Precise and reliable data are unavailable because of radical shifts in prices, changes in the consumption basket, and the unreliability of the bureaucratic process by which statistics are gathered in Russia.) Recovery did not begin until 1997—and then, with an anemic GDP growth of 0.8 percent. The second disturbing trend was the slump in federal tax revenues, which fell from 25–30 percent of GDP in 1989 to 10–12 percent by 1997, while federal spending was still running at 15–18 percent of GDP. (Regional and local governments raised and spent another 10–15 percent of GDP.)

The reformers tended to breezily explain away these problems. The slump in GDP, they argued, was partly the result of changes in statistical reporting. During Soviet times managers had overreported output to maximize plan bonuses, and now they were underreporting output to minimize taxes. Alternatively, reformers argued that to the extent that the output fall was real, it reflected an end to the production of goods without any value in a market economy, like nuclear submarines and busts of Lenin. Likewise, the fall in government revenue was regarded as nothing to be too concerned about. For the IMF, the Russian state's share in GDP was still considered "too large" for an economy at its level of development. The government had to learn that it must stop subsidizing factories and farms and stop paying the utility costs of residents living in cities irrationally located north of the Arctic Circle.

Privatization was the third leg of the reform triad. It involved the transfer of economic assets into private ownership in order to unleash entrepreneurship and create competitive markets.[13] State enterprises should be sold off, and those firms that stayed in state hands should be weaned off subsidies and given hard budget constraints. State and collective farms should be broken up and people allowed to buy and sell land. Bankruptcy legislation should be introduced and enforced to ensure the closure of loss-making firms and the redistribution of their resources (machinery, premises, and labor) to more efficient producers.

Privatization was soon to be hailed as a major victory for the reformers. Within a few years, up to 70 percent of productive assets were transferred out of state ownership into "private" hands. The first phase of "spontaneous privatization" in 1989–1991 was followed by the voucher privatization program of 1992.[14] Citizens were given vouchers that they could use to bid for shares in former state enterprises, which had to re-register as private corporations. One important difference between the Russian approach and the model of voucher privatization introduced in Czechoslovakia in 1991 was that Russian workers and managers were given the option of acquiring a majority of the shares in their own firms, using a combination of vouchers and plowed-back profits. The head of the State Privatization Committee, Anatolii Chubais, introduced this option as a concession to opponents of privatization in the Supreme Soviet in June 1992.[15] As a result of this political compromise, the voucher privatization program was one of the few reform measures to actually be passed into law. The worker/manager buyout proved the most popular privatization method, with 70 percent of firms choosing this option. In most of these firms control over the shares quickly became concentrated in the hands of a small group of managers. However, many firms resisted involvement in the voucher program, preferring to swap their shares with other companies or regional governments. Overall, less than one-third of the shares in privatized firms were distributed for vouchers.

The third wave was that of privatization through cash sales, which began in 1994. The government was reluctant to sell to foreign investors, since they wanted control of the most valuable assets to stay in Russian hands (or more exactly, in the hands of their cronies); but Russian buyers lacked the capital to buy shares in cash auctions. For this reason, Chubais, the privatization tsar, decided in 1995 to go with the idea of swapping packets of shares in a dozen leading oil and metals companies in return for loans from Russian banks (popularly known as the "loans-for-shares" scheme).[16] These transactions reeked of corruption: The prices were very low relative to the firms' earnings and assets, and most of the auctions were "won" by an affiliate of the bank organizing the bidding. It also became increasingly clear that much of the money that the banks were "lending" to the government in fact came from state coffers. The loans-for-shares scheme enabled the Moscow-based banks to move into the industrial sector in the provinces and take control of some of the major revenue-generating assets of the economy, such as the Norilsk nickel mine, Murmansk shipping fleet, and Sidanko oil company.

After the hiatus of the 1996 presidential election campaign, during which the oligarchs circled their wagons to ensure Yeltsin's reelection, privatization sales resumed in 1997, including more oil companies and shares in the Svyazinvest telecommunication conglomerate. The 1997 sales, unlike those in 1995, were more competitive, and this triggered fierce rivalry between the oligarchs. As a result of the ugly political feuding, privatization sales were effectively halted at the end of 1997. Privatization remained high on the agenda of Russian politics, however. On one hand, the international financial institutions were still pressing for the further privatization and breakup of monopolies like Gazprom and Unified Energy System (EES) (the formerly state-owned gas and electricity companies). On the other hand, the oligarchs lost control of some firms, due to their failure to fulfill contractual obligations to invest in the plants; because of tax arrears and debts to suppliers; or because of legal challenges by disaffected minority shareholders.[17] Thus some previously privatized enterprises came back into political play.

The Politics of the Russian Transition

Democratic theory is of only limited use in explaining the chaotic transition to capitalism in Russia. Western observers and Russian liberals alike initially assumed that the main barrier to reform would be opposition from groups with a vested interest in the pre-1991 system, such as communist bureaucrats and workers in state-subsidized industries and farms. One of the major Western books on the transition from socialism argued that it would be very difficult for the countries of Eastern Europe to simultaneously introduce democracy and capitalism, since the newly empowered citizens would not be willing to transfer common state property into a small number of private hands.[18] Nor would they want to replace subsidies and price controls with free-market pricing, which could put some goods beyond their reach.

However, most of the countries of Eastern Europe did indeed see the rapid and simultaneous introduction of both pluralist democracy and capitalist markets. Elites saw little or no alternative to embracing these models, which were being urged on them by the international community. Joel Hellman and Steven Fish have argued that the countries that introduced the quickest and most successful market reform were the same ones that had experienced truly competitive elections at the start of their democratic transitions and had developed into competitive, open pluralist systems (with parliamentary systems being more successful than presidential ones).[19] Some countries entered a virtuous circle in which political pluralism reinforces successful market reform, whereas others plunged into a vicious circle of declining state capacity and creeping authoritarianism. Russia seems to be an anomaly (although Hellman and Fish prefer not to treat Russia as a special case), in that Russia did liberalize, privatize, and stabilize fairly quickly—but cannot really be described as a healthy, pluralist democracy. In Russia, the backward-looking elites and social groups with a large stake in the old system of state-owned industry and subsidies were politically stunned by the rapid collapse of communism. They proved totally unable to make use of the nascent democratic system to defend their interests in the transitional economy. The workers in these sectors also were politically inert due to shattering social changes, a massive fall in living standards, and tremendous uncertainty about their future. As a result, a much narrower group of social actors—state bureaucrats, bankers, and energy barons with a strong interest in a distorted (or what Hellman terms "partial" reform)—were able to hijack the transition. And the key political agency was a less-than-democratic, strong presidency.

The Emergence of the Superpresidency

The Russian market transition was driven by the rapid emergence of a strong executive branch, rooted in Yeltsin's presidential apparatus. The speed and severity of the economic collapse in Russia left almost no opportunity for the democratic process to pass judgment on the state's economic policy. The legislature (before 1993, known as the Congress of People's Deputies) and executive (President Yeltsin) were elected before the collapse of the Soviet Union (in March 1990 and June 1991, respectively). Yeltsin and the congress were united in opposition to Gorbachev's efforts to hold together the Soviet Union. But after the Soviet collapse in 1991, Yeltsin and the congress disagreed over what sort of constitution Russia needed (presidential or parliamentary) and over how fast to push the pace of economic reform.

Yeltsin moved into the Kremlin, and the presidential administration swelled to over 7,000 officials—even more than in the old Soviet Communist Party Central Committee.[20] Yeltsin refused to become the leader of a political party, claiming that as head of state he was "above" party politics. In following years the Russian legislature was treated not as a source of laws and a vehicle for democratization but as an annoyance that was to be ignored or outmaneuvered. Governments and ministers were changed at the whim of the president. Most of the economic liberalization measures were introduced by presidential decree—a power that the congress granted the president on an emergency basis for one year in November 1991. In December 1992, when Yeltsin's emergency powers expired, the congress refused to confirm reformer Yegor Gaidar as prime minister. Instead it endorsed Yeltsin's compromise choice, Viktor Chernomyrdin, a bland bureaucrat who had headed the Soviet gas industry. Yeltsin called a referendum in April 1993, in which he won a narrow majority in support of his policies. The fact that 53 percent of Russian voters endorsed Yeltsin's economic policies despite the punishing fall in living standards and 2,000 percent inflation shows that people were voting not on the basis of a narrow evaluation of their own economic interests in the present or immediate past, but on a perception of where their interests would lie several years down the road.[21] Yeltsin's liberal reformers were able to convince voters that their program still offered the prospect of a brighter future, despite (or perhaps because of) the sacrifices already made. The Communist opposition was still struggling to rebuild their political organization after the banning of the

Communist Party of the Soviet Union in the wake of the August 1991 coup, and meanwhile were offering a reactionary, retrospective political program involving a halt to reforms and the restoration of the Soviet Union, which only a minority of the electorate found credible or attractive.

Despite his referendum victory, Yeltsin was unable to bend the congress to his will. So with an unconstitutional decree he dismissed the parliament in September 1993, sending in the army to dislodge recalcitrant deputies. Elections to a new parliament, consisting of the State Duma (lower house) and the Federation Council (upper house) were held in December 1993, but again produced a victory for Yeltsin's communist and nationalist opponents. A simultaneous referendum on the new constitution passed by a narrow majority, giving more powers to the president and in effect creating a superpresidential system. Yeltsin became a kind of elective tsar: ruling like an autocrat, but constrained by the need to seek reelection in 1996.[22]

Thus, although some reform programs were passed into law, most were introduced by presidential decree. Implementation was in the hands of bureaucratic institutions such as the Central Bank or the State Privatization Committee, which emerged as very powerful institutions, insulated from parliamentary scrutiny. They were run by cliques with close ties to the presidential administration and with minimal legal or public accountability. The presidential administration set up a network of bureaucracies in the center and the provinces, with ad hoc presidential commissions paralleling the work of government ministries.

Winners and Losers Among the Sectoral Lobbies

Most surprising in the Russian context was the political passivity of the two largest interest groups inherited from the Soviet economy—the military-industrial complex and the agroindustrial complex (referred to respectively by the Russian acronyms VPK and APK).[23] Each of these sectors employed about 20 percent of the Russian workforce and received subsidies from the state budget to the tune of about 10 percent (APK) and 20 percent (VPK) of Russian GDP in 1990. Yet despite their votes (and their guns); their political networks deeply entrenched in the national and regional bureaucracies; and their blocs of representatives in the parliament, these groups' interests were completely crushed by the unbridled capitalism of 1992 and found only a marginal niche in the system of oligarchic capitalism that was constructed thereafter.

Initially, in 1992, the farm and military lobbies were quite well represented in the ranks of the reformist government. The problem was that they were still thinking within the context of the old, planned economy and were lobbying for money and assistance from the state—money that the state was in no position to provide.[24] Indeed, this lobbying may have had a negative effect, preventing the sector from undergoing radical restructuring and privatization that might have enabled some of the firms to carve out a more stable niche for themselves in the emergent system of oligarchic capitalism. The VPK was pushing for weapons orders, for conversion of plants to civilian production, and for help in promoting exports, but the state budget was simply in no condition to deliver help in these areas. Planned military spending fell from 7.9 percent of GDP in 1990 to 3.8 percent in 1997; and actual spending was at least one-third lower.[25] By 1993 the VPK had only marginal influence in the government (illustrated by the dismissal of its main advocate, Deputy Prime Minister Georgii Khizha, in May 1993), and was heavily dependent on the US$2–3 billion it was able to earn from arms exports, which probably accounted for half of its total revenue. There was a fierce struggle for control over these export earnings, with the presidential apparatus directly represented in the management of the main arms export company, Rosvooruzhenie.[26]

The farm lobby was slightly more successful in clinging to subsidies and in blocking radical land reform. Most collective and state farms re-registered under new names but did not alter their structure or operations.[27] Although a legal opening was created for independent private farmers, they faced a variety of bureaucratic barriers, and more importantly, a hostile economic climate. Their numbers peaked at about 280,000, accounting for less than 3 percent of Russian food production.[28] The first farm minister in 1992, Viktor Khlystun, was inclined toward reform; but Deputy Prime Minister Aleksandr Zaveryukha, appointed in January 1993, was an outspoken defender of the "traditional" farm structure and a determined opponent of land privatization. In October 1994 he was joined by a new minister of agriculture, Aleksandr Nazarchuk, appointed directly from the ranks of the Agrarian Party. The Agrarian Party, which had been formed out of the rural branches of the former Soviet Communist Party, still controlled a large proportion of the rural electorate. They had a strong presence in regional legislatures and did well in the December 1993 State Duma elections. Even though they failed to pass the 5 percent threshold in the December 1995 Duma elections, they had sufficient deputies from the single-mandate races to form their own faction (with help from the Communist Party). Each spring the farm lobby managed to wring US$300–400 million worth of state-backed loans to buy fuel and fertilizer for the planting and harvest seasons—credits that everyone knew were unlikely to be repaid.[29] (In the subsidy game, the farm lobby came in second to the coal miners, who were able to pull about US$1 billion a year.[30]) However, this partial success in lobbying also came at a price. The farm lobby was unable to prevent the marketization of the chemical, agricultural machinery, and wholesale trade networks upon which their capital-intensive farming pattern crucially depended. The collapse of those other elements in the agroindustrial complex, plus the lack of real reform of the farms themselves, meant that Russian farms sank still deeper into debt and inefficiency.

The energy sector (commonly referred to in Russian sources by its acronym, TEK [for *toplivo-energeticheskii kompleks*]) was well able to protect its interests in the transition to the market, since the natural resources it controlled opened up a rich source of export revenue for Russia. Its interests in maximizing export revenue coincided with the free trade objectives of the reformers. The TEK was in effect "the milk cow of the reforms," and it was rewarded by direct representation in government and the ability to write its own reform agenda.[31] After his appointment as prime minister in December 1992, Viktor Chernomyrdin brought in Tyumen oil boss Yurii Shafranik as minister for fuel and energy and Gazprom's Vladimir Kvasov as government chief of staff. In August 1996 Shafranik was replaced as minister by Petr Rodionov, the former head of the Leningrad branch of Gazprom. Even after Chernomyrdin's departure, the pattern of direct representation continued. Sergei Generalov, former vice president of the Yukos oil company (and later, deputy head of Menatep bank) was appointed minister for fuel and energy by Prime Minister Sergei Kirienko in March 1998.[32] However, there were some points on which the interests of the TEK and liberal reformers diverged. The TEK fought off repeated efforts by the liberals to increase TEK tax payments, and became increasingly unhappy with the real appreciation of the ruble after 1995, which ate into the domestic buying power of their earnings. Gazprom occupied a pivotal position, since it was active in both the monetized economy (earning some US$8 billion in gas exports) and the nonmonetized economy (supplying gas to domestic consumers at one-fifth of the export price, and tolerating widespread arrears).[33]

Generally speaking, therefore, one can see that stabilization and the policy of the strong ruble, introduced in 1995, benefited the lobbies on the revenue side of state activity (such as the TEK and banks) and disadvantaged the sectors on the expenditure side (such as the farms and military industry). Likewise, the liberalization of foreign trade favored the fuel lobby at the expense of the farmers and the manufacturing industry. The latter were hit by a flood of imports following the lifting of import quotas and duties between 1993 and 1995, by which time the average import tariff had been reduced to 13–14 percent.[34] Apart from the fuel exporters, the main beneficiaries of trade liberalization and the strong ruble were Russian consumers, who gained access to a cheaper and more varied range of products, due in part to increased imports. Hence, for example, Russian production of televisions dropped from 2.2 million to 100,000 sets a year, whereas about 4 million sets were imported annually.[35] Consumer interests had been largely ignored by the Soviet state, beyond a concern for the provision of basic staples at low cost. Consumers were not organized politically: They are a classic example of a numerous and dispersed interest group, as opposed to, say, the workers of a particular industrial plant, who are fewer in number, more concentrated, and hence in principle easier to organize. One factor working in favor of import-friendly consumers was the fact that in the Soviet era domestic manufacturers of consumer goods had no national ministry of their own that might have tried to defend their interests in the transitional period.

But after 1989, consumers were empowered with the right to vote in contested elections, and keeping the emergent middle class satisfied was an important factor in the consolidation of powerful city bosses such as Moscow's mayor, Yurii Luzhkov. But it would be an exaggeration to talk about consumers as a powerful

political bloc. After all, the economic interests of ordinary citizens had been severely damaged by the inflation of 1992, which wiped out their life savings, and
by various pyramid schemes in 1992–1994 (many of them connected to privatization voucher funds), the collapse of which led to an estimated 20 million people
losing their savings a second time. Various efforts to lobby for the defense of the
"defrauded investors" produced few concrete results.

Almost the only manufacturing sector that was able to save itself behind tariff barriers was the auto industry, which persuaded the government to keep tariffs on new car imports at levels between 40 and 65 percent. (Used cars were
exempt, and were imported at a rate of half a million a year.) Auto production
was concentrated in a handful of massive factories in Togliatti, Nizhnii
Novgorod, and Moscow, and their directors had close personal ties to the Yeltsin
administration.[36] The heavy engineering industry, once the backbone of Soviet
modernization, was the main victim of trade liberalization. Domestic demand
collapsed with the slump in investment, at the same time as the cost of raw materials (steel and energy) rocketed. In 1992 the former heavy machinery ministry was turned into the Energomashinostroitelnaya Korporatsiya (EMK), a
holding company uniting 25 firms scattered across the country and with 60,000
workers and annual sales of US$3 billion; but its main hope for revival seemed
to be waiting for contracts from Gazprom and the oil industry.[37]

The Features of Oligarchic Capitalism

Russian capitalism has developed in a distinctive direction and has built up its
own, unique institutional structure, which differs both from Anglo-American,
stock-market-based capitalism and German or Japanese corporate capitalism,
where the state and banking system play a key role in guiding industrial companies. What is surprising is that Russia's distinctive model was established at the
same time that the country was opening its doors to the global economy. Many
observers assumed that under liberalization Russia's economic institutional structure would converge on the model of the developed capitalist countries. Only if
Russia maintained protectionist barriers and price controls, it was thought, would
the country be able to preserve some of the distinctive features of the Soviet economic system.

However, liberalization did not produce convergence, or at least not as much as
had been anticipated. Russia dismantled trade barriers, introduced world market
prices to most domestic markets, and saw foreign trade as a proportion of GDP
rise from 10 to 30 percent over the course of the decade. But Russia nevertheless
created its own distinctive pattern of capitalist institutions (variously called
"Kremlin capitalism," "comrade capitalism," and "crony capitalism"). The
Russian model combines elements of the old and the new, fusing some Soviet-era
practices with the new capitalist opportunities.

Enterprise Survival Strategies

The privatization program succeeded to the extent that the bulk of state firms were transferred into private ownership. But it failed to enforce hard budget constraints on these firms and to expose them to market competition. Unlike capitalist firms, these companies did not pursue profit maximization. And unlike Soviet firms, they no longer had plan targets to fulfill. So what was their objective function? Their strategy was simply physical survival as a going concern, or in Russian parlance, the "preservation of the work collective."[38] Firms facing cash shortages resorted to barter to keep supplies flowing in. Managers could not pay all the taxes and wages that were owed; but if they could pay a fraction of the sums due the government and the workers, these recipients seemed to think that half a loaf was better than none. Even a firm operating in survival mode required some cash income, however, so as to be able to buy inputs not available through barter (imported machinery, for example) and to pay some taxes in cash to the federal government. Some cash income was also welcome to factory managers, who in many cases were siphoning off part of the proceeds to satisfy their personal incentives. Although a bankruptcy law was introduced in 1993 (and revised in 1998), it has not been used to close down major loss-making enterprises.[39] In the few cases where a court did declare a major firm insolvent (e.g., the Rostov Agricultural Machinery plant), the worst that happened was that the factory was put into receivership and a new director installed.

Factories in survival mode did shed some labor—although this was often the result of the more skilled and entrepreneurial workers' voluntarily quitting in order to find work at firms that paid higher wages, without arrears.[40] They also made some effort to introduce new products and find new markets, including export markets (a vital source of reliable cash earnings). However, these positive signs of adaptive behavior did not mean that the logic of capitalism had infused the whole industrial structure.

Workers, managers, and local political leaders saw the survival strategy as a rational and morally defensible reaction to the challenges of transition. Economic efficiency was weighed against social stability. Partly this was a reflection of the deep roots that paternalistic values had struck in Soviet society, a value system that carried over into postcommunist Russia. Partly it was a reflection also of the geographical realities of the country: the fact that many enterprises provided the only major source of employment in isolated towns. Lack of savings (wiped out by the 1992 inflation) and rigidities in the housing market meant that it was difficult for workers to migrate from these towns.

Rent-seeking

A key feature of Russian capitalism is the creation of oligopolistic markets (that is, markets controlled by a small number of sellers) rather than free markets, and the pursuit of rents rather than profits. Against the background of firms following the survival strategies described above, managerial elites were able to extract rents from their firms' activities.

Russia's main comparative economic advantage lies in its vast natural resources, and the main source of profit for nascent capitalists is selling those resources on world markets. Natural resources yield what economists term "rent," meaning that the price customers are willing to pay considerably exceeds the cost of production and that the supply of the good is limited. Saudi Arabia produces oil at US$2 a barrel and sells it at $20; Russia's production costs are higher, at roughly $5–7 a barrel (Russian accounting practices do not yield a reliable figure), but still low enough to provide lucrative rents.[41] A similar logic applies to natural gas, metals, precious stones, and even timber and fish.[42]

There are two threats to rent-seeking. Rents can be taxed away by governments, or they can be competed away by the entry of new firms into the market. In Russia the government progressively lost its capacity to levy taxes, thanks to the spread of barter and firms' energetic efforts to hide cash earnings from tax authorities. The government also voluntarily yielded some of its lucrative tax opportunities, most notably by slashing duties on exports and imports—at the behest of the international financial institutions, who saw tariffs and quotas as barriers to the energizing logic of free trade. Thus, duties on natural gas were slashed from 24 ECUs per metric ton in January 1992 to 2 ECUs by December 1995; on rolled steel, from 92 to 1; aluminum, from 232 to 10; copper, from 400 to 200; nickel, from 1,600 to 640; timber, from 41 to 6; and nitrogen fertilizer, from 30 to 2.[43] This represented a colossal transfer of rents from government to industry, and to the metal-ore sector in particular, represented in the government at that time by Deputy Prime Minister Oleg Soskovets. The steepest cuts in duties came during the calendar year 1993, after Chernomyrdin took over as prime minister and when Soskovets was most influential. It was also a time when Yeltsin, locked in combat with the parliament, was looking for allies among the industrialists.

The second challenge to rent-seeking is the entry of new firms that can undercut the oligopolistic prices of existing producers and still make a profit. Unfortunately this process had only a very limited impact on the Russian economy. Some of these sectors were not open for competition at all but were preserved as national monopolies (most notably Gazprom, the railways, and the electricity monopoly, EES).[44] Other producers were split up at the national level but preserved as regional monopolies (such as telecommunications, which was split into 89 firms, and the oil industry, split into 16, mostly regionally based companies). In the case of sectors such as metals and chemicals, output was concentrated in a dozen or so giant plants whose owners were usually more than happy to collude in the preservation of oligopolistic pricing and informal division of markets among themselves. This was often true even where foreign investors took ownership, as with the case of the U.K.-based Trans-World Group, which acquired about 40 percent of Russia's aluminum capacity.[45] Ironically, one of the sectors most exposed to competition was the weakest sector of the Soviet economy—farming. Imported foodstuffs quickly acquired a large share of sales in the major cities, in part because the domestic food-processing industry and wholesaling network were painfully slow to modernize.

The emergence of an oligopolistic economy was a deliberate policy, encouraged and endorsed by Chernomyrdin during his long tenure as prime minister (1992–1998). For example, in endorsing the merger of oil giants Yukos and Sibneft in January 1998 (a deal that later collapsed), Chernomyrdin said, "Russian companies must compete on the outside [market], but within the country they should cooperate."[46]

Clan Structure

Russia's industrial structure has developed into a complex, murky, but nonetheless distinct pattern. In order to manage the exigencies of life in the semi-market economy, firms rely upon personal networks of political and economic contacts. Firms are grouped together in blocs of interdependent operators. In many cases these ties are formalized in share ownership; but other forms of mutual obligations within these groups are informal, based on patterns of favor-giving that have built up over time.

Within the framework of the highly institutionalized (indeed, *over*institutionalized) Soviet political economy, a network of personal contacts and mutual obligations arose that lubricated the wheels of Soviet bureaucracy and resolved the inevitable conflicts between contradictory sets of regulations and commands. These contacts were vertical (clientelism) and horizontal (the "shadow economy").[47] This pattern applied from the highest levels of political decision making (the Politburo) to the relations between managers and workers on the shop floor. Economist Vitalii Naishul, whose ideas influenced reform leader Yegor Gaidar, argued that these informal ties in the "administrative market" were more powerful than the formal planning institutions, and that the reform must not only dismantle the apparatus of central planning, but also shatter the informal networks through exposing them to market competition.[48] However, the networks proved more adaptable than Naishul anticipated, and much of this pattern of personalized relationships has been carried over and adapted to the conditions of a market economy.

The dominant form of structuring industry in the Soviet era was the national ministry. These vertical agencies were dismantled through the privatization process, and no dominant institutional structure has arisen in their place. One formal structure that is fairly widespread is the financial-industrial group, or FIG. These groups emerged in response to changes in the tax regime favoring the creation of holding companies, whose shares are usually jointly held by the member companies (who also swap shares among themselves). There are some 100 major FIGs, with the top ten controlling between 25 and 30 percent of the economy.[49] These firms develop ties with each other through cross-ownership, lending, and long-term contracts, and hold seats on each other's boards of directors. Although the birth of these corporate institutions was legally opaque and based on back-room dealings, they are slowly acquiring a more respectable and transparent public face. The leading corporations have their accounts audited by major international accountancy firms. They sell shares and float bonds in domestic markets—and prior to August 1998, did so also in international markets. The banks belonging to these corporations were receiving international credit ratings. The FIG structure has the advantage of spreading the group's activities through a range of sectors. This spreads risk, increases the company's pool of managerial skills, and hopefully encourages managers to develop a broader and more long-term outlook. However, in focusing on the FIG structure, one might overestimate the importance of formal ownership ties and underestimate the degree to which fluid personal networks shape decisionmaking. Lists of shareholders are typically not publicly available; the terms of privatization of state-owned blocks of shares are often rigged to favor certain firms; and there is an absolute lack of transparency in the allocation of government credits, the floating of state bonds, and the circulation of strange securities and other forms of surrogate money.

By 1996, the attention of Western and Russian analysts had shifted away from FIGs toward "clans"—networks of personal trust established by people who had worked or studied together—emerging at the national level.[50] One can map the lattice of personal networks—"clans"—that individual figures have constructed as they moved up into the economic and political elite. These groups often originated in a specific region and then went together to Moscow when one of their number was tapped for high office. Chubais brought with him to the capital a group of young economists from Leningrad; Boris Nemtsov likewise promoted a dozen former colleagues from Nizhnii Novgorod when he moved to Moscow.[51] This pattern of regional teams moving up together in the bureaucracy was also characteristic of the Soviet era.

The use of the word *clan* is a bit misleading, however, since these groups are not based on blood ties but on personal loyalty, and perhaps also on a shared sense of regional identity. Thus the "clans" of contemporary Russia are a quite different phenomenon from clans in the anthropological sense of the term, which are based on birth into an extended family, ethnic group, or region. Such genuine clans are still present in parts of the former Soviet Union (from Kazakhstan to the North Caucasus) and play an important role in the political life of those regions. The Moscow "clans," in contrast to the ethnic variety, are pragmatic coalitions of convenience, which may break apart under pressure or simply as conditions change.

By late 1997, the media had begun to refer to the Russian business elite as "oligarchs," and there was a growing recognition that Russia had created a system of oligarchic capitalism.[52] *Ekspert* magazine began publishing a regular rating of oligarchs from September 1997, based on evaluations by experts. An important characteristic of these oligarchic formations or clans is that they are formed and headed by one or two dominant personalities. Each group is perceived as having a single, dominant leader who runs the group as his personal fiefdom. For obvious reasons, no detailed study of decisionmaking within these groups has yet been carried out; however, power is presumably more dispersed than the image of one-man rule that the oligarchs project in public. This trend represents a personalization of economic power that parallels the personalization of political power under Yeltsin. The two phenomena are directly connected: the patrimonial ties that Yeltsin used to run the Kremlin spread out into the industrial sector.

The Interpenetration of State and Economy

Another feature of Russia's oligarchic capitalism are the close ties between the state apparatus and economic leaders. Most of the major oligarchic groups on the eve of the August crisis had their roots in the party-state apparatus of the Soviet era (see Table I.1). Gazprom, LUKoil, and EES are the direct descendants of Soviet industrial ministries. Even though the state continues to own a large bloc of shares in these firms, the state does not act as an owner but rather delegates control over these firms to the incumbent directors. For this reason, the state's attempts in 1997 to extract more taxes from Gazprom and to revoke the 1994 agreement under which chairman Rem Vyakhirev acts as a trustee for the state's 40 percent stake in the company came to naught, not least because Vyakhirev had the support of parliamentarians (whose regions depend on the continuation of subsidized gas supplies).

Alfa Group, Inkombank, Rosprom, SBS-Agro, and Rossiiskii Kredit all had their origins in enterprises formed under the auspices of the Communist Party of the Soviet Union or its youth branch, the Komsomol. Vladimir Potanin's Oneksimbank came out of the apparatus of the former foreign trade ministry and Vneshekonombank, but grew into the most extensive and diversified of the oligarchic holdings.[53] Only Vladimir Gusinskii's Most and Boris Berezovskii's LogoVAZ can be regarded as relatively independent start-up operations, but they soon migrated toward sources of political power—the Moscow city authorities in the case of Most Group, and the presidential administration itself in the case of Berezovskii.

This close interpenetration of political and economic decision making can be understood as a systemic feature inherited from the Soviet era. In the absence of a tradition of private property and rule of law, "power and money were reciprocally fungible," as Simon Kordonskii put it.[54] Oligarch Mikhail Khodorkovskii explained: "We understand that we are part of this state and depend on the state and that the state depends upon us, and that we can attain our goals only through joint work."[55] The liberal economists supervising the introduction of the market themselves became civil servants, creating new bureaucracies and redistributing property as their predecessors had done, while using ideology for justification and looking for political enemies to explain economic failure. As one Russian scholar observed, "In the proper oligarchic countries, oligarchs are not dismissed or appointed, and it is impossible to remove an oligarch from his post, as happens in

TABLE I.1 The Oligarchs (as of August 1998)

	Leaders	Banks	Industrial Holdings*	Media Holdings*
Alfa Group	Mikhail Fridman Petr Aven	Alfa Bank	Tyumen (#5 oil company) West Siberian Metals	ORT, Muz (television)
Gazprom	Rem Vyakhirev	Imperial National Reserve Gazprombank ties to Inkombank	Gazprom, subsidiaries: Mezhregiongaz Gazeksport Stroitransgaz Perm Motors engines	NTV, Prometei (TV) *Rabochaya tribuna, Trud, Profil*
Inkombank	Vladimir Vinogradov	Inkombank	Samara aluminum Babaev food processing Magnitogorsk Steel	*Vek*
LogoVAZ/ Sibneft	Boris Berezovskii Roman Abramovich	Obedinennyi Bank Avtovazbank	LogoVAZ auto dealership Sibneft oil (#6 oil company) Aeroflot AvtoVAZ auto plant National Sport Foundation	ORT, TV6 (TV) *Nezavisimaya gazeta Novye izvestiya*
LUKoil	Vagit Alekperov	Imperial Neftyanoi Nikoil	LUKoil (#1 oil company)	Ren-TV (television) *Izvestiya*
Media-Most	Vladimir Gusinskii Boris Khait	Most-Bank Rosbiznesbank	Media-Most Spasskie vorota (insurance) Most Development (real estate)	NTV, TNT (television) *Segodnya, Itogi* Ekho Moskvy (radio)
Moscow city government	Yurii Luzhkov	Bank Moskva Guta bank Mosbiznesbank	Sistema holding company. (telecom, hotels, oil, etc.) ZIL auto works Moskvich auto works	TV-Tsentr (television) Govorit Moskva (radio) *Moskovskaya pravda Obshchaya gazeta*

(continues)

(continued)

Oneksimbank	Vladimir Potanin Mikhail Prokhorov	Oneksimbank (Interros) MFK/Renaissance Capital	Norilsk nickel Novolipetsk, Kuznetsk steel Sidanko (#4 oil company) Svyazinvest telecom Perm Motors aircraft engines Sukhoi aircraft Severnaya verf shipbuilding North-West Merchant Fleet	*Komsomolskaya pravda* *Izvestiya, Russkii telegraf* *Ekspert* Europa plus (radio)
Rosprom-Yukos	Mikhail Khodorkovskii Aleksandr Zurabov	Menatep Promradtekhbank	Yukos (#2 oil company) Vostochnyi (#11 oil company) Ust-Ilimsk pulp mill Volzhskii pipe works Apatit fertilizer plant Krasnoyarsk metal works	ORT (television) *Moscow Times, Kapital*
Rossiiskii Kredit	Vitalii Malkin	Rossiiskii Kredit	Lebedinskii, Stolinskii, and Mikhailovskii ore mines Orlovskii, Bezhetskii steel mills	none
SBS-Agro	Aleksandr Smolenskii	Stolichnyi Bank Agroprombank (acq. 1996)	Ural Precious Metals	ORT (television) *Kommersant* *Sel'skaya zhizn'* National News Service
Unified Energy System (EES)	Anatolii Dyakov (till May 1997) Boris Brevnov (till April 1998) Anatolii Chubais	none	EES (electricity)	none

*Includes partial ownership and indirect financing. Media are newspapers and magazines unless otherwise stated.

SOURCE: based largely on the "Register of Oligarchs" prepared by Panorama (Moscow) and available at http://www.leader.ru/cgi-bin/lnk?bank/15/17.

Russia."[56] This interdependence of business and the state also reflected the relative weakness of both of these actors vis-à-vis society as a whole.[57] Fearing social protests or communist revanche, business and the state leaned toward mutual cooperation, especially in times of crisis.

It was not supposed to be this way. The privatization program was intended to end, once and for all, the politicization of economic decision making through the introduction of private ownership.[58] Once ownership had shifted from state to private hands, the flow of subsidies was supposed to cease: Private owners, unlike state companies, would be able to shed the social spending burden that made subsidization necessary. Unfortunately, the hasty, chaotic, and corrupt privatization program had the opposite effect. It institutionalized the idea that it is acceptable for people in positions of political power to divide up economic assets with their cronies. As Andrei Shleifer and Daniel Treisman have acknowledged, new rents had to be created in order to forge political coalitions to dislodge the groups with a stake in the old structures.[59] They have concluded that this devil's bargain was a worthwhile endeavor overall—but they did not consider alternative strategies or essay a systematic evaluation of the costs and benefits of an oligarch-led transition.

The oligarchs' political ties have involved more than the simple cultivation of good relations with officials in the government and the presidential administration. Gaining control of media outlets was also an important part of the process. (See Chapter 2 in this volume.) Money can buy media, and media can be used to make or break political reputations, to boost or destroy the chances of candidates in elections. The self-styled "seven bankers" first came to prominence in the lead-up to the presidential elections of 1996, when they agreed to pool their financial and media resources to engineer a Yeltsin victory.[60] Yeltsin's campaign managers painted the election as a stark choice between a communist past and a democratic future, and a sophisticated media campaign drove home this message—along with lavish pork-barrel government spending in a bid to cut wage and pension arrears, and a hastily patched-together cease-fire in Chechnya.

In the wake of Yeltsin's election victory, some of the oligarchs reaped a reward in the most direct way, through personal entry into the ranks of state service. Oneksimbank chief Vladimir Potanin became a deputy prime minister, and Berezovskii became a deputy secretary of the Security Council (and later, head of the Commonwealth of Independent States' secretariat).[61] However, rivalry between the oligarchs intensified in spring 1997, as they fought off efforts by the new first deputy prime ministers Nemtsov and Chubais to launch a second wave of liberalization and cuts in subsidies to consumers of gas and electricity. The oligarchs also started fighting among themselves over the spoils of the next wave of privatization. The "bankers' war"—fought mainly through personal attacks and corruption allegations in rival oligarch-controlled newspapers—became so intense in summer 1997 that Yeltsin felt obliged to summon the six leading bankers to a meeting that September and persuade them to declare a truce.[62] As economic indicators worsened in summer 1998, Yeltsin once again called the top ten oligarchs to a meeting at the Kremlin, to publicly display their support for the government's policies in defense of the ruble.[63] There was even talk of forming a permanent Council of Economic Cooperation, which would serve as a kind of parallel government of oligarchs—but such dreams were shattered by the August 1998 financial crash (see Chapter 7).[64]

A further dimension of political activism is the search for a regional power base. For all of the "virtual" nature of the modern Russian economy, with earnings being hidden in offshore banks through multiple electronic transfers, territory still matters to those in search of a fortune. In this era of globalization, capital might be footloose and infinitely mobile, but natural resources are not. Especially in the Russian case, questions of economic policy must be viewed through a regional prism: 66 percent of Russia's oil and 90 percent of its natural gas come from the Yamalo-Nenets and Khanty-Mansi autonomous *okrug*s (districts) of northwestern Siberia. Not only mines but also factories and farms, and for that matter newspapers, television stations, and corporate headquarters are all located in some specific physical space. That space has local inhabitants, politicians, courts, police, and of course, criminals. (Organized crime is primarily organized on a territorial basis, since protection rackets revolve around control of a specific locale.) Disputes over ownership of a specific factory often boil down to the willingness of a private security firm and/or the local police to enforce a given court order and physically expel the incumbent managers from the plant. Such pushing-matches at the gates of disputed enterprises are a staple of Russian television news.[65]

Most of the oligarchs were based in Moscow, so most of them felt it wise to negotiate a working relationship with the city administration headed by Luzhkov, a regional oligarch in his own right. (See Chapter 3 in this volume.) Attempts by oligarchs to break out of Moscow and find a regional base elsewhere have not always been successful. Berezovskii, a bitter enemy of Mayor Luzhkov, bankrolled the successful election campaign of ex-General Aleksandr Lebed for the governorship of the resource-rich Krasnoyarsk territory in April 1998. As Lebed explained it: "Businessmen have had enough of living in a country where to be rich is dangerous for your health. They've had enough of having to duck and run from their armored cars to their protected offices. That is why they are financing me."[66] Krasnoyarsk is an interesting case, since the presence in the region of a range of revenue-generating assets (including coal mines, a hydroelectric power plant, a clutch of aluminum smelters, and the Norilsk nickel combine) has led to fierce competition within the regional elite.[67] In most regions there are fewer sources of wealth, and political and business elites are more likely to collude in order to advance their collective interests vis-à-vis the center.

The Pattern of Lobbying

The Western political science literature generally assumes that interest groups are formally organized and that they have origins and existence separate from or outside of the state; but neither of these assumptions holds true for Russia.[68] Russia's oligarchic capitalism is very distant from Western-style corporatism, a model that is defined by the institutionalization of relationships between the state and business and between the state and organized labor. Business-state relations in developing countries are also much more likely to be characterized by interpenetration than by insulation.[69] The Russian pattern is closer to that found in Southeast Asia, where informal, personal ties are decisive. In places like Japan and Malaya, these are channeled through a dominant ruling party; in the Philippines, they are structured around family clans.[70] In some cases these ties fall prey to clientelism and corruption, and in others they can be conducive to strategic cooperation and growth. The state can help business elites overcome their collective action dilemma and work cooperatively for long-term development.[71]

Russia's personalized power networks are closer to the clan model of oligarchy than to the ruling party model. President Yeltsin half-heartedly tried (and failed) to create a "party of power" to fill the vacuum caused by the demise of the Soviet Communist Party. The Democratic Russia movement, which helped Yeltsin become president and rallied behind him in August 1991, broke apart due to personal rivalries and disagreements over the pace of economic reform and Yeltsin's authoritarian tendencies. Despite institutional support from the presidential administration, it performed poorly in the December 1993 Duma elections. The party Our Home Is Russia, led by premier Chernomyrdin and formed in April 1995, received a dismal 8 percent of the vote in the December 1995 Duma elections. If a stable "party of power" had been created, then the legislature might have become a more important forum for lobbying by business and other interests.

The fusion of political and economic power in Russia means that it is even a little misleading to talk about "lobbying," since this implies a set of economic interests outside the state, seeking to influence public policy. In fact, lobbying in Russia is a two-way process—and more top-down than bottom-up, since the state creates and sustains most business groups.[72] It follows from the pattern of Russia's political economy presented above that business-state interactions are personalistic, nontransparent, and based on the porous nature of the political-economic boundary. As in Soviet times, they still have a hub-and-spoke pattern, centered in Moscow—since most favors come out of the nation's capital. The exchanges are particularistic and not universal: Businessmen lobby for exemptions from laws rather than for laws per se. Leading government officials spend more time signing decrees granting exemptions than trying to pass laws establishing general rules of the game.

Throughout the 1990s, the pattern of lobbying stayed more or less the same, although the list of favors changed. In Soviet times the lobbying was for investment resources and access to scarce physical goods; in 1992–1993, the list was led by soft credits, budget subsidies, and import/export licenses. During those years, hundreds of millions of dollars were channeled to dubious organizations such as the National Sports Fund, which were granted permission for duty-free exports of oil and metals and for imports of alcohol and tobacco. When such quotas were abolished in 1995, these organizations were actually compensated from the state budget for the new taxes they had to pay.[73] Subsequently the action shifted to lobbying for tax arrears waivers, access to shares in firms undergoing privatization, cheap energy, and state purchasing orders. (Competitive auctions for government purchases are almost unknown, and state contracts can be an important source of business for the newly privatized enterprises.) Even where efforts were made to cut the opportunities for lobbying, new possibilities often emerged. For example, formal oil export quotas and duties were abolished in 1996; but restricted pipeline capacity meant that the government still played a role in deciding how much oil companies were allowed to export.[74]

The main targets of business lobbying have been the presidential apparatus and powerful government agencies such as the State Tax Service and the Federal Energy Commission. Business executives meet with leading state officials on a regular basis, not only in their offices but also at exclusive private restaurants, tennis clubs, bathhouses, and each other's dachas. Discreet loans and research contracts also have been extended to senior officials: In 1997, Chubais was obliged to resign after it was revealed that he had been paid $90,000 for writing a chapter for a nonexistent book, and that he had been granted a $3 million interest-free loan in early 1996 by the SBS-Agro bank to create his own civil society research foundation.[75] Not only have some business executives been directly recruited to government, but it has also become common for officials to be hired in senior positions in the oligarchs' organizations after leaving state service. (For example, Andrei Vavilov, deputy finance minister from 1992 to 1997, later became head of the Moscow Finance Corporation [MFK], part of the Oneksimbank group. Viktor Ilyushin, a longtime presidential adviser and then deputy prime minister, became vice president at Gazprom after losing his government job in March 1997.)

The parliament is of secondary importance compared to the presidential and governmental apparatus, but it is nonetheless a significant arena of political activity for Russian business. Growing numbers of executives have been seeking election to parliament, not least because of the immunity from criminal prosecution that deputies enjoy. (In December 1999, Berezovskii and Roman Abramovich, the head of the Sibneft oil company, were elected to the Duma.) And although the State Duma is generally weak vis-à-vis the Kremlin (e.g., in the appointment of prime ministers), its role as a lawmaking institution should not be overlooked. The Duma obstinately refused to pass legislation enabling the private sale of land—a right guaranteed by the 1993 constitution. In November 1995 the Duma passed a highly restrictive law allowing production-sharing for foreign investors in natural resource projects, but three years later they had approved only seven out of 300 proposed sites under the legislation. In May 1998 the Duma passed a law restricting foreign owners to 25 percent of the electricity giant EES, causing shares in EES (and the stock market as a whole) to tumble.

Most of the business connections to the legislature consist of personal ties to individual deputies—the bankrolling of particular candidates' election campaigns and the buying of deputies' votes on specific issues. Duma first deputy chairman Vladimir Ryzhkov described the process as "getting together, having a drink, chatting—and a law comes out."[76] There are some regional lobbies in parliament (such as the Siberian deputies), but generally speaking, attempts to create organized groups among the deputies have fared badly. Parties claiming to represent the interests of business, from the liberal-oriented Party of Economic Freedom under Konstantin Borovoi to Arkadii Volskii's heavy industry–based Civic Union, have gone nowhere, although they have served as launching pads for individual careers. Grigorii Yavlinskii's Yabloko party was reportedly the most successful at raising money from private business, but even it was stuck at 6–7 percent support.[77] The Agrarian Party, as noted above, lost its place in the proportional representation race in 1995 but continued to maintain an official deputies' faction in the Duma. The Communist Party of the Russian Federation has some ties to the farm sector and to defense plants, and the liberal Democratic Party also has connections to the latter.

The government has sporadically made an effort to regulate and channel the pattern of business lobbying. The dominant strategy has been incorporation—from the setting up of consultative committees, to the hiring of individual business leaders into the ranks of government. None of these consultative arrangements have developed into effective corporatist structures. Most were little more than paper entities that made no real decisions and that merely provided an opportunity for personal networking (and impressive-sounding titles and passes for the participants). A more ambitious but less successful strategy has been to try to undermine the power of business lobbies through the creation of parallel structures more loyal to the government. (For example, in 1992, Chubais created the Association of Private and Privatized Enterprises to counter Yurii Skokov's League of Commodity Producers.)

Conclusion: Temporary Fix, or the Shape of Things to Come?

The emergent pattern of business-state relations in Russia seems unsatisfactory to both sides. Businesses compete for individual favors from state agencies and are constantly fearful that their privileges might be revoked. The government finds itself swamped by a tide of special pleading and deal-making, and it is unable to design and implement an effective development strategy. It seems like a classic case of the collective action dilemma, where the pursuit of individual self-interest fails to create conditions for the provision of public goods such as rule of law, reliable contract enforcement, and a rational, transparent state bureaucracy.

The economic reformers initially assumed that creating a system of market incentives would lead to the emergence of economic agents who would have a vested interest in establishing institutions to protect their long-term property rights. Thus, in a neat display of recursive logic, the rule of law was treated as endogenous to the transition model. The "demand" for secure contracts would create the "supply" of institutions to provide them. This approach grossly underestimated the weakness of rule of law in Russia and the problems that would be caused by the absence of a framework of market-friendly commercial laws and courts to enforce them. Crime and corruption were similarly assumed to be minor irritants. In fact, they quickly emerged as one of the most important forces driving the post-Soviet political and economic system.

A second problem with this approach is that it assumes that the agents are known in advance. The question of institution building is treated as an optimization exercise facing existing, known actors, who have to decide whether to internalize or externalize transaction costs, how principals can secure compliance from agents, and so on. Political scientists also tend to assume that interest groups are known in advance: They mobilize resources, create organizations to overcome the collective action dilemma, form coalitions, and do other predictable things. In the post-Soviet transition, however, we are faced with the puzzle that the people sitting on all the resources at the beginning of the transition saw their power collapse. Many of the most sizeable business interests existing at the time proved unable to organize themselves to protect what they could—to introduce protectionism for domestic manufactures, for example. Efforts to create political vehicles for the collective representation of business interests (such as the Civic Union) also failed.

The explanation probably lies in the dominant role of systemic change variables: the triumph of structure over agency. The collapse of the Soviet system meant a completely new logic to the political economy, and eventually, a new set of actors. Powerful players like the commercial banks, the State Privatization Committee, and the oligarchic business empires emerged seemingly from nowhere. In the face of sweeping systemic change, existing agents seemed powerless: They could delay change only temporarily and at a high social cost. The systemic explanation may also be couched in more global, universal terms—for example, the growing interdependence of national economies through globalization and the international triumph of liberal political values (as in Francis Fukuyama's *The End of History*[78]).

Perhaps it is a mistake also to assume that business *should* shape its political environment and create a political shell for itself—an assumption that might be indicative of the residue of Marxism in Western social science. Looking at the politics of business in an international context, it is clear that corporations want to make money—but do they want to spend time and effort in trying to create political institutions, even institutions reflecting their broader collective interests? Businesses want to buy decisions from politicians, which sometimes means buying politicians, but they do not appear to want to create politicians. Perhaps individual businesses only take on the task of creating public political institutions when they feel under direct threat. The cozy corporatist systems existing in Europe and Latin America, where government and business work hand-in-glove, evolved mostly as a response to pressure from organized labor. This factor is largely absent in the Russian case. So a full understanding of the flawed pattern of business-state relations in Russia must be rooted in a broader explanation of the slow pace of development of civil society and the character of interactions between state and society as a whole.

Notes

I would like to thank Timothy Colton, Oleg Kharkhordin, Mitchell Orenstein, and Barney Schwalberg for their comments at the seminar where the first draft of this chapter was presented.

1. Lilia Shevtsova, *Yeltsin's Russia: Myths and Reality* (Washington, D.C.: Carnegie Endowment, 1999).

2. Jeffrey D. Sachs and Katharina Pistor, eds., *The Rule of Law and Economic Reform in Russia* (Boulder: Westview, 1997); Stephen Handelman, *Comrade Criminal: Russia's New Mafiya* (New Haven: Yale University Press, 1997).

3. *World Bank Development Report 1996: From Plan to Market* (Washington, D.C.: World Bank, 1996); John Williamson, "Democracy and the 'Washington Consensus,'" *World Development,* vol. 21, no. 8, pp. 1329–1337.

4. David G. Tarr and Constantine Michalopoulos, *Trade Performance and Policy in the Newly Independent States* (Washington, D.C.: World Bank, 1996); Oleg Davydov, *Inside Out: The Radical Transformation of Russian Foreign Trade, 1992–1997* (New York: Fordham University Press, 1998).

5. For data on economic performance see the quarterly and monthly reports *Russian Economic Trends,* published by the Working Center for Economic Reform, in Moscow.

6. Sergei Pavlenko's analysis of 300 decrees giving special privileges to economic interests in the course of 1992 found that 45 percent of the decrees favored individual firms; 15 percent, individual regions; 15 percent, the energy sector; and 12 percent the farm sector. "Pravitel'stvo reform i dotatsionnogo koryta" [The reform government and the subsidy trough], *Moskovskie novosti,* 18 April 1993.

7. Andrei Shleifer and Daniel S. Treisman, *Without a Map: Political Tactics and Economic Reform in Russia* (Cambridge: MIT Press, 2000), p. 54.

8. David Woodruff, *Money Unmade: Barter and the Fate of Russian Capitalism* (Ithaca: Cornell University Press, 1999).

9. According to the government commission on tax arrears chaired by Petr Karpov, in the 210 leading tax debtor companies only 27 percent of their receipts were in cash (*Russkii telegraf,* 31 January 1998).

10. Daniel S. Treisman, "Fighting inflation in a transitional regime: Russia's anomalous stabilization," *World Politics,* vol. 50, no. 2, 1998; Shleifer and Treisman, *Without a Map,* chs. 3–4.

11. These are end-of-year rates. Inflation dropped to 11 percent in 1997 before rising to 85 percent in 1998 (European Bank for Reconstruction and Development, *Transition Report 1999* [London: EBRD, 1999]).

12. Gaddy and Ickes refer to the barter system as a "virtual economy" because it is based on subsidized, value-destroying enterprises. But one can also argue that the financial sector was the virtual economy—particularly in light of the collapse of the banking system in August 1998. See Clifford Gaddy and Barry Ickes, "Beyond the bailout: Time to face reality about Russia's 'virtual economy,'" *Foreign Affairs,* no. 77, 1998, pp. 53–67.

13. Roman Frydman, Andrzej Rapaczynski, et al., eds., *The Privatization Process in Russia, Ukraine, and the Baltic States* (Budapest: Central European University Press, 1993); Lynn Nelson and Irina Kuzes, *Property to the People: The Struggle for Radical Economic Reform in Russia* (Armonk, N.Y.: M.E. Sharpe, 1994).

14. Peter Rutland, "Privatization in Russia: Two steps forward, one step back?" *Europe/Asia Studies,* vol. 46, no. 7, 1994, pp. 1109–1132.

15. The full title of this agency was the State Committee for the Management of State Property.

16. Yekaterina Borisova and Tatyana Degtyareva, "The privatization train left the station along with the money," *Rossiiskaya gazeta,* 9 June 1999.

17. Menatep was ordered to give up its stakes in the Volzhskii Pipe Factory and Apatit chemical plant, and Oneksimbank lost control over the chemical giant Azot (Mark Whitehouse, "Rosprom ordered to return two stakes," *Moscow Times,* 19 March 1998).

18. Adam Przeworski, *Democracy and the Market* (Cambridge: Cambridge University Press, 1991). Indeed, a majority of Russian citizens remained opposed to private ownership of large enterprises throughout this period, according to the regular polls of the All-Russian Center for the Study of Public Opinion (VTsIOM), available on line at www.wciom.ru.

19. Joel Hellman, "Winners take all: The politics of partial reform in post-communist transitions," *World Politics,* no. 50, January 1998, pp. 203–234; M. Steven Fish, "The determinants of economic reform in the post-communist world," *East European Politics and Societies,* vol. 12, no. 1, 1998, pp. 31–78.

20. The 7,000 estimate is from *Trud,* 21 July 1995, cited in John Willerton, "Presidential power," in Stephen White et al., eds., *Developments in Russian Politics 4* (Durham, N.C.: Duke University Press, 1997), pp. 35–60. On the politics of Yeltsin's court, see Tatyana Netreba, "Players on the president's team," *Argumenty i fakty,* no. 49, December 1997.

21. William Mishler and Richard Rose, "Trajectories of fear and hope," *Comparative Political Studies,* vol. 28, no. 4, 1996, pp. 560–564.

22. Igor Klyamkin and Liliya Shevtsova, "Eta vsesil'naya, bessil'naya vlast'," [This all-powerful, powerless power], *Nezavisimaya gazeta,* 24 June 1998.

23. VPK = *voenno-promyshlennyi kompleks;* APK = *agro-promyshlennyi kompleks.*

24. Yakov Pappe, "Otraslevye lobbi v pravitel'stve Rossii" [Sectoral lobbies in the Russian government], *Pro et Contra* (Carnegie Endowment), 1996, no. 1, pp. 61–78.

25. Mikhail Gorokhov, "General retreat," *Profil',* no. 22, June 1997, pp. 28–31; *Krasnaya zvezda,* 18 September 1998.

26. Ilya Bulavinov, "Weapons of selective destruction," *Kommersant-Daily,* 13 March 1998.

27. Don Van Atta, "Agrarian reform in post-Soviet Russia," *Post-Soviet Affairs,* 1994, no. 10, pp. 159–190.

28. In addition to private farms, the small garden plots of individual citizens and farmers continue to provide about 60 percent of food production (Stephen Wegren and Frank

Durgin, "The political economy of private farming in Russia," *Comparative Economic Studies,* vol. 39, no. 3, fall 1997, pp. 1–24).

29. They were granted 1.8 billion rubles for 1998, or about US$300 million at the exchange rate then prevailing (*Kommersant-Daily,* 3 April 1998).

30. Tatyana Lysova, "Portet uglyem" [A portrait in coal], *Ekspert,* 16 March 1998.

31. Pappe, "Otraslevye lobbi v pravitel'svte Rossii."

32. G. Baranov and Ye. Kiseleva, "An insider in the government," *Kommersant-Den'gi,* 15 May 1998, pp. 13–16.

33. Peter Rutland, "Lost opportunities: The political economy of Russia's energy sector," *Bulletin* of the National Bureau of Asian Research, November 1997.

34. Import tariffs were raised by 3 percent in July 1998, in the face of a looming trade deficit (*Kommersant-Daily,* 21 July 1998).

35. *Russkii telegraf,* 25 April 1998.

36. For example, the director of the AvtoVAZ plant in Togliatti, Vladimir Kadannikov, was Yeltsin's second choice for prime minister, after Viktor Chernomyrdin, in December 1992, and later became a deputy prime minister. AvtoVAZ was allowed to run up US$1.3 billion in federal tax arrears (Reuters, 2 October 1997). The truck industry, in contrast to personal autos, saw output plummet 90 percent due to a slump in demand from its traditional customers: the army and farms (*Kommersant-Daily,* 21 October 1997).

37. Bloomberg (financial news wire service), 20 January 1998.

38. Simon Clarke, ed., *Management and Industry in Russia* (London: Edward Elgar, 1995); Barry Ickes and Randy Ryterman, "From enterprise to firm," in Robert W. Campbell, ed., *The Postcommunist Economic Transformation* (Boulder: Westview, 1994), pp. 83–104.

39. In 1997, 4,600 cases were filed (compared to 300,000 in the United States), out of Russia's 2.5 million enterprises (*Moscow Times,* 4 March 1998).

40. For example, the coal mines shed half of their 900,000-strong workforce in the 1990s (see Chapter 5 of this volume).

41. Dow Jones, 2 December 1998.

42. According to Security Council Secretary Ivan Rybkin, unreported fish exports transferred to foreign factory ships on the high seas were running at $2.5 billion a year (Interfax, 16 January 1998).

43. Davydov, *Inside Out,* p. 25. In July 1996, export tariffs on oil, then 20 ECUs per ton, were abolished, but they were replaced with an excise tax payable by domestic as well as foreign customers. The ECU, or European Currency Unit, was the forerunner of the Euro.

44. The railways and EES were split into regional companies, but the national agency holds a controlling stake in the regional subunits (with the exception of the Irkutsk and Krasnoyarsk regional electricity companies, whose shares were given to regional authorities in 1993).

45. *Moscow Times,* 10 June 1998.

46. *Kommersant-Daily,* 20 January 1998.

47. M. N. Afanas'ev, *Klientilizm i rossiiskii gosudarstvennost'* [Clientelism and Russian statehood] (Moscow: Obshchestvennyi nauchnyi fond, 1997).

48. See, for example, Vitalii Naishul, "Communism: Death or transformation?" delivered to the Mont Pelerin Society in Cannes, 25–30 September 1994, available at www.libertarium.ru/eng/library.

49. Juliet Johnson, "Russia's emerging financial-industrial groups," *Post-Soviet Affairs,* vol. 13, no. 4, pp. 333–365.

50. Thomas Graham, "The new Russian regime," *Nezavisimaya gazeta,* 23 November 1995.

51. Andrei Chugunov, "The Nizhnii Novgorod accent in the government," *Kommersant-Daily,* 20 May 1997. In one interview, Nemtsov helpfully listed the government officials who belonged to his clan: In fact, only two of the seven people he named came from Nizhnii Novgorod (*Izvestiya,* 20 January 1998). In mid-1997, Nemtsov himself began using the Russian phrase for "oligarchic capitalism," claiming that he wanted to turn that variant into "people's capitalism." See, for example, Boris Nemtsov, "Oligarkhiya ili demokratiya?" [Oligarchy or democracy?], *Nezavisimaya gazeta,* 17 March 1998.

52. Aleksei Zudin, "Oligarkhiya kak politicheskaya problema rossiiskogo postkommunizma" [Oligarchy as a political problem of Russian postcommunism], *Obshchestvennye nauki i sovremennost',* no. 1, 1999, pp. 45–65; Vladimir Lepekhin, "Ot administrativno-politicheskoi diktatury k finansovoi oligarkhii" [From administrative-political dictatorship to financial oligarchy], *Obshchestvennye nauki i sovremennost',* no. 1, 1999, pp. 66–82. Our attention here is focused on big business. For a look at the political ties of small entrepreneurs, see N. Lapina, *Biznes i politika v sovremennoi Rossii* [Business and politics in contemporary Russia] (Moscow: INION, 1998).

53. Tatyana Lysova, "Reforma oligarkhov" [Reform of the oligarchs], *Ekspert,* 18 March 1998; Paul Klebnikov, "An enthusiastic convert," *Forbes,* 1 December 1997; "Dawn raiders turn into gentlemen," *Euromoney,* November 1997.

54. Simon Kordonskii, "The structure of economic space in post-perestroika society," in Klaus Segbers and Stephan de Spiegeleire, eds., *Post-Soviet Puzzles,* vol. 1 (Baden-Baden: Nomos, 1995), pp. 157–204. On the pre-1991 system, see Peter Rutland, *The Politics of Economic Stagnation in the Soviet Union* (New York: Cambridge University Press, 1993).

55. Quoted in Jonas Bernstein, "Enter the corporate state," *Moscow Times,* 18 September 1997.

56. Policy Foundation Director Vyacheslav Nikonov, quoted in Olga Pestereva and Irina Shkarnikova, "Club of science-fiction fans," *Kommersant-Daily,* 19 March 1998.

57. Zudin, "Oligarkhiya kak politicheskaya problema," p. 48.

58. As argued in Maxim Boycko, Andrei Shleifer, and Robert Vishny, *Privatizing Russia* (Cambridge: MIT Press, 1995).

59. Shleifer and Treisman, *Without a Map,* p. 19.

60. Dmitrii Dokuchaev, "The 'Big Seven' of Russian business are named," *Izvestiya,* 5 January 1997.

61. The Security Council is an advisory body that reports to the president. It comprises the foreign minister and the heads of the main "power" ministries.

62. Dmitrii Pinsker, "Anti-Davos in Moscow," *Itogi,* 23 September 1997.

63. Andrei Bagrov, "They were expecting a penalty," *Kommersant-Daily,* 3 June 1998. This group included those listed in Table I.1, with the exception of Berezovskii and Vinogradov, and also included Vladimir Bogdanov, the head of the Surgutneftegaz oil company.

64. Andrei Piontkovsky, "Oligarchy has ministers at its beck and call," *Moscow Times,* 25 June 1998.

65. An early example was the Lebedinskii Iron Ore Works in Belgorod: In 1994, Rossiiskii Kredit bank, which held 24 percent of its stock, fell out with director Anatolii Kalashnikov. Kalashnikov used local police to kick the shareholders out of the plant's offices, and then diluted their stock to 5 percent. In 1997 a local court gave control over the plant to the Belgorod governor (*Moscow Times,* 28 October 1997).

66. He was talking to a French newspaper reporter, as reported in Johnson's Russian List, 3 May 1998. Within a year, Lebed and Berezovskii had become enemies.

67. Galina Kovalskaya, "There will be no replacement," *Itogi,* 13 July 1998, pp. 35–37.

68. Sergei Peregudov, Natalya Lapina, and Irina Semenenko, *Gruppy interesov i rossiiskoe gosudarstvo* [Interest Groups and the Russian State] (Moscow: Editorial URSS, 1999); Andrei Neshchadin et al., *Lobbizm v Rossii: Etapy bol'shogo puti* [Lobbyism in Russia: Main Stages] (Moscow: RSPP, 1995).

69. Peter Evans, "State structures, government-business relations, and economic transformation," ch. 3 in Sylvia Maxfield and Ben Schneider, eds., *Business and the State in Developing Countries* (Ithaca: Cornell University Press, 1997).

70. Peregudov, Lapina, and Semenenko, *Gruppy interesov i rossiiskoe gosudarstvo,* p. 36.

71. Sylvia Maxfield and Ben Schneider, "Business, the state and economic performance," ch. 1 in Maxfield and Schneider, eds., *Business and the State in Developing Countries.*

72. Vladimir Chervyakov, "The Russian national economic elite in the political arena," in Segbers and de Spiegeleire, eds., *Post-Soviet Puzzles,* vol. 1, pp. 205–281; Peter Rutland, "Business lobbies in contemporary Russia," *International Spectator* (Rome), vol. 32, no. 1, January 1997, pp. 1–15.

73. Vladlen Maksimov, "Distribution of benefits in particularly large amounts," *Novaya gazeta,* 1 September 1997.

74. *Kommersant-Daily,* 17 October 1997.

75. The book eventually was published: Anatolii Chubais, ed., *Privatizatsiya po-rossiiski* [Privatization, Russian-Style] (Moscow: Vagrius, 1999).

76. He said both businesses and government ministries operate this way (ITAR-TASS, 14 October 1997). He was responding to a press conference statement made the day before by deputy Konstantin Borovoi, who said that "huge money" was being spent by corporations buying deputies' votes, citing examples from the aluminum industry.

77. Menatep, Most, and SBS-Agro were reportedly Yabloko backers (*Kommersant-Daily,* 6 December 1997).

78. Francis Fukuyama, *The End of History and the Last Man* (New York: Free Press, 1992).

CHAPTER 1

How Russia Is Ruled

Donald N. Jensen

After nearly a decade of rule by President Boris Yeltsin, the character of the political system that he headed is still the subject of wide—and often bitter—dispute. Observers have adopted various perspectives in trying to answer the two central questions about Russian politics: Who governs, and to what end? Russia is alternately described as a democracy, a republic, an oligarchy, a criminalized state, or simply a mess (in Russian, *boloto,* or swamp). To those interested in comparisons, Russia has been likened to nineteenth-century America, Germany in the 1920s or the 1930s, France in the 1950s, Spain in the 1970s, Colombia in the 1990s, and even Pakistan. There is general agreement only on two points: that there will be no return to Soviet communism, and that the road since the end of the USSR has been unexpectedly and painfully rocky. Such varied impressions reflect the complex processes simultaneously buffeting the country: the continued collapse of the remnants of the Soviet system; the renewal, though not always along Western lines, of key parts of the state and society; the stagnation of still other elements, which remain largely untouched by change; and continuity with key elements of the Russian past.

This chapter examines these complex processes and attempts to answer the question of who governed Russia on the eve of the August 1998 crisis, and moreover, what difference it makes who governs. These questions can be answered only by linking the analysis of governmental institutions and political processes to an explanation of how and why major policy decisions are made as they are. Conclusions about a "democracy," an "oligarchy," or a "criminalized state" are little more than conjecture if they are not based on a careful examination of how Yeltsin, the government, leading bankers, the State Duma, the media, regional leaders, and other major actors actually affected, or failed to affect, a wide range of policy questions. In this regard I believe today's Russian government is not a new regime arising out of the old Soviet Union but a successor to it. Russian politics should be seen not as the product of a revolution that introduced a radically new set of political institutions and behaviors but rather as an evolutionary process growing out of Russian political culture: the distinctive set of beliefs, behaviors, and institutional arrangements about how governing ought to be carried out.[1] These factors will almost certainly shape the country's politics long into the future.

The Importance of Political Culture

There is indeed much that is new in Russian politics. Public opinion polls show, for example, that Russians display more political tolerance and support for civil liberties than ever before.[2] The constitution that Russia adopted in December 1993 borrows heavily from the West. However, continuities with Russia's political culture and the Soviet past are everywhere evident:[3] in the support for a strong leader, for example, and the more widespread preference for order even if it comes at the expense of democratic rights.[4] Three elements of that culture have special importance today because of their implications for the institutionalization of a democratic regime:

An underdeveloped state. Contrary to the popular image of an all-powerful Leviathan, the state has traditionally been weak in Russia. The few state institutions that did exist were cumbersome and inefficient. Their authority was poorly defined and they had trouble implementing their decisions. Laws guaranteeing property or power once it was obtained were nonexistent or poorly enforced. Instead, authority was personal and informal. The idea of civil society—the recognition by the state of the right of nonofficial social groups to legal status and a legitimate sphere of free action—was poorly developed. Indeed, the distinction between private and official action itself was often blurred.[5] Institutions in today's Russia also have vague, often overlapping authority: The boundaries between federal and regional authority, for example, are poorly defined, as is the separation of powers at the federal level. The boundary between "official" action and the private activity of ordinary citizens is hazy. Laws are inconsistently enforced. Despite a large official bureaucracy, the government cannot implement many of its decisions—even "routine" functions such as tax collection. Thus, the state cannot easily act as a catalyst for social development by taking resources and devoting them to the public interest.

Patrimonialism. Political authority was viewed by traditional Russian elites as closely related to property ownership. The tsar—who identified the state with himself—"owned" the nation, its vast resources, and its citizens. He concentrated in his hands the most profitable branches of commerce and industry and granted favored nobles economic privileges in exchange for their support. The civil service practiced a by-product of patrimonialism (kormlenie, or "feeding," in the figurative sense), administering the tsar's lands, collecting taxes, and keeping a portion of what it collected for itself. Today, patrimonial attitudes characterize many Russians, especially the elites. Especially influential entrepreneurs have gotten rich, with government support, by stripping Russia of oil, natural gas, and other resources and salting away profits abroad

rather than reinvesting them in the country's development. Corruption—
the modern equivalent of *kormlenie*—is widespread. The government
continues to hold large blocks of shares in key industries, often in natural resource extraction.

The culture of the imperial court.[6] The culture of the Russian ruling elite traditionally centered on the tsar, who refereed and balanced the competition
among elite and princely clans for his favor as well as for political, coer-
cive, and economic advantages. Decisionmaking was collective and reflected a workable consensus among members of an inner circle, the dy-
namics of which were controlled by tradition, a balance of interests, and
the regulating fiction of the tsar's unlimited power as a source and justification for the clans' authority.[7] Political competition in Russia from 1991
through 1999 similarly centered on Yeltsin's "court." Yeltsin avoided iden-
tifying with any single faction and instead balanced off ministers, business tycoons, and security chiefs, who in the absence of selected political
rules of political competition, were in perpetual competition with one another for his favor. Ties between members of the "court" and society at
large, as before 1917, were minimal. Yeltsin's divide-and-rule strategy
fostered oligarchic infighting and inconsistent policymaking but enhanced his authority.

Crime Integral to the Political System

These trends have contributed to the criminalization of the political system.
Today the normal business of the state, of law enforcement, and of the courts cannot be conducted without resort to what in many Western democracies would be
considered official illegality and corrupt and criminal interests.

Crime and illegality are not threats to the system. They are part of it. Since the
state is weak and authority is informal and personal, commitment to the rule of
law is feeble. Hundreds of Yeltsin's decrees, for example, violated the constitution
or decisions of the legislature and the courts. Law enforcement has been ineffective and inconsistent—so much so, that the government has been unable to mo-
nopolize punishment for violations of accepted norms of behavior. Thousands of
private security firms—some resembling private armies—exist in order to protect
property rights and ensure contract compliance, in the absence of a state able to
perform these functions.

Patrimonialism fosters corruption—the use of public resources for private
gain. With few institutional or legal restrictions on their activity, many public officials engage in untrammeled *kormlenie*. Since the line separating ownership
from sovereignty is poorly defined or nonexistent, the Russian state facilitates insider trading, the granting of preferential licenses, and the illegal banking of state
funds. Moreover, the widespread illegal or underground markets growing out of
the state's inability and unwillingness to create the preconditions for legal eco-

nomic activity have blurred any moral difference between illegally generated capital and income earned through legitimate means.

The highly fluid, personalized nature of Kremlin politics encourages a reliance on favors from the "tsar"—today, the Russian president—rather than the rule of law. The system also fosters the use of compromising material *(kompromat)* as a tool in the leadership struggle, with contending leaders jockeying for Yeltsin's favor by selectively publicizing allegations of their rivals' corruption. Government officials conduct business in an atmosphere in which state service is routinely used—and indeed expected—to advance personal material interests, often in the name of "reformist" economic goals or revenue raising. What would be denounced in Western societies as a conflict of interest appears to the elite as a natural and agreeable state of affairs.[8] In 1998 surveys by the European Bank for Reconstruction and Development (EBRD) and the Control Risks Group, Russia ranked among the top three countries in the world in corruption.[9] In the past two years dozens of corruption cases have been uncovered in the Procurator-General's office, the Federal Agency for Government Liaison and Information (FAPSI), the Ministry of the Interior, the State Customs Committee, the State Tax Service, the Central Bank of Russia, the Ministry of Foreign Economic Relations, the former Committee on Precious Metals, the Ministry of Health and Medical Industry, and the Russian Statistics Agency.

The Audit Chamber—the nonpartisan, independent state auditor analogous to the U.S. General Accounting Office—has extensively chronicled the pervasiveness of the problem. The Chamber recently found that at least one-sixth of Russia's budget in 1997 was misspent due to mismanagement and corruption—a loss estimated at more than US$10 billion. The Chamber's head, Venyamin Sokolov, surmised that the actual amount lost may have been twice that sum. In 1995 and 1996, he added, "Not a single article of the federal budget law was observed."[10] The Audit Chamber determined in 1995–1996 that the Russian government had conducted $160 million in gold sales without the required approval by the legislature. Two government agencies illegally retained almost $100 million in commissions, and one-third of the cash generated by unauthorized gold sales was spent on perquisites for high-ranking officials. In July 1997 the Audit Chamber found illegal the government's 1995 auction of Norilsk Nickel shares to Oneksimbank, controlled by Vladimir Potanin, an ally of Anatolii Chubais, who was then first deputy prime minister. Of $3 billion earmarked for reconstruction of Chechnya's economy in the aftermath of the 1994–1996 war, the Chamber found documentation for only $2 billion. Less than $150 million actually reached Chechnya. Also in 1998 the Audit Chamber reported numerous financial irregularities that had occurred in the management of the state-owned Russian Television Network (RTR), largely between 1990 and 1996. The State Property Committee, according to the Chamber, failed to monitor the finances of RTR, leading to the misappropriation of property, precious metals, and funds.

Organized Crime

It is the centrality of official crime and illegality to normal political activity, not organized crime, that is the major threat to democratic development; but Russian organized crime is nevertheless a major problem. The Russian interior ministry has estimated that in 1996 there were 8,000 criminal gangs in the former Soviet Union, and 300 operating internationally. The ministry has estimated that 40 percent of private business, 60 percent of state-owned enterprises, and more than half of the country's banks are controlled or influenced by organized crime. Russian organized criminal groups have in many ways supplanted the state in providing protection, employment, and even social services.[11] The majority of private enterprises are compelled, by force if necessary, to pay protection fees of up to 30 percent of their profits to organized crime.

The criminal groups built themselves up on foundations laid in Soviet times— on the "thieves-in-law" *(vory v zakone),* who ran underground criminal networks from inside the penal system, specializing in activities such as robbery and prostitution. During the Brezhnev era, some of the thieves-in-law made common cause with members of the Communist Party, who grew rich through bribes, payoffs, and underground barter exchanges providing goods that the socialist system had banned or could not supply.[12] Today organized crime includes these thieves-in-law, officials, and entrepreneurs who got their start illegally during Soviet times, and new groups that arose during the perestroika years, sharing experiences (such as service in the Afghan war), membership in sports clubs, or loyalty to a particular leader. Ethnic groups composed of Chechens, Armenians, Azeris, Dagestanis, Georgians, and Ingush are also important players in the criminal world.

The weakness of the state requires that businessmen have protection, known as a "roof" *(krysha),* to be able to operate. Linking criminal and legal economies, this "shelter" can take the form of a criminal overlord protecting the members of his organization or of a criminal group providing security to a private businessman in exchange for regular payments. Often the *krysha* provided by a criminal group includes other services, such as protection of property, debt collection, customs assistance, legal and business advice, and banking privileges at banks controlled by the group. A *krysha* also can include forms of corrupt government protection involving the militia, tax, police, military, customs, and border guards.[13]

In a developed democracy, these abuses would be mitigated by the workings of democratic government or by protests from an aware and active civil society. In Russia, however, the pervasiveness of crime has undermined the country's already weak political institutions and civil society, contributing to the fraying of the social fabric. Crime is also the main reason why the economy still shows only the faintest signs of improvement. The standard of living, the health, and the future prospects of the majority of Russian citizens have deteriorated while the wealth made by its business elites has been siphoned off abroad, often illegally. The fact that crime is embedded in Russia's system of governance does not necessarily mean that it cannot be reduced through a combination of sound public policies and effective leadership. Its deep roots, however, suggest that it cannot be effectively combated without fundamentally changing the way the regime itself works.

Continuity of Elites

Within this cultural framework, the continuity of the current political establishment with the more dynamic and adaptable fragments of the old Soviet administrative elite—the *nomenklatura*—is the central fact of Russian politics. The Soviet system did not end because of a revolution from below but because portions of the *nomenklatura* decided to abandon the old ruling institutions, from the Communist Party to Gosplan, and formally to embrace a market democracy. Today this small oligarchy of political leaders, bankers, media tycoons, industrialists, and bureaucrats—popularly referred to as the "Party of Power"—dominate the "commanding heights" of Russia's politics and economy: its key government positions, financial and industrial assets, mass media outlets, and instruments of coercion.

Between 1989 and 1991, opposition groups with bases in the intelligentsia and favoring a democratic political system and civil liberties formed a loose, anti-Soviet coalition with ethnic nationalists and members of the Soviet managerial elite who were convinced that the old command-administrative system was no longer working.[14] The alliance broke apart quickly after the August 1991 coup as these managers resisted the efforts of the government of acting Prime Minister Yegor Gaidar to implement radical economic and political reforms—which, had they been carried out, would have deprived the *nomenklatura* of its influence and status.[15] The managerial elite gradually drove the radical intellectuals from positions of influence and consolidated its hold on power.

Studies of the new Russian elite show that the majority of its members are drawn from the second rank of the Soviet-era *nomenklatura*. According to one such study, 19 percent of the 1988 elite were in leading positions of private business in 1993; and 48 percent of the 1988 group were still in the political elite in 1993.[16] A large proportion of today's ruling class are products of the same prestigious academic institutions that spawned the Soviet leadership, or they worked in the Communist Party's youth branch, the Komsomol, under whose sponsorship they were allowed to start businesses well before the "official" demise of communism and often in violation of the law. Still others—industrial managers, ministers, and enterprise directors—came to power by "privatizing" their sectoral economic ministries during the latter years of Soviet rule. Despite the removal of their enterprises from government control, they continued to profit from their official contacts. This core group has been joined by new elements that now constitute one-third of the whole—entrepreneurs without government money and contacts, and people with links to organized crime, who did not occupy leadership roles in the Soviet system. In addition to the tensions between the old and the new groups, there are crosscutting rifts within individual groups.[17]

Although democratic institutions have taken root in Russia since 1991 (to the extent that regular elections have been held and certain institutions have proven minimally effective), they are not strong enough to consolidate elite rule. This elite, formerly unified around Marxism-Leninism, is divided now over rival policies and on how to divide the Soviet patrimony. It also lacks an ideology that legitimizes its rule. Moreover, the elite has failed to come up with a political formula to win over the masses. The government feels little accountability to the public for its actions. The public, in turn, feels little responsibility for the actions of the government.[18] Yeltsin's reelection in 1996 was secured with the support of the financial elite, whose media outlets demonized his Communist opponent, Gennadii Zyuganov. The key question, therefore, is whether in the transition away from Soviet communism, Russia's elites will succeed in creating a new set of values, a durable set of institutions, and accepted rules of the political game.

The post-Soviet transition has also generated a large numbers of "losers." Only 1–2 million "new Russians" earn more than $2,000 a month; a middle class of 5–10 million people earn more than $500 a month; and some 80 million adults make less than that, and spend more than half of their earnings on food. The ruling elite pays lip service to the plight of the majority, but there are few effective ways for most Russians to influence elite decisionmaking. Opposition generally takes the form of personal protest, as in the individual's failure to pay taxes, alcoholism, and suicide—all nonpolitical, or politically ineffective, means. The most influential opposition force is the Communist Party of the Russian Federation (KPRF), which claims half a million members and has regularly drawn between 25 and 30 percent of the vote in recent elections, mainly from the elderly. The Communists and their allies now have a majority of seats in the State Duma, the lower chamber of parliament. Despite the party's constituency among the elderly and the working poor, the KPRF's leaders share many values with the ruling elite, especially the perception that there is a gulf between the elites and the masses. The party also has a strongly statist orientation, inherited from its Soviet Communist Party predecessor, which inclines it toward pragmatic cooperation with the government.[19]

Institutions of Government

A "superpresidency"—a constitutional system providing for an extraordinarily strong chief executive, a weak national legislature, and an only partially developed judiciary—dominates Russian politics at the national level.

The Presidency

Elected by popular vote for a four-year term, the president is in charge of foreign and defense policy and is commander-in-chief of the armed forces. The three "power" ministries—of defense, of the interior, and of foreign affairs—report directly to him. The president nominates the prime minister, subject to approval by the State Duma, who chairs the Council of Ministers or government. If the Duma rejects the presidential nominee three times, however, the president can dissolve the Duma and call for new parliamentary elections. The president can submit draft laws to the Federal Assembly and can veto legislation, subject to an override by two-thirds of both houses of parliament (the Federation Council and the State Duma). He also has the power to legislate by decree on matters not directly covered by existing federal legislation.

The presidency was created in December 1993, after Boris Yeltsin's draft constitution won popular endorsement in a national referendum. Russian voters' support stemmed from a general desire to be rid of the stalemate between the president and parliament that had paralyzed the national government much of the time since 1991 and that had culminated in a bloody insurrection in the streets of Moscow in October 1993. A strong executive, many liberal politicians and intellectuals believed, would be the best guarantor of economic and social reforms. Popular approval of the referendum thus reflected Russia's cultural and historical preferences for a strong leader, which coincided with Yeltsin's understandable desire to maximize his political power.

The president heads a sprawling, multilayered, multifaceted bureaucracy, the Presidential Administration, that many have compared to the old Central Committee bureaucracy of the Soviet Communist Party. (This comparison is encouraged by the fact that the administration physically occupies the former Central Committee offices on Staraya Ploshchad.) The president rules through a network of official representatives in the regions and a number of shadowy commissions that monitor the work of government ministries. Yeltsin's presidential entourage included policy experts, courtesans, family members, and others, not all of whom occupy official positions. (In perhaps no other industrialized country have a former car salesman, and the president's daughter, personal bodyguard, and tennis coach, become trusted policy advisers.)

The Kremlin bureaucracy includes the department known as the Administration of Affairs, which under Yeltsin was headed by Pavel Borodin. This department provides logistical support for the executive branch. It includes 200 firms with more than 50,000 employees; manages 2,000 buildings, including the 3 million square meters of office space and buildings that it occupies in Moscow; and owns the Rossiya airline, a medical center, a restaurant chain, five motor transport depots, several construction complexes, and a consumer service center. There are a large number of other agencies of executive power that nominally are subordinate to the Council of Ministers but in which the president often takes an interest. In addition to the 22 federal ministries there are 11 state committees working on issues such as sports, film, antimonopoly policy, statistics, and customs; 2 federal commissions (on securities and energy); 17 various federal services covering such issues as roads, migration, and forests; 3 agencies (patents and trade, space, and government communications); and 2 oversight agencies. The number of officials whose appointment must be approved by the Kremlin is now about 30,000.

The central organ of the executive branch, the Presidential Administration comprises about 1,500 staff members and was reorganized at least seven times in the six years of its existence under Yeltsin. Depending on Yeltsin's preferences and who was serving as chief of staff (Sergei Filatov, Nikolai Yegorov, Yurii Petrov, or Anatolii Chubais), it variously acted as a routine bureaucracy, an appendage of the president, and the center of power in the executive branch. Duplication of effort and competition within departments were widespread. With the appointments in 1997 of Yeltsin's friend Viktoriia Mitina, the coauthor of his memoirs Valentin Yumashev, and his daughter Tatyana Dyachenko to high posts in the Presidential Administration, the administration increasingly came to resemble an extended presidential family. Dyachenko was present at all important meetings, according to press reports, and accompanied her father on all important trips. Yeltsin reportedly relied on her to be a channel of accurate information. The influence of the Presidential Administration has largely eclipsed that of the government staff, with which it uneasily coexists and whose authority it overlaps and overshadows. Important decisions by the Council of Ministers have generally been approved by the Presidential Administration before they enter into force.

During the years following the adoption of the new constitution, Yeltsin did not so much exercise power as try to hold onto it against all potential challengers. In large part this was due to his increasing physical incapacity, due to various ailments ranging from pneumonia to heart disease. Yeltsin's periods of greatest political visibility and activity coincided with efforts to prevent any rival from emerging. In doing so he managed, through his own strong personality and political skills, to expand his presidential powers even beyond those specified in the constitution.

Yeltsin largely ruled by decree rather than persuasion: Instead of proposing new laws and persuading the Federal Assembly to adopt them, Yeltsin signed about 1,500 decrees per year, and many key government programs were introduced through such decrees. Although the first, 1992 privatization program (through vouchers) was voted into law, the second phase of "cash" privatization, including the notorious 1995 loans-for-shares auctions (in which leading oil companies were auctioned off at bargain prices to favored banks), were carried out by presidential fiat. Yeltsin determined the strategic course of policy, though he clearly had neither the health nor the inclination to involve himself in the elaboration or micromanagement of policy once its general direction was set. Considerable power therefore devolved into the hands of Yeltsin's advisers and leading figures within the Presidential Administration—although they still had to convince Yeltsin to change policy direction and to continue trusting their capacity to act on his behalf. Conversely, Yeltsin was able to prevent general policy initiatives by the government or Duma that he opposed.[20]

Yeltsin constantly shuffled ministers and advisers and reorganized government structures. The number of government ministries fluctuated wildly under his rule, as did the scores of largely ineffectual commissions and committees set up to address various policy questions. In response to failed policies—and sometimes for purely political reasons—Yeltsin fired a wide range of political friends and enemies. In March 1998, for example, he dismissed Prime Minister Viktor Chernomyrdin, who by all accounts had been loyal to the president for more than five years—apparently, for showing too much independence. At other times he brought in leaders with popular appeal (e.g., Aleksandr Rutskoi, Ruslan Khasbulatov, Aleksandr Lebed, and Boris Nemtsov), only to discard them when they outlived their usefulness.[21]

Behind such juggling was Yeltsin's desire to maintain his hold on power. He carefully balanced competing leaders, interest groups, and cliques against one another. In the early 1990s, for example, he used Soviet-era industrialists such as Viktor Chernomyrdin and Oleg Soskovets to balance off the radical reformers in the team of Anatolii Chubais and Yegor Gaidar. He strengthened the police and interior ministry (MVD) troops to balance off the regular army. He steadfastly refused to identify with any particular political party or legislative faction.

Yeltsin also used material incentives—money, apartments, dachas, and limousines—to co-opt officials over whom he did not have the power of appointment, such as legislators. Evidence of this practice was suggested by Yeltsin's request to longtime aide Pavel Borodin, made publicly during the debate over the confirmation of Prime Minster Sergei Kirienko in April 1998, to take care of the "needs"—a clear reference to material incentives. Yeltsin also used compromising information to get legislators' backing.[22]

Within Yeltsin's entourage, power was wielded by those closest to the president and who saw him most often. Yeltsin by most accounts was open to a wide variety of advice before he made a decision, and by many accounts was famous for agreeing with the last person in his office to have argued for a particular position. Yeltsin's immediate entourage included four categories: those responsible for providing services directly to the president (press liaisons, speech writers, and administrative staff); policy advisers on matters such as foreign affairs and economics; representatives to other bodies of power (the Constitutional Court, political parties, the Duma, and the regions); and his immediate circle of friends and family. The State Legal Administration, in 1998 headed by Ruslan Orekhov, performed the critical of role of gatekeeper, controlling the paper flow to the president's office.

The Government Ministries and the Council of Ministers

The Council of Ministers is responsible for the formulation and implementation of economic and social policy, including policies on credit and monetary supply, culture, science, education, health, social security, and ecology. The government also manages federal property and is charged with fighting crime. Although the constitution in principle gives the government some responsibility over foreign affairs, defense, and national security, in practice the president has clearly dominated in these areas.

The president, subject to Duma confirmation, appoints the prime minister, who heads the Council of Ministers. If the president dies or is incapacitated, or simply decides to resign (as Yeltsin did in December 1999), the prime minister is to become acting president for a three-month period, after which new elections are to be held. If the Duma rejects three times the president's nominees for prime minister or votes no confidence in the government twice within three months on its own initiative (or once, if the government itself requests the confidence vote), the president can dissolve the Duma, appoint a new prime minister, and call for new parliamentary elections. Contrary to the rule in Western parliamentary democracies, where there is bargaining for ministerial portfolios during the formation of a new government—often managed by the party that has won the largest number of seats—in Russia the president and the prime minister are under no obligation to hand out portfolios to the most influential parties. In practice, a few members of rival parties are often invited to fill ministerial seats. A large apparatus of more than 1,000 functionaries directly supports the work of the government ministries.

The Council of Ministers has failed to establish full viability for a number of reasons. Because the constitution vests executive power in both the government and the presidency, the two institutions often work in parallel. There has been a constant struggle between them over power and policy. Yeltsin used the government as a lightning rod to deflect criticism of unpopular policies, but he was uncomfortable with any assertion of political independence by the prime minister. According to most observers, this is why he had Viktor Chernomyrdin removed as prime minister in March 1998. Similarly, in 1994, Yeltsin insisted that Chernomyrdin's deputy Vladimir Kvasov resign because he believed Kvasov was not active enough in implementing presidential instructions to the government.[23] These actions by the president effectively deprived the government of the backing it needed to build the coalitions necessary to implement its program.

The government has been internally split into several camps: advocates of anti-inflationary monetary policy, largely in the ministries of the economy and finance, the State Property Committee, and the State Antimonopoly Committee; ministries representing raw material industries such as oil, natural gas, timber, gold, and diamonds, which seek to maximize exports; sectoral ministries such as agriculture and industrial manufacturing, which seek state subsidies, cheap energy, and protection from foreign competition; and champions of increased spending on social welfare, in ministries such as health, science, and education. Strains were exacerbated by chronic revenue shortages and lobbying by regional leaders for special favors. As a result of these pressures, the prime minister had to balance the often overlapping demands of these constituencies as well as cope with the interference of a president whose agenda was sometimes quite different from that of the government. When new Prime Minister Sergei Kirienko began work in May 1998,

Yeltsin, in a departure from general past practice, signed a decree empowering the government to take decisions without channeling them first through the Presidential Administration. It is not clear whether this statement of intent actually lessened the power of the Kremlin vis-à-vis the ministries, and Kirienko was in any case swept out of office by the financial crash of August 1998.

The Legislature

The legislature, the Federal Assembly, is divided into two chambers, the upper being the Federation Council, and the lower, the State Duma. The Federation Council, created to represent Russia's 89 regions or "federation subjects," has 178 deputies—two from each region. One of these deputies is from the locally elected executive branch, and the other is the head of the regional legislature, elected by regional deputies. In addition to voting legislation approved by the lower house, the Federation Council has the power to confirm border changes within the federation; approve the introduction of martial law or a state of emergency by the president; approve the appointment of Constitutional Court and Supreme Court judges; and approve or dismiss the Procurator-General.

The State Duma consists of 450 seats and is elected through two types of mandate: 225 seats are allocated through a national party-list vote, with the seats divided among those parties that clear a 5 percent vote threshold. The other 225 seats are distributed through single-member constituencies on a first-past-the-post basis. Deputies serve four-year terms and are not allowed to hold other types of employment.

Most federal laws require a simple majority to pass a bill in the Duma. The Federation Council has the option of voting on most bills passed by the Duma, but must do so within 14 days. Although most laws submitted by the lower house, the State Duma, do not require the approval of the Federation Council before being sent to the president, both houses must ratify some laws, including laws on the federal budget, taxes, foreign currency, credit, customs regulation and money emissions, the ratification of international treaties, the status and protection of the country's borders, and declarations of war and peace. If the Council rejects a law passed by the Duma, committees comprising representatives of both houses may try to reconcile differences before sending it back to the full body for another vote. Alternatively, the Duma can pass a bill over the objections of the Federation Council if two-thirds of the deputies vote for it again in the same form. If the president vetoes a law, the Duma and Federation Council can override the veto by a two-thirds vote in both houses. The Duma's other powers include approving the president's choice of prime minister and voting no confidence in the government. The Duma also confirms the president's nomination for head of the Central Bank, declares amnesties and pardons, and brings impeachment proceedings against the president.

During its short history the Federal Assembly has largely been an appendage of the executive branch. The presidential veto and decree power have made the presidency and to a lesser extent the government the primary sources of major laws and rules. Although the constitution vests the power of legislative initiative in either chamber of parliament as well as in the president and the government, the Federal Assembly has considered far fewer bills than many legislatures in other countries. The executive branch has far more resources than the legislature to prepare bills. The parliament's committee system is weak, and its oversight of the executive branch is feeble. Even with the threat of a no-confidence vote and dismissal of the government, the Duma has been offset by the power of the president to dissolve the parliament and call new elections. Yeltsin, moreover, often refused to obey the legislature's wishes, especially over the budget, unilaterally withholding spending to advance his preferred economic program. (Shortfalls in tax revenue in the course of the year force the government and the Presidential Administration to sequester spending on programs to varying degrees, depending on the executive branch preferences.)

Despite its weakness, the Duma has sometimes been a useful public forum for debating national issues such as NATO expansion and the war in Chechnya, and it occasionally even overruled Yeltsin. It also delayed the passage of important pieces of legislation that Yeltsin wanted to see adopted (such as the law on production sharing, long awaited by foreign investors) or blocked them altogether (such as laws allowing the unencumbered buying and selling of agricultural land). In the wake of the 1993 and 1995 parliamentary elections, moreover, Yeltsin made changes in the cabinet to bring it more into line with voters' apparent preferences.

After the opposition's triumph in the 1995 Duma elections, the Kremlin sought to block legislation it opposed by cultivating ties with the Federation Council, many of whose members owed their appointments as heads of local administration to Yeltsin. As governors began to be directly elected in the following two years, however, the Federation Council began to distance itself from the executive. With independent political bases and constitutional protection against dissolution, Council members began more aggressively to lobby the federal government for favors. During the consideration of Kirienko as nominee for prime minister, moreover, many members lobbied (unsuccessfully) against his confirmation by the Duma, though they had no constitutional right to participate in the process.[24]

The legislature's institutional weaknesses vis-à-vis the president have been exacerbated by the ineffectiveness and inexperience of the parliamentary leadership. Although opposition factions have dominated the Duma and have frequently denounced the president's policies, they have disagreed among themselves over strategy and tactics and often appeared more interested in maintaining their privileges than in standing up to the president. The Duma has tried unsuccessfully on several occasions to impeach the president. It passed a preliminary vote of no confidence in Prime Minister Chernomyrdin's government in June 1995, but backed down a few days later. In its most assertive stance toward the president to date—its rejection of the candidacy of prime minister–designate Kirienko in the first two rounds of voting in March and April 1998—the Duma eventually buckled to pressure from the president.

Although the Duma often denounced Yeltsin's policies and individual members of the government, relations were nevertheless sometimes constructive. The Duma passed some elements of Yeltsin's economic program, such as the first two parts of the Civil Code, and reached a compromise with the president on a new electoral law. The federal ministries frequently lobby Duma deputies for approval of favorite bills. Yeltsin and the prime minister regularly met with the chairman of the two chambers to discuss matters of common concern.

The Law on Government, signed by Yeltsin in December 1997 as the price for the Duma cancellation of a no-confidence vote, was a small step toward more equal relations between the branches. The bill for the first time gave the parliament some control over the Council of Ministers. It specifies the division of responsibility between president and prime minister in running the government, and establishes that the resignation of the prime minister must be followed by the resignation of the government as a whole. Government ministers also will be obliged to appear before the Duma at the latter's request. (Previously they could avoid appearing by citing the pretext of other pressing business.)

Russian Federalism

Russia's 89 regions include 52 *oblast*s (regions), 6 *krai*s (territories), 21 republics, and 10 autonomous *okrug*s (districts). Each republic—nominally the "homeland" of a non-Russian minority, such as the Tatars or the Bashkirs—has the right to its own constitution and to elect its own president. Oblasts and krais are run by governors, most of whom were presidential appointees until elections became mandatory in 1996. Autonomous okrugs are ethnic subdivisions of oblasts or krais that have claimed special status either because they are very rich (e.g., the Yamalo-Nenets autonomous okrug in Tyumen, which has 53 percent of Russia's oil reserves) or because they are so poor that they can survive only with federal financial support.[25]

The regions display considerable and growing political, economic, and social diversity. From the contested elections in the USSR in 1989 to the first Duma elections in December 1993, a clear regional pattern of voting has emerged. Northern and central areas of European Russia, the Urals, and parts of Siberia have tended to be more supportive of Yeltsin and reformist parties. More conservative areas, roughly forming an arc from the western border of Russia eastward through parts of the North Caucasus, the Volga region, and southern Siberia (the so-called Red Belt), generally opposed Yeltsin.[26] Urban areas have voted strongly in favor of Yeltsin, whereas rural areas have tended to prefer the opposition Communist Party. Voter turnout has tended to be higher in areas that support the opposition. The large percentage of the economy that has become demonetized, surviving on barter and the circulation of various types of securities (which together account for more than 50 percent of domestic industrial transactions), deters the formation of national markets. Similarly, housing shortages, the close link between the workplace and social services, and other constraints on labor mobility have tied most workers to their place of employment and impeded the development of regional and national labor markets.

The gap between the richest and poorest regions is vast and is increasing. The average Muscovite's salary is more than 17 times that of inhabitants of the North Caucasus republic of Ingushetia. In 1997, 46 percent of all money in the federal budget was contributed by taxpayers headquartered in the city of Moscow. Apart from Moscow, St. Petersburg, and a few other regions rich in natural resources (such as Tyumen) or possessing export-oriented metals plants (such as Vologda), the vast majority of federation subjects are little differentiated by income.[27]

Many governors have used popular election to legitimize rule with an iron hand. In a number of regions, fundamental questions about the distribution of economic and political power remain unresolved. Executive and legislative branches are in frequent conflict. In several jurisdictions (such as Primorskii krai, Buryatiya, and Udmurtiya), the regional governor and the mayor of the region's capital city are in conflict. Moreover, the role of the presidential representative in each federation subject is not clearly defined. The representative in principle is supposed to help resolve regional personnel questions, supervise the disbursement of aid sent from Moscow, and oversee the activity of federal bodies in the region. In practice, Yeltsin's representatives have encountered fierce resistance. In several regions there is a rivalry between several centers of power representing sectoral (agricultural, military, fuel and energy), territorial, or ethnic lobbies.[28] In many instances, close ties between political and business elites allow elected officials to acquire needed budgetary funds.

The most contentious issue between the federal government and the regions is the division of power between federal and regional authorities, especially power over tax and budgetary matters. More than 40 republics, krais, oblasts, and autonomies have so far signed bilateral treaties delimiting authority between themselves and the federal center, commencing with the treaty signed by Tatarstan in February 1994. (Tatarstan was the only republic, along with Chechnya, to refuse to sign the federation treaty in March 1992.) Although many such treaties are in conformity with the Russian constitution, which vaguely provides for joint federal-regional control over many areas, some of these agreements, such as the treaties with Tatarstan, Bashkortostan, and Sakha/Yakutiya, are confederal, exempting signatories from the operation of certain federal laws, and thereby violating Article 5 of the constitution, which defines all federation subjects as equal. Some subjects, moreover, have attempted to assume jurisdiction over areas such as foreign policy, which are constitutionally federal concerns. In 19 of Russia's 21 republics, 29 of 49 oblasts, and 4 of 10 autonomous okrugs, constitutional laws have been passed that conflict with the Russian Federation's constitution. The justice ministry reported in 1997 that in the previous two years 16,000 laws examined by that ministry violated the federal constitution. The city of Moscow, Russia's most politically and economically powerful region, has struck a de facto understanding with the federal government that gives it substantial political and economic autonomy. It resolves problems with the federal authorities through direct negotiations.[29]

Growing regional autonomy, which began well before the end of the Soviet Union and was a key reason for its demise, continued unchecked under Yeltsin. Yeltsin's decrees were routinely ignored in the provinces. Numerous regions adopted charters that blatantly violated the constitution and federal law. Nevertheless, the federal government needed the support of regional leaders to implement many policies. Although strong ethnic kinship, economic, and cultural ties ensure that the Federation will likely hold together, federal efforts to slow the flow of power away from Moscow have been largely reactive and have brought mixed results, from relative equilibrium between center and periphery (Tatarstan, Moscow city) to disaster (the Chechen war).

Several events spurred the decentralization of power:

- The weakening of the federal state—accelerated by the constant internecine battles in Moscow—created opportunities for ambitious regional leaders to seize more power and authority, and compelled the more timid to assume greater responsibility for the local political and economic situation. Although more than half of all federal ministries and agencies have regional branches,[30] no structure has yet replaced the Soviet Communist Party and its auxiliary organizations as a nationally unifying structure.[31] In some of the 89 federation subjects, relations between regional ministries and their federal counterparts are based on agreements that clearly define jurisdiction and the rules of cooperation. The implementation of such agreements depends, however, on the willingness of regional leaders to implement them.
- As a result of a 1995 reorganization of the Federation Council, governors and regional Duma chairmen occupied all seats in the chamber.
- After the 1996 presidential election, in which regional bosses played a key role in organizing Yeltsin's victory (graphically demonstrating the president's political dependence on them), the governors acted far more independently.
- The direct elections, beginning in 1996, of the governors of Russia's 68 oblasts and krais (Russia's 21 republics had been electing their presidents since 1991) strengthened the hand of regional leaders in power conflicts with the center. Yeltsin's abortive effort in 1997 to sack Yevgenii Nazdratenko, the popularly elected governor of Primorskii krai, showed the limits of Moscow's power.[32]

Relations between the center and the regions have been built on direct, bilateral lobbying and on compromise and "horse trading," as regional leaders have generally preferred to press their own parochial concerns rather than to work in concert with other governors or to fortify the Federation Council as an institution. Nevertheless, the three groups of leaders that proved most likely to form alliances to affect federal policy in the Yeltsin era were:

- Yeltsin loyalists, such as Dmitrii Ayatskov in Saratov, who were appointed by the president in 1991 and continued to support him after their popular election;
- governors like Ivan Sklyarov in Nizhnii Novgorod and Luzhkov in Moscow—strong managers who supported Yeltsin at crucial times; who had well-established, independent political bases; and who governed largely without reference to ideology; and
- "crossover governors" (e.g., Yegor Stroev in Orel, and Aman Tuleev in Kemerovo), who were formerly in opposition but had been co-opted by the federal establishment.

Two other groups, which tended to be headquartered in the poorest regions, had far less political clout in negotiating with federal authorities. These included failed managers, such as Leonid Gorbenko in Kaliningrad, who came to power on nonideological platforms, lost control over events, and were largely abandoned by Yeltsin; and supporters of opposition political parties (e.g., Yevgenii Mikhailov in Pskov, a member of Vladimir Zhirinovsky's Liberal Democratic Party; and Communist Aleksandr Chernogorov in Stavropol).[33]

The federal government largely seeks control over the regions on those questions it regards as important, but it also needs the cooperation of regional elites in order to implement many of its decisions. Interregional financial transfers are the main levers of control available to federal authorities. The center subsidizes between 75 and 80 of the 89 federation units via cash transfers and loans. Only the remaining dozen or so are net contributors to federal coffers. The amount of aid a region receives is in most cases determined by a region's budget deficit—often an imprecise indicator of its actual economic situation—and the regional governor's connections in Moscow. Examples of federal aid include arrangements to allow the regions to retain a larger share of tax revenue (e.g., Sakha/Yakutiya, the Siberian region that produces almost all of Russia's diamonds, is allowed to buy 20 percent of the gems mined on its territory at cost and to use profits for extra-budgetary spending). The main expenditures in territorial budgets are usually on housing, utilities, education, health, and social security.

The regions seek to maximize their political and economic autonomy, press to keep as much local tax money as possible at home, and often try to take over objects belonging to the federal government. Many regions also lobby for additional federal assistance with as few strings attached as possible. The influence the regions can bring to bear on the federal government is highly dependent on their geographic position, economic significance, financial potential, ethnic composition, and population size, as well as the clout of their governors. Local governments also extensively borrow money at home or abroad or engage in barter deals or the mutual offsetting of debts to garner additional resources beyond the center's control. The eight interregional associations have been slow to develop because of vast differences among neighboring regions and because individual governors are jealous of yielding any of their own personal power. Tellingly—with the exception of the group Siberian Accord—these associations were primarily formed at the initiative of Moscow, and not that of the regions themselves.

Informal Politics

In Russia, as elsewhere, interest groups actively try to influence policy; however, pressure group lobbying activity in Russia has several distinctive qualities: Firstly, in Russian society there are few legally recognized lobbying associations with a large membership comparable to the National Rifle Association or the American Association of Retired Persons in the United States.[34] Instead, members of the elite, many of whom have economic and politics interests at stake, lobby other members of the elite.

Secondly, although lobbying is focused on all centers of political power, the superpresidential system of government means that lobbying is especially intense in the federal executive branch and the Russian president's entourage. Thirdly, due to the weakness of the rule of law in Russia, lobbies often have particularistic goals: They want special favors and exemptions from laws, rather than the passing of legislation. Russian lobbyists usually seek privileges such as tax deferrals, customs benefits, the right to engage in certain kinds of activity, licenses, and state orders (which may guarantee funding). Lobbying also can sometimes reverse a presidential "no."[35]

Lastly, interest group lobbies in Russia are especially powerful because political parties there are weak. Without the intermediating influence of political parties, the lobbies—often representing private firms—can bring their influence directly to bear on state policy. Government ministries, instead of political parties, sometimes perform a mediating role among various interests.

Soviet Precedents

In the highly centralized Soviet system, lobbying was concentrated in centralized and officially authorized groups representing functional interests. For example, the nine ministries supervising the production of military hardware actively represented the interests of the military-industrial complex. Since resources were usually allocated on the basis of the annual plan, lobbying by these authorized groups meant a constant struggle for priority in access to resources. Although the relative clout of various lobbies was constantly evolving, in general the military-industrial complex and the construction industry were on top. In exchange for favored status in the struggle for resources, however, the state guided a lobbying group's activity and selected its leaders.[36]

Soviet lobbies at first supported the reforms initiated by Mikhail Gorbachev. They hoped that these reforms would result in a relaxation of control over their activities by the state and party administrative bureaucracies—for example, that they would be freed of the obligation to make deliveries to the state at artificially low prices, and that they could find their own customers and charge them real market prices. Instead, perestroika hastened the breakdown of the system in which they had long benefited, since the favored lobbies now had to compete for resources and access with a variety of others: entrepreneurs, former state employees, and criminal structures. These competitors—many operating illegally—were creating their own stock exchanges, banks, and export companies and had their own access to state resources. The disintegration of the old lobbying system was further encouraged by the increasingly assertive Russian government, which sought to undermine the authority of the Union authorities by handing out privileges to a wide array of regions and enterprises, especially to those businesses loyal to them. By 1989–1991, the old lobbying system, with its formal, hierarchical system of interest representation, had virtually collapsed.

Lobbying in the Russian Federation

The policies of the new government established under Gaidar in 1992 restored a measure of order in the system of lobbying but forced interest groups to realign. Severe budget shortfalls demanded radical reductions in subsidies to sectors heavily dependent on state largesse during the Soviet period, especially agriculture, heavy industry, and the military-industrial complex. Lobbying groups in the ascendance were largely those that could profit by selling abroad or in close association with the government—exporters of raw materials such as oil, natural gas, diamonds, and gold, as well as the financial sector, where a few large banks amassed huge profits because of inflation, the ruble's devaluation, and their ability to become "authorized banks" handling state budgetary transfers.

In 1991–1993, a large number of associations based on shared economic interests also emerged. One group of industrialists, largely in charge of obsolete enterprises in heavy industry and dependent on state deliveries of raw materials, sought state subsidies to protect them from the effects of the market. Prominent associations included the Russian League of Industrialists and Entrepreneurs, which was created in 1989 by the Communist Party and which represented heavy industry and the military-industrial complex, as well as organizations claiming to speak for the new class of businessmen, such as the International Association of Enterprise Managers, the League of Cooperatives and Entrepreneurs, and the Association of Russian Banks. Although most of these groups were not very influential, some met with limited success. The enterprise directors managed to squeeze continuing subsidies out of the government, and secured the replacement of economic "radicals" such as Mikhail Poltoranin, Gennadii Burbulis, Petr Aven, and eventually Gaidar himself, by officials more sympathetic to their interests.[37]

Since the Gaidar period, the key lobbies have expanded and consolidated their positions. Among the most influential groups today are economic sectoral interests such as oil, natural gas, banking, and the precious metals industries, as well as the other so-called "natural monopolies" controlling areas such as electricity production and the railways. These sectors usually bring revenue to the federal budget, are relatively competitive on international markets, and have patrons in the elite. The agrarian lobby, one of the few strong holdovers from the Soviet period, continues to be influential in that it is one of the few lobbies to secure regular, direct subsidies from the federal budget (i.e., guaranteed credits for spring sowing campaigns). The elites of regions such as Moscow city, Moscow oblast, St. Petersburg, Nizhnii Novgorod, Krasnoyarsk, and the Yamalo-Nenets autonomous okrug—which either donate money to the federal budget or are otherwise strong economically—also have been relatively successful in their lobbying efforts at the centers of federal power.[38] Other active lobbyists predictably include foreign and international granters of economic and financial aid to Russia, such as the U.S. government, the World Bank, and the International Monetary Fund, as well as foreign firms with a substantial investment stake in the Russian economy.

In March 1998, a presidential spokesman openly chastised several high-ranking ministry officials for lobbying the Duma on behalf of draft laws that contradicted government policy. Subunits of the federal government (especially government ministries) and committees of the Duma clearly are beholden to and influenced by lobbying groups to some degree. In the absence of laws regulating their activity, the lobbies have used a wide variety of tactics to advance their agendas.

. *Financing of electoral activity.* The major lobbies have lavished large sums of money on candidates and factions running in the Duma elections, although contributing large sums of money did not necessarily result in the election of the candidates the lobbies supported. In 1996 the oligarchs bankrolled President Yeltsin's reelection campaign win. Interest groups also have financed regional races.

Backroom politicking. Elected politicians at all levels are bombarded with requests for favors from interest groups. In the Duma, they submit draft bills or petitions for customs exemptions or other benefits to sympathetic members or factions, often bypassing the appropriate committees. In the Presidential Administration, lobbies seek to further favorable decisions or prevent unfavorable ones by cultivating key individuals, using planted media stories to shape the decisions of those individuals, or preventing a decision by swamping the relevant departments with proposals. Moreover, lobbies often can exploit loopholes in presidential decrees by acting unilaterally.

Performing services for the government. Russia's large financial-industrial groups (FIGs) perform important services for the government. In lieu of a strong state treasury, firms have managed—and profited from—government money. At least one large financial-industrial group also provides regular analytical reports to the Council of Ministers.

Bribery. Interest groups freely pay money to Duma members and other government officials to secure favorable votes as well as to determine which laws are discussed first and which are tabled. According to press reports, some Duma deputies also sell positions on their staff to raise money.[39]

Making trouble. Despite the general absence of mass interest groups, public displays and disruptive tactics such as the coal miners' strike in May 1998, which involved the blockade of train lines, have been effective in pressuring the government.

Public diplomacy. Spokesmen for interest groups appear in the press to explain their positions, frequently in the news media they control.[40]

Privatizing the State: Financial-Industrial Groups

Financial-industrial groups (FIGs)—the networks of politicians, banks, industrial firms, private security forces, and media organs that constantly struggle with one another over policy and resources—are by far the most influential lobbies. In May 1998 there were more than 80 registered FIGs, including 1,000 industrial enterprises and 100 banks, and there were thousands more de facto FIGs, largely representing small or medium-sized businesses and their in-house banks.[41] The government needs the financial-industrial groups for revenue, personnel, and expertise; the FIGs depend on the state for access to ownership of significant public assets, protection from attempts to challenge past illegal privatizations, and preferential state loans and tax concessions.

A few large FIGs are especially important, not because they are necessarily better run than their competitors but because of their privileged origins in the Soviet *nomenklatura* and continued close relationship to the state. Unofficially, experts claimed in 1996 that Russia's eight largest FIGs controlled between 25 and 30 percent of GNP.[42] Many top government officials have been recruited from the leading groups and return to the FIGs at the end of their tenure in public office. They became an essential component of the political system as it developed under Boris Yeltsin: It is hard to imagine a Russian president being able to rule without their support.

The financial-industrial group controlled by the natural gas monopoly Gazprom, for example, brings in about one-fourth of the government's hard currency earnings, controls a quarter of the world's natural gas reserves, has a market capitalization estimated at about US$50 billion, and has a major say in Russian foreign policy due to the fact that it controls pipelines that are vital to the economic well-being of neighboring ex-Soviet republics. Former Prime Minister

Chernomyrdin was the founding president of Gazprom, and its interests are represented in the government by the fuel and energy ministry. The payment of part of the firm's nearly $2 billion in tax arrears in December 1997 enabled the state—which still owns 40 percent of the firm's shares—to meet conditions laid down by the IMF for the release of a $670 million tranche of a total $10.2 billion structural adjustment loan. For political reasons, Gazprom has tolerated a large number of unpaid bills, but it also benefits from many legal or de facto privileges.

Of the ten most politically influential FIGs in 1998, five (Alfa, Inkombank, Rosprom-Yukos, SBS-Agro, and Rossiiskii Kredit) got their start between 1987 and 1991, with the direct political and financial support of the Soviet Communist Party or its youth branch, the Komsomol. Two others (Gazprom and LUKoil) are based on the "privatized" remnants of the old Soviet oil and gas ministry. One (Most Group) was created during the final days of the Soviet Union and grew rich on its business dealings with the city of Moscow. (The capital's new leaders had taken over much of the wealth amassed by the old Moscow Communist Party, not least its physical premises.) The two remaining major FIGs, LogoVAZ and Oneksimbank, were founded after 1991; but Oneksimbank, which was established by former members of the Soviet *nomenklatura* from the foreign trade bureaucracy, relied heavily on commercial relationships forged during the Soviet era.[43]

After 1991, the large FIGs further prospered due to the immaturity of Russia's institutions, the impact of the government's uneven "reform" policies, and Yeltsin's own governing style.[44] Many FIG leaders got rich from the privatization process of 1992–1994, when state-owned enterprises were converted into joint-stock companies. Most were taken over by consortia of managers and workers, though in effect managers controlled the enterprises and often bought up the shares distributed to the workers. Many managers then sold to or went into partnership with outside interests, including criminal organizations and FIGs.

During this period the government also handed out tax breaks, import-export licenses, and other privileges to raw materials exporters and trade and financial interests in order to secure their support in the face of increasing political opposition. In the absence of a strong treasury system, the government ensured large profits for many banks with close ties to the regime by "authorizing" them to manage state funds for a wide variety of government agencies.

In the second wave of privatization (known as "loans-for-shares"), in 1995, large banks were given shares in some of the most desirable corporations through staged auctions, as collateral in return for huge loans to the financially strapped government. One year later, when the government failed to repay the loans, these company shares became the property of the banks that had made the loans. In this way, banks acquired controlling interests in many leading oil and metals producers at a fraction of their potential market value had competitive auctions been held with foreign participation.

In return for financing Yeltsin's reelection campaign in 1996, Oneksimbank obtained direct representation in the government, with director Vladimir Potanin becoming a deputy prime minister, allowing Potanin's group to advance their agenda without having to work through intermediary organizations such as political parties.

Structure. The most important FIGs straddle the government and private sector. They include a large bank acting as a holding company; substantial interests in industry, the service sector, and the media; a private intelligence service; a security force; and influential political patrons in the Kremlin or the Russian government (as well as former government officials among senior corporate managers). Although the FIGs constantly battle one another for control over state property, they are linked by extensive cross-ownership. Inadequate financial reporting often makes it difficult to say with certainty who owns what, since formal ownership sometimes rests with a subsidiary or affiliated company as well as with the FIG. Many smaller FIGs are clustered around regional power structures, where they often seek to resist the encroachment of Moscow-based FIGs and to profit from performing business services for the local government. Regional FIGs are more likely than those tied to the federal government to have industrial rather than financial holdings. Many also have direct links to organized crime and military units based in the region, according to a wide variety of sources.

FIGs based on sectoral economic interests, such as Gazprom and LUKoil (oil), have relatively constant business interests and strong internal structures. FIGs based on the entrepreneurial and leadership skills of a single person, such as Boris Berezovskii's LogoVAZ empire, are more unstable and heavily dependent on the political clout of their captains. These leaders do not build independent structures but instead seek to spread their influence within existing firms and institutions such as the finance ministry, or to acquire existing firms (Berezovskii's use of the financial assets of Russia's giant car manufacturer, the Togliatti-based AvtoVAZ, and the international airline Aeroflot, are examples). FIGs with especially large industrial holdings, such as Rosprom-Menatep and Oneksimbank, though founded by influential captains and sometimes unstable, are beginning to build structures independent of their leaders.

The city of Moscow controls its own FIG. (Other regional jurisdictions have their own FIGs, but only Moscow is a consistent player at the national level.) Mayor Luzhkov's easy access to Yeltsin enabled the city to pursue its own brand of municipal capitalism, including its own privatization policy and the encouragement of imports, with revenue from city real estate deals (from which it earned $3 billion in 1997) and the mayor's office's direct participation in more than 100 joint-stock companies. The city owns a share of almost every major commercial enterprise in the capital—luxury hotels, office buildings, fast-food restaurants, grocery stores, shopping malls, gas stations, food processors, and even an oil refinery. Moscow's political clout also derives from Luzhkov's connections with leading banks, most of which are headquartered in the city. Although it has only 7 percent of Russia's population, Moscow provides about one-third of the country's tax revenues and accounts for 20 percent of its foreign trade. Moscow's financial resources are also a reserve for federal authorities, who draw on them in politically delicate cases or when the executive branch seeks to avoid dealing with the Duma.[45]

Differences Over Power and Policy. Relations among the major FIGs have been opportunistic and unstable. Vladimir Gusinskii's Most Group has in the past been close, in turn, to Luzhkov, Gaidar, and Chernomyrdin, each of whom was a rival of the others. Boris Berezovskii over the years was close to Gaidar, Aleksandr Korzhakov, and Soskovets, before throwing his support to Soskovets's onetime rival, Chernomyrdin. Berezovskii and Gusinskii were bitter rivals until they joined forces to support Yeltsin in 1996. There have been many instances where the FIGs have cooperated to advance joint interests: in blocking penetration of the Russian market by foreign banks; in proposing the loans-for-shares auctions; in supporting Yeltsin during the 1996 campaign; and in denying confirmation to Tatyana Paramonova, former acting director of the Central Bank.[46] In general, however, they are fierce rivals for the largesse of the state and differ on key issues: the role of government in the economy (and conversely, the role of big business in governing the state); the extent to which Russia's economy should be open to foreign investment; and into which sectors, if at all, their profits should be reinvested.

Yeltsin As Arbiter. Yeltsin served as the umpire of this system, in which constant competition by elites for power, resources, and the favor of the executive strongly resembled politics at the tsar's court. Although he generally sided with the economic liberals in the government, Yeltsin tried to avoid allying himself with any single FIG and seemed to balance off the FIGs to prevent any group from attaining too much power. He brought representatives from competing FIGs into the government and made sure that the sale of state property was widely distributed among competing groups and their foreign partners.

During his second term, however, Yeltsin was much less effective. Public warfare among the oligarchs occurred more frequently, erupting with particular vigor after the sale of 25 percent of the shares in Svyazinvest in July 1997. (The winner was a consortium of Potanin's Oneksimbank and George Soros's Quantum Fund.) Although his faltering health undoubtedly played a role, Yeltsin's increasing reliance on family members and close associates in governing apparently led him to make decisions with their financial welfare in mind. Berezovskii was thus able to exploit his apparent friendship with Yeltsin's daughter to his own personal financial and political benefit, and he often used it to upset the balance of power. Former Prime Minister Chernomyrdin effectively stepped into the breech for a time; but he was fired in March 1998, apparently because Yeltsin saw Chernomyrdin's increasingly assertive and public performance as arbiter as a political threat.

The Politics of Policymaking

Now that we have seen how Yeltsin, the Federal Assembly, regional leaders, and interest groups and other political actors have functioned, we should be able to explain how policies were made. Some observers argue that the system always has operated more or less consistently to serve the interests of those in power: the president and the oligarchs. Let us see whether these generalizations are valid.[47]

One way to understand how an issue is shaped by and affects the distribution of political power is to examine what appear to be the costs and benefits of the proposed policy. Among the costs one would count any burden, monetary or non-monetary, that individuals must bear, or think they must bear, if the policy is adopted. The costs of a government spending program are the taxes it requires to fund the program. The costs of a foreign policy initiative may be the increased chance of having the nation brought into war.

Benefits are any satisfactions, monetary or nonmonetary, that persons believe they will enjoy if the policy is adopted. The benefits of a spending program are the payments, subsidies, or contracts received by particular persons. The benefits of a foreign policy initiative may be the enhanced collective security of the nation or the protection of a valued ally.

Costs and benefits are what people believe them to be, whether or not these beliefs turn out to be accurate. Moreover, not every policy will fit neatly into one category or another. A complex issue such as the passage of an IMF loan program might attract the participation of the president and the Presidential Administration, the government, the Duma factions and committees, the Federation Council, regional government leaders, the business oligarchs, sectoral lobbies, international financial institutions, Western governments, and foreign investors. Viewing politics in this way enables us to highlight key distinctions among policies, which is an essential step toward answering the question "Who governs?" This approach sheds light on each stage of policymaking: (1) establishing the political agenda (how perceived costs and benefits determine what politics is to be about); (2) decisionmaking (how the perceived costs and benefits of a policy proposal are distributed, and what the government intends to do about it); and (3) implementation (how perceived costs and benefits determine whether and how the people and institutions affected by a decision modify their behavior).

In the sections that follow, we will discuss the politics, not the merits, of four types of policies: majoritarian politics, interest group politics, client politics, and entrepreneurial politics.

Majoritarian Politics

Majoritarian politics promises benefits to large numbers of persons at a cost that large numbers of persons will have to bear. Almost all Russians at some point in their lives receive pension benefits, live in apartments with subsidized heating, and ride subsidized public transport. Everybody who works has to pay social security taxes. National defense and state-provided medical care offer the prospect of a distributed benefit that all pay for through taxes.

Such issues tend to be put on the agenda because they are visible or dramatic. Even in Russia, where public opinion is weak, they tend to get resolved in favor of the position that has a majority of citizens on its side—although in most cases these majoritarian policies are basically inherited from the Soviet era. Policymakers are aware that public opinion exists even in Russia and that they ignore it at their electoral peril. Although most Russians have little incentive to join interest groups or political parties, they nevertheless vote for or against politicians based on the stands the latter take on questions of national defense, health care, and education. In the 1996 presidential elections, Yeltsin skillfully and convincingly defined the issue before voters as an ideological choice between market and democratic reforms—which he represented—and communism, represented by his opponent Gennadii Zyuganov. However, public opinion on a broad issue provides few details to policymakers. Even though most Russians oppose NATO expansion, they do not feel strongly about it, and they disagree as to how expansion should be countered. In such instances, elites tend to formulate policies based on their ideology or worldview, or in reaction to crises.

The fact that perceived costs and benefits of majoritarian politics are widely distributed means that few interest groups feel strongly enough to organize and become involved. Thus, interest group activity (pro and contra) is relatively low in these cases. Debates about putting such policies on the agenda and what to decide about them largely take place within formal institutions such as the Duma or the Federation Council. Although President Yeltsin may have cared about a policy—for example, ratification of the START II Treaty—he did not usually perceive the costs or benefits as important enough to expend significant political capital on getting the outcome he wanted.

Interest Group Politics

Interest group politics promises benefits to a relatively small, identifiable group and the imposition of costs on a different, equally identifiable group. A government decision to sell a state enterprise to a particular FIG at a price below fair market value will benefit that group, but it will hurt other FIGs interested in bidding for the enterprise. A law allowing foreigners to invest in Russian oil firms will benefit some companies, but not those that can compete effectively using domestic capital alone. An example of interest group policies are the loans-for-shares auctions in 1995. Though many examples of interest group politics involve monetary costs and benefits, this need not be the case.

A notable recent example of interest group politics was the 1997 "bank war," which began when Yeltsin infuriated the oligarchs who had supported his reelection, by announcing that the state-owned industries in the next round of privatization auctions would go to the highest bidder in transparent, competitive auctions instead of through an ordered division of spoils. The oligarchs saw this new policy as one that might impose concentrated costs on them and benefits on their business competitors. The result was an intense political and economic struggle among financiers, fought largely by mudslinging in the media, which was stopped only by Yeltsin's halting of the auctions in September.[48]

Public opinion usually plays little role in interest group politics. The groups that are likely to be affected feel strongly enough about the issue to organize themselves. Since many important interest groups have media organs under their control, the press also often plays a prominent role. President Yeltsin and Russia's successive prime ministers actively mediated among interest groups, usually ensuring that benefits were apportioned in a way that would maintain the status quo; but parts of the government also sometimes act as allies of particular groups. Interest group politics, moreover, does not end with the passage or defeat of the initial proposal. The struggle typically has continued during implementation—in the bureaucracy, the courts, the Audit Chamber, or even with the president's further intervention.

The Stolichnyi Bank (now SBS-Agro) purchase of Agroprombank in 1996 was an example of interest group politics involving rival parts of the government. In this instance one interest group, the FIG controlled by Stolichnyi Bank, thought it would profit by the sale; Agroprombank, backed by the collective farm *(kolkhoz)* lobby, thought it would be harmed by the sale and opposed the takeover. The matter was settled when the government, acting as arbiter, forged a compromise: The sale was approved after Stolichnyi agreed to maintain the bank's agricultural profile and turned over to the agriculture ministry, which often speaks for the interests of the farmers, enough shares of stock that it could block any drastic change. There was little involvement by the Duma or the courts.

The politics of the presidential court, a kind of interest group politics, results not from policies that promise concentrated costs and benefits but from the ability of members of the elite to help confer potential costs or benefits on other members of the elite. In 1997, for example, Anatolii Chubais left the government after reports published in media outlets controlled by his political and business rivals, led by financier Berezovskii, that he had illegally received a $90,000 advance to write a book. To Berezovskii, Chubais represented a potential political and economic threat. Court politics is usually marked by competition within the elite for political and economic power and status. As in other interest group politics, the president usually has acted as arbiter in these struggles. Since the opinion of the president and other elite members matters, compromising material is often used to discredit rivals.

Client Politics

Client politics promises benefits to an identifiable group, with costs distributed over a substantial portion of society. Because the group that is to benefit has a strong incentive to organize and lobby for that benefit, but because costs affect everyone only slightly, those who must pay have little incentive to organize and may be indifferent to or ignorant of the proposal. Russian farms benefit substantially from agricultural subsidies; each consumer, however, pays only a small amount of these subsidies in the form of higher taxes. Royalties paid by European airlines to the Russian civil aviation industry for the right to fly through Russian airspace give considerable financial benefits to Aeroflot and to aviation officials, who are not interested in using the fees for a distributed public good such as modernization of air traffic control or air safety improvements. There is little incentive for citizens interested in air safety to organize. Other examples of client politics are the use of "authorized" banks to manage government money, the granting of preferential export licenses, and the dependence of many regional governments on money handed out by Moscow. In foreign policy, LUKoil and other firms with commercial interests in Iraq have pressured the government to work for the lifting of international sanctions against Baghdad. The costs of this policy—the greater isolation of Russia in the international community and increasing tensions in Russia's relations with the United States—are widely distributed. The benefits are greater profits for the firm.

Client politics does not always involve material benefits. Certain groups, such as the Russian Orthodox Church and Soviet Army veterans, may have special legal protection from the government or have their values specially honored. Several ethnic enclaves—for example, Tatarstan—have special constitutional protection.

Client politics often takes place away from the public eye. Neither the public at large nor the mass media have much interest in or knowledge of the policies involved. In order to protect their favored relationship with the government, client groups must find strategically placed patrons in the government or the legislature. Often clients can exert influence in the cumbersome process by which the Presidential Administration makes policy decisions. The Duma's agriculture committee, for example, is a strong advocate of financial support for Russian agriculture. Because of the importance of a client having a sponsor, corruption tends to be far more widespread in client politics than in majoritarian politics. Implementation is likely, since it involves a group receiving a benefit.

Entrepreneurial Politics

Entrepreneurial politics promises benefits for society as a whole or for some large part of it, and a substantial cost for some small, identifiable part of it. This kind of politics includes many policies that are intended to restructure the legacy of the Soviet system: military reform, which promises improved national defense by contracting the army's size and moving to a voluntary force; contraction of the coal industry, which promises a more efficient, economically competitive coal industry if mines are shut down and state subsidies ended; and land reform, which proposes improved agricultural production through the reduction of low-interest credits, subsidies, state purchase of agricultural products, and direct investment. Compliance with international agreements limiting the spread of nuclear technology promises a benefit to Russian society: the avoidance of sanctions that would undermine Western financing of the Russian Space Agency. However, compliance imposes a high cost on Russian firms whose livelihood depends on sales of such technology to clients in Iraq, China, or Iran.

If the beneficiaries are the public at large and the public has little incentive to press for what it thinks are its interests, then one would expect that organized *opponents* of a policy would usually win. Moreover, since the Russian political system provides ample opportunity to block policies that threaten organized interests, it is remarkable that these policies are passed at all. The natural gas monopoly Gazprom, for example, has successfully lobbied in the Duma against bills it opposes. Since the public is not organized to act for itself in order to put an issue on the agenda, a policy "entrepreneur" must act on its behalf; but an entrepreneur may not actually be representing the public's interests and may be acting partly for selfish reasons. Yeltsin often acted as a policy entrepreneur, such as when he pushed privatization, the freeing of prices, and the elimination of the budget deficit, all policies that imposed costs on specific interest groups. Nemtsov, Chubais, and the U.S. government have frequently been policy entrepreneurs on issues toward which the Russian public was indifferent or that it was too unorganized to pursue for itself. The IMF, a policy entrepreneur, has tried to break up monopolies such as Gazprom and the electric utility United Energy Systems, even though there is little domestic support for doing so. The World Bank, another entrepreneur, has led the fight to restructure the coal industry.

Policy entrepreneurs often try to achieve through emotional or symbolic appeals what narrow appeals to self-interest cannot. They present the rationale for a new policy in dramatic terms: to advance "reform," "stop a return to communism," or "prevent the business oligarchs from gaining control of the country." Legislative and administrative action based on such appeals was often cast in equally bold terms, with strict standards, stern penalties, short deadlines, threats by Yeltsin to dissolve the Duma or rule by decree, and conversely, calls from the Duma for impeachment of the president. The mass media are of great importance in entrepreneurial politics, especially key journalists who decide to give exposure to the proponents of a policy. Interest groups often vigorously oppose entrepreneurial politics; but to the extent that media images and slogans are powerful, special interests nevertheless publicly give policy entrepreneurs lip service.

Even if policy entrepreneurs get what they want, however, interest groups can often undermine a policy by refusing to implement it or by weakening the administration of that policy. This is especially true of decisions that affect many layers of bureaucracy or that involve negotiations among powerful actors. Although the government has gradually reduced budget subsidies to the agricultural sector in recent years, the agricultural lobby has sometimes found other funding sources in the agriculture ministry. Army commanders have resisted the federal government's attempts to reduce the size of the armed forces by forging alliances with regional governors, whose jurisdictions would be economically harmed by reductions in the size of the armed forces. In 1992 the management at major oil firms was sufficiently organized to resist the general privatization plans drawn up by the Gaidar government.

Despite his considerable formal authority, there were serious limitations on Yeltsin's ability to be a successful policy entrepreneur. Yeltsin did not have the time, interest, attention span, or political popularity to secure implementation by himself. Implementation is dependent on the building of coalitions with groups affected by a particular decision, and Yeltsin's vigorous use of his presidential powers tended to prevent the building of such coalitions. Yeltsin delegated the task of overseeing implementation to deputies such as Chubais, Nemtsov, or Yevgenii Primakov; but his inconsistent support for those individuals undermined their efforts to see that policies were carried out.[49]

Although a Russian president may be able to carry out specific policies and to change the people who participate in the policy process, it is doubtful that he can change the structure of politics itself, redistribute the society's wealth, encroach on the fundamental interests of the oligarchs, or eliminate corruption.[50] The success of interest groups in resisting the implementation of entrepreneurial policies is a major reason why many of the government's "reform" policies have been unsuccessful.

To What Ends?

At the end of the Yeltsin era, the absence of legal protection for the oligarchs' business empires, the lack of rules governing the elite's political activity, and the uncertainty surrounding the presidential succession created considerable nervousness among FIG leaders. They were particularly concerned about whether their immense profits of the previous decade would be undone, and whether the new president could or would take Yeltsin's place as umpire of their interests. Figures such as Berezovskii and Chubais, whose clout had depended on their personal ties to the Yeltsin entourage, were especially vulnerable. Gusinskii's arrest on corruption charges, soon after Vladimir Putin's election to the presidency, sounded alarm bells in many quarters, although Gusinskii was subsequently released. Russia's ongoing transition under its new president is clearly testing the stability and longevity of the structures of power that emerged in the decade under Yeltsin; and in time, it will reveal the extent to which power has been institutionalized or hinges critically on personal rule.

Notes

1. J. Q. Wilson, *American Government: Institutions and Policies* (Lexington, Mass.: D.C. Heath, 1980), p. ix.

2. V. A. Kolosov and R. F. Turovskii, "The electoral map of contemporary Russia," *Russian Social Science Review,* vol. 39, no. 1, January–February 1998, pp. 67–69. See also, *Trud,* 18 March 1998, pp. 1–2.

3. Wilson, *American Government*, p. 81.

4. For a more detailed discussion of political culture and these concepts, see E. L. Keenan, "Muscovite political folkways," *Russian Review*, vol. 45, 1986, pp. 46, 156–157.

5. Richard Pipes, *Russia Under the Old Regime* (New York: Collier, 1974), pp. 70–71.

6. Keenan, "Muscovite Political Folkways," p. 132.

7. Ibid., pp. 156–157.

8. Virginie Coulloudon, "The criminalization of Russia's political elite," *East European Constitutional Review*, fall 1997, p. 74.

9. See also the regular ratings of Transparency International at www.transparency.de.

10. *Financial Times*, 9 June 1998.

11. Louise I. Shelley, "Transnational organized crime: An imminent threat to the nation state," *Journal of International Affairs*, winter 1995, vol. 48, no. 2, p. 484.

12. John Lloyd, "Red alert," *New York Times Magazine*, 31 January 1998.

13. CSIS Task Force Report, "Russian organized crime" (Washington, D.C.: Center for Strategic and International Studies, 1997), pp. 29–31.

14. Peter Rutland, "After August: Elite consolidation, institutional decay, and political stability in Russia," in Bruce Parrott, ed., *Systemic Crisis in Russia* (forthcoming). I am indebted to Peter Rutland for much of the analysis in this section.

15. "Memorandum for the Russian Government," *Nezavisimaya gazeta*, 1 April 1992.

16. Rutland, "After August"; see also Olga Kryshtanovskaya, "Nomenklatura of our time," *Obshchaya gazeta*, 23–29 January 1997; O. Kryshtanovskaya, "The real masters of Russia," *Argumenty i fakty*, no. 21, May 1997.

17. Rutland, "After August"; see also A. Plutnick, "Narrow is the circle of these revolutionaries," *Izvestiya*, 4 July 1997.

18. "Still most awkward partners," *Economist*, 9 May 1998, p. 26.

19. Rutland, "After August," p. 9.

20. George Breslauer, "Presidential leadership and elite stability," unpublished paper, November 1997, p. 2.

21. Peter Rutland, "Boris Yeltsin: The problem, not the solution," *National Interest*, fall 1997, pp. 36–37.

22. Breslauer, "Presidential leadership and elite stability," p. 2.

23. *Moscow Tribune*, 12 November 1994.

24. *Kommersant-Vlast'*, 16 June 1998.

25. "Russia's other governments," *Economist*, 3 January 1998, p. 25.

26. Robert W. Orttung and Anna Paretskaya, "Presidential elections demonstrate rural-urban divide," *Transition*, vol. 2, no 19, 20 September 1996; R. S. Clem and P. R. Craumer, "The regional dimension," in Laura Belin and Robert Orttung, *Russia's 1995 Parliamentary Elections: The Battle for the Duma* (Armonk, N.Y.: M.E. Sharpe, 1997), p. 137.

27. K. Ivanov, "Russian regions: More different than alike," *Ekonomika i zhizn'*, no. 18, May 1997.

28. V. Mironov, "Regional differences in systems of local government: Why do they occur?," *Jamestown Foundation Prism*, vol. 4, no. 4, 20 February 1998.

29. See Chapter 3 in this volume, "Moscow city management," by Virginie Coulloudon.

30. *Segodnya*, 21 March 1998.

31. Thomas Graham, "Prospects for Russia," unpublished paper, February 1998, p. 4.

32. *Economist*, 3 January 1998.

33. Robert Orttung, "Anatomy of a dinosaur: Russia's new regional elite," meeting report, September 1997, Kennan Institute for Advanced Russian Studies, Washington, D.C.

34. Michael McFaul, "Democracy unfolds in Russia," *Current History,* October 1997, p. 24.

35. "Political lobbies in Russia," *Business in Russia,* June 1995, p. 46.

36. "Political lobbies," p. 46.

37. V. Lepekhin, "A new hegemon: How entrepreneurs are preparing to seize power," *Novaya yezhednevnaya gazeta,* 18 June 1993; A. Anichkin, "Entrepreneurial organizations are dividing up the Soviet inheritance," *Izvestiya,* 17 June 1993; A. Luzin, "Consolidation around anticrisis program is needed," *Rossiiskie vesti,* 1 December 1992, p. 2; V. Borodulin, "It is very difficult to force them to work not for the homeland," *Kommersant-Daily,* 2 March 1995.

38. *Nezavisimaya gazeta,* 21 January 1997.

39. *Izvestiya,* 3 May 1997; "Lobbyists in disguise invade Russian parliament," AFP [Agence France–Presse], 14 May 1997.

40. See Chapter 2 of this volume.

41. S. Blagov, "Conspiracy theorists disappointed by 'Oligarchy,'" Interpress Service, 14 April 1998.

42. See McFaul, "Democracy unfolds in Russia," p. 24. An expert from the Association of Russian Banks claimed that Russia's top 25 banks, which included all of the banks belonging to the leading FIGs, controlled 85 percent of the total assets in the country, 86 percent of enterprise funds, 94 percent of deposits, and 88 percent of budget resources (*Vek,* no. 24, June 1998).

43. See Juliet Johnson, "Russia's emerging financial-industrial groups," *Post-Soviet Affairs,* vol. 13, no. 4, pp. 333–365; Juliet Johnson, "Carving up the bear: Banks and the struggle for power in Russia," *CSIS: Post-Soviet Prospects,* March 1997, pp. 1–4.

44. A. Fadin, "The joint-stock company as a party of a new type: Is the reconversion of money into power possible?," *Obshchaya gazeta,* 12 August 1994.

45. V. Razuvaev, "The time of independent local princes? Sketches for a portrait of Yurii Luzhkov," *Russian Social Science Review,* vol. 39, no. 1, January–February 1998, pp. 34–36.

46. Johnson, "Russia's emerging FIGs," pp. 358–359.

47. For the application of these ideas to an American government context, see Wilson, *American Government,* ch. 14.

48. Blagov, "Conspiracy theorists disappointed by 'Oligarchy.'"

49. Breslauer, "Presidential leadership and elite stability," p. 2.

50. A. Buzgalin and A. Kolganov, "Lebed: Just one bullet out of a big clip," *Jamestown Foundation Prism,* vol. 4, no. 13, 26 June 1998.

CHAPTER 2

The Distorted Russian Media Market

Laura Belin, with Floriana Fossato and Anna Kachkaeva

The media business in Russia has developed along two somewhat contradictory lines in the post-Soviet years. At the micro level, economic change has forced media outlets to adapt to market realities. Soon after the collapse of the USSR, production costs rose sharply, and with few exceptions, revenues from sales and advertising did not keep pace. At the same time, state subsidies for the media, which had been abundant during the Soviet period, were sharply curtailed. Within a few years, the new economic conditions had brought about major changes in patterns of media ownership and financing. Whereas in the early 1990s most non-state-run publications were managed by their own editorial collectives; this was no longer the case by 1998.[1] Even those print media that remained formally independent were usually reliant on some sort of outside financing. For the electronic media, high start-up costs meant that few new outlets were created without financing from government or private investors.

Yet at the macro level the media business has not developed according to the normal principles of a market economy. Despite the persistent unprofitability of most outlets, relatively few of the "central" (i.e., Moscow-based) media have gone under. On the contrary, new newspapers, magazines, and television companies have been created each year, even as most existing ones operate at a loss. Three newspapers (*Rossiya, Parlamentskaya gazeta,* and *Vremya-MN)* began publication during the first half of 1998 alone.

What is causing this distortion in the market, which keeps many more media afloat than can be supported by consumer demand? The answer relates to the political use of the media. The media have become weapons used in struggles among political and financial groups, and a battleground on which those disputes are waged. For the country's elite, media are valuable assets not because of their balance sheets but because they are instruments for injecting viewpoints into the political discourse. Consequently, even newspapers with relatively small circulation and no prospect of breaking even have found sponsors outside the journalistic community. In effect, subsidies from private businesses have taken the place of federal government subsidies, keeping Moscow's media market crowded and making it appear robust.

In many cases, the money that supports the media comes with strings attached. Although Soviet-style censorship is gone, reliance on outside financing constrains the autonomy of journalists. A diverse spectrum of opinions can be found in the Russian media as a whole, but news coverage in individual outlets is frequently slanted toward the viewpoints of owners or financial backers, who thus get a "return" on their investment in these unprofitable enterprises.

Media Outlets As Prized Commodities

Private enterprises have been paying for media exposure since the early 1990s. Sometimes this practice has taken the form of "hidden advertising," such as when individual journalists, editors, or television producers have arranged flattering news coverage in exchange for payoffs. In other cases, the relationships between corporations and media were out in the open; for instance, the gas monopoly Gazprom extended loans to the daily *Komsomol'skaya pravda*. The Most Group became the first business empire to own several media outlets, founding a newspaper and television station in 1993 and purchasing a controlling stake in Ekho Moskvy radio the following year.

The pace of media acquisitions by business groups accelerated after the 1996 presidential election. It cannot be proven through sociological analysis that the media were the decisive factor in Boris Yeltsin's victory over Communist challenger Gennadii Zyuganov; but within the Russian political and journalistic communities, it is considered self-evident that the media were the linchpin of Yeltsin's campaign strategy.[2]

How much did the Russian media actually influence voters in 1996? The barrage of favorable coverage did not turn large numbers of people into enthusiastic supporters of the president. Less than two months after the election, the All-Russian Center for the Study of Public Opinion found that one-third of respondents who voted for Yeltsin described themselves as "indifferent" to his victory. By late September 1996, just 12 percent of those surveyed by the same organization said they trusted Yeltsin.[3] Nor was it the few months of anti-Zyuganov coverage in the media that persuaded people that a return to Communist rule would be undesirable. Opinion polls long predating the presidential campaign showed that Zyuganov and his party evoked a high number of negative responses.

The media boosted Yeltsin's chances during the months leading up to the election by framing the campaign as a two-man contest between the incumbent and his Communist challenger. Research conducted in other countries has suggested that news reporting can strongly affect candidates' electoral prospects. For instance, undecided voters are more likely to support the candidate they expect to win the race. Consequently, coverage that portrays candidates as nonstarters can dissuade citizens from "wasting" their votes on them. In addition, the media can influence voters through "priming": If news reports focus on a particular set of issues during a campaign, citizens become more likely to use those issues as a basis for evaluating their leaders.[4] By depicting Yeltsin again and again as the only alternative to a Communist return to power (as opposed to concentrating on his policy record), the Russian media may have helped direct the votes of Zyuganov's opponents toward Yeltsin rather than toward other rivals.

Journalists aided the president's campaign in many other ways as well. Between the first round on June 16 and the runoff election on July 3, reporters and commentators did their best to bring voters to the polls by stressing repeatedly that Zyuganov's only chance for victory was a low turnout. Perhaps most important, journalists colluded to keep the public from learning that Yeltsin nearly died as a result of a heart attack one week before the second round of the election. It is impossible to quantify the contribution of such media coverage to Yeltsin's victory; but the election result fueled the widespread perception that the media are a powerful tool for popular persuasion. In addition, the turnaround by some journalists, who changed from sharp critics to vocal supporters of the president in a matter of weeks, showed that it was possible to quickly mobilize journalists to support a particular viewpoint.

The media's power should not be overstated: The capacity of news coverage to influence political events does have its limits. A classic example is the war in Chechnya, which dragged on for more than 20 months despite the media's nearly unanimous condemnation of the fighting from the beginning.[5] Still, journalists can sometimes place issues on the radar screen and affect the public image of prominent individuals.

If the potential to influence public opinion has been the main attraction for prospective media magnates, one might ask why they would care to own Moscow-based newspapers, since most Russian citizens get their news from nationwide television channels.[6] Although local and regional media have growing audiences, few "central" newspapers are available outside the capital.

The print media's agenda-setting role helps explain why investors have been willing to spend millions of dollars to support newspapers with circulations under 100,000, mostly confined to the Moscow area. Even if newspapers reach far fewer consumers than do television networks, they have an important audience among political elites and opinion-makers. A highly controversial article can provoke comments from senior officials and even draw prime-time attention from television networks. For example, in July 1998, a front-page *Nezavisimaya gazeta* editorial advocated the creation of a Provisional State Council to run the country and oversee early presidential elections.[7] Within hours, Yeltsin was shown on television ruling out any chance of a "coup." Although the president rejected the newspaper's proposal, the prospect of an early end to his term gained new salience and was discussed on several television networks. It is difficult for officials to ignore sensational articles about purported policy plans or corruption allegations, even those published in small-circulation newspapers, because such reports frequently prompt journalists (foreign as well as Russian) to seek official comment.

Financial Links with Government and Business

Some of the central media—a relatively small number of outlets in the capital city—are still state-owned and -operated.[8] Most others, however, are privately owned and funded: Nearly every major financial-industrial group in Russia is involved in the media business, as are several leading companies in the energy sector. In some cases, businesses founded their own media. Others purchased shares in (or informally began paying the bills for) established outlets that were struggling. The following section describes the media holdings of Russia's most important political and business organizations.[9]

Federal Government and the Media

Only one Russian television company is fully owned by the state: Russian Television (known as RTR), which is part of the All-Russian State Television and Radio Company (VGTRK). RTR broadcasts nationwide on Channel 2 and also manages the Kultura network, which was created in 1997 and airs primarily educational and cultural programming. RTR's editorial policy generally supported the Kremlin and the government throughout the Yeltsin years, although the network's negative coverage of the war in Chechnya and certain other issues prompted Yeltsin to replace RTR's chairman at the start of the 1996 presidential campaign. Members of the political opposition have for the most part received unflattering coverage on RTR, with the exception of a special weekly program on parliamentary activities.[10]

In May 1998, the Kremlin took steps to strengthen RTR's position vis-à-vis the Channel 1 broadcaster, Russian Public Television (ORT). (At the time, RTR news coverage was sympathetic to government ministers and policies that were under fire on other television networks.) Yeltsin signed a decree ordering the creation of a new holding company under the aegis of VGTRK, to include all fully state-owned electronic media. Some 89 state-owned regional television and radio companies became affiliates of VGTRK, as did the Moscow-based radio stations Radio Rossiya, Radio Mayak, and Radio 1. One of the most controversial aspects of the decree was the subordination of some 100 local television and radio technical centers to the new holding company, as subdivisions thereof. (More than 90 percent of private radio and television companies in Russia were already reliant on the center's transmission services for broadcasting, due to the assertion of central control of all media during the Soviet period.) Executives from several other television networks complained that the decree granted unfair privileges to RTR over private or semiprivate networks.

It remains to be seen whether the increased political support for VGTRK will translate into more budget funding for the network. Like many other budget-funded entities in Russia, state-owned television and radio have been chronically underfinanced in recent years, receiving far less money than the amount theoretically allocated to them in the federal budget. Thousands of RTR employees and other communications workers have suffered delays in the payment of wages. But Yeltsin's May 1998 decree had handed VGTRK a potentially important source of revenue in the form of the technical centers, which charge other electronic media fees in exchange for vital transmission services.

In the early 1990s, the state also was the sole owner of Russia's Channel 1 broadcaster, Ostankino. That situation changed in November 1994, when Yeltsin decreed the transformation of Ostankino into ORT. Even though the state retained a controlling 51 percent stake in ORT, the network's editorial policy on some matters—especially the actions and statements of controversial government ministers—was markedly different from RTR's (as is discussed later in this chapter).

The few newspapers that are fully state-owned do not boast wide circulations and are chiefly of interest to bureaucrats and legal practitioners. *Rossiiskaya gazeta,* the official government daily, publishes some government resolutions and occasionally other official documents, such as Constitutional Court decisions and presidential decrees. *Parlamentskaya gazeta,* which began publication as a weekly in May 1998, is the official newspaper of the State Duma and Federation Council. Established in concession to opposition politicians who objected to the prevailing news coverage of parliamentary affairs, it publishes favorable reporting on legislators along with the texts of some laws and nonbinding parliamentary resolutions.[11] The Presidential Administration is without an official newspaper, as *Rossiiskie vesti* broke off its ties to the Kremlin in April 1998. Newspaper staff complained of long-standing funding shortfalls.[12]

The state retains full ownership of two major news agencies: ITAR-TASS and RIA-Novosti. In addition, the official point of view often finds its way into reports published by the private news agency Interfax. This was particularly true during the 1996 presidential campaign, and the trend has deepened since August 1997, when Mikhail Komissar, one of the founders of Interfax, became a deputy head of the Presidential Administration.[13] Control over the news agencies is important, since they often break stories and carry exclusive comments from high officials. Being privy to some briefings that are closed to other correspondents, the major news agencies to some extent set the tone for coverage appearing in other Russian and even foreign media.

Media and the Moscow City Government

The Moscow city government has been involved in the media market since the early 1990s, giving subsidies to some newspapers (notably, the popular daily *Moskovskii komsomolets*) and helping many others indirectly by charging them preferential rates for rent and utilities. As Boris Yeltsin's second term of office progressed, the number of media outlets formally linked to the Moscow city authorities increased, a development almost certainly linked to preparations for a presidential bid by Mayor Yurii Luzhkov.[14] At a ceremony to mark the launching of the weekly *Rossiya* in March 1998, Luzhkov expressed the hope that the newspaper would publicize important Moscow city policies to Russians living outside the capital.

Among the most important media assets controlled by the Moscow government is the television network Center TV (in Russian, TV-Tsentr), which began broadcasting in June 1997 under the leadership of longtime RTR general director Anatolii Lysenko. Center TV currently reaches few localities outside the Moscow area, but its executives have spoken of plans to broadcast nationwide in the future. The Moscow government owns two-thirds of the shares in the Center TV consortium, which includes Center TV itself, a pool of Moscow cable networks, and a satellite-cable project, Meteor TV.

Most of the other media outlets linked to the Moscow authorities are part of a separate holding company, Center Media Consortium SMM. That company is a subsidiary of the Sistema corporation, which is headed by Vladimir Yevtushenkov and has close ties to Mayor Luzhkov. Center Media Consortium SMM's assets include several Moscow radio stations and the television company TeleExpo, which produces programs for the state-owned Channel 5 network and broadcasts the music channel MTV. The consortium also manages the Metropolis publishing house, which the Moscow city government created as a subsidiary of Sistema in April 1998. Metropolis purchased the weekly *Literaturnaya gazeta* from Menatep Bank and publishes newspapers including *Rossiya*, *Moskovskaya pravda*, *Vechernyaya Moskva*, *Tverskaya 13*, *Vechernii Klub*, *Kul'tura*, and several free newspapers including *Metro* and *Tsentr-Plyus*.

The Moscow city government has financial ties to some media that remain outside the Center Media Consortium SMM and its parent corporation, Sistema. In particular, the government owns shares in the private television network TV-6 and has provided subsidies to the weekly newspaper *Obshchaya gazeta*.[15] The creation of the private network REN-TV in 1996 was reportedly financed through a multimillion-dollar loan from the Bank of Moscow, which is controlled by the city government. However, REN-TV has paid off that loan.[16] Although *Moskovskii komsomolets* editor-in-chief Pavel Gusev no longer holds a post in the city government (he was Moscow's information minister from January 1992 to October 1997[17]), his newspaper still consistently supports the mayor. *Moskovskii komsomolets* manages several businesses with the consent of the city authorities.

LogoVAZ Financial-Industrial Group

Boris Berezovskii's experience demonstrates that influence over the Russian media depends not so much on the form of ownership of media outlets as on the degree of their reliance on outside financing. One of Russia's wealthiest businessmen, he served as deputy secretary of Russia's Security Council from November 1996 to November 1997 and was appointed executive secretary of the

Commonwealth of Independent States in April 1998. He has also long wielded more influence on editorial policy than anyone else at ORT. Yet Berezovskii does not own a majority stake in the 51 percent state-owned network, which broadcasts nationwide on Channel 1. His LogoVAZ group owns 8 percent of ORT shares, and Berezovskii controls another 8 percent through the Obedinennyi Bank, which belongs to the LogoVAZ group. That bank is part of a four-bank consortium that owns a combined 38 percent of the shares in ORT.

Berezovskii's influence has eclipsed that of the other ORT shareholders, in large part because at the same time as the state was amassing arrears to the network worth millions of dollars, his businesses were paying the salaries of top ORT executives and some journalists.[18] Consequently, even after First Deputy Prime Minister Boris Nemtsov vowed in 1997 to increase the state's role in managing the network, the majority on the new board of ORT directors chosen in February 1998 were Berezovskii loyalists.[19]

Obedinennyi Bank also owns 37.5 percent of the shares in the private network TV-6, which broadcasts to much of European Russia. The network has for the most part featured entertainment programming designed to appeal to younger viewers, although since 1997 it has also broadcast a weekly current-affairs program on Sundays.[20]

Berezovskii has long been involved in the print media as well. He is most closely associated with the daily *Nezavisimaya gazeta,* which has a small readership outside Moscow but has a steady audience among political elites. The newspaper devotes extensive resources to covering foreign news, especially countries in the Commonwealth of Independent States. After refusing to accept funding from "sponsors" for years, *Nezavisimaya gazeta* folded in May 1995 and resumed publication four months later thanks to an investment from the Obedinennyi Bank. Vitalii Tretyakov, the newspaper's editor, has admitted that his newspaper is "almost completely dependent" on structures linked to Berezovskii for funding.[21]

LogoVAZ owns shares in the glossy news magazine *Ogonek,*[22] and in 1997, Berezovskii helped finance the creation of *Novye izvestiya,* a newspaper staffed mainly by journalists who fled *Izvestiya* in July of that year, following conflicts with the newspaper's shareholders.

Media-Most

Vladimir Gusinskii's Media-Most holding company, founded in January 1997, manages one of Russia's most powerful media empires. Gusinskii, founder of the Most-Bank, became involved in the media world earlier than most other Russian businessmen. Most-Bank founded the television network NTV and the newspaper *Segodnya* in 1993, and expanded its holdings in subsequent years. In early 1997, Gusinskii gave up his post as chief executive of the bank to concentrate on running Media-Most. He controls about 70 percent of the shares in the holding company. Other shareholders include senior NTV executives and journalists.

NTV is the flagship of the Media-Most empire. Although it was initially on the air for just six hours a day and only accessible to viewers in parts of European Russia, NTV quickly became the country's most influential private television network. Its bold coverage of the war in Chechnya cemented its reputation.[23] Throughout most of 1995, NTV cultivated a defiant stance vis-à-vis the authorities, ridiculing official lies concerning President Yeltsin's health and criminal cases opened against the network in connection with the satirical puppet program *Kukly* and an NTV journalist's interview with a Chechen hostage-taker.[24]

Recognizing the credibility NTV had established with its audience, Yeltsin's administration actively sought the network's support before the 1996 presidential campaign. An informal deal struck in January 1996 with the State Communications Committee allowed the network to pay government rates for transmission services, rather than the much higher commercial fees charged to other private broadcasters.[25] Two months after the presidential election, NTV was granted a license to broadcast around the clock. That license also enabled NTV to reach all major cities nationwide, and two years later, it was still the only private television network in Russia with the technical capacity to do so. In late 1996, NTV launched the satellite networks NTV-Plyus and NTV-Kino. Igor Malashenko, first deputy chairman of the Media-Most board of directors and previously the top executive at NTV, said that NTV was running a profit in 1998, before the August economic crisis.[26] Not only did the network attract healthy advertising revenues, it continued to pay lower transmission fees than other private networks.

Media-Most also controls the regional television network TNT Teleset, which started broadcasting in January 1998. More than 70 private television stations signed partnership agreements with TNT, some of them in major cities such as Yekaterinburg, Novosibirsk, Tomsk, and Krasnoyarsk. By February 1998, the estimated number of potential TNT viewers was 30 million.[27]

. Another important electronic media outlet controlled by Media-Most is the radio station Ekho Moskvy. Founded in 1990, the station sold a controlling stake to the Most Group in 1994. Its news and interview programs attract a wide audience in the Russian capital and can be heard in major cities in European Russia and Siberia. Ekho Moskvy is often the first news organization to report a story: For instance, in August 1996 the station broke the story that Yeltsin had undergone a brief examination in the hospital, contrary to official statements that claimed he had made a one-day trip to the Valdai resort. (The flip side of this distinction is that Ekho Moskvy occasionally "breaks" stories that turn out to be false, such as a May 1998 report that the IMF had agreed to a $10 billion bailout package for Russia.)

Through the Sem Dnei publishing house, Media-Most also owns the daily newspaper *Segodnya,* the weekly news magazine *Itogi* (a joint venture with the U.S. publication *Newsweek*), the entertainment magazines *Sem'dnei* and *Karavan istorii,* and the television guide *Karavan. Itogi* was launched in spring 1996 and quickly became influential. In September of that year it broke the story that Yeltsin had agreed to have open-heart surgery.

A few other newspapers have received funding from the Media-Most empire, although they are not part of its holdings. Media-Most has invested in the weekly *Novaya gazeta* and the monthly *Iskusstvo kino*. Most-Bank services the accounts of the weekly *Obshchaya gazeta* and provided a capital investment in 1997 to allow that newspaper to revamp its format.

Oneksimbank

Oneksimbank, founded by Vladimir Potanin, was a relative latecomer to the media market. The bank's media holdings are mostly concentrated in newspapers and magazines. In the first half of 1997, Oneksimbank acquired significant stakes in the dailies *Izvestiya* and *Komsomol'skaya pravda*. Unlike most Moscow-based newspapers, both of those dailies are distributed outside the capital and reach hundreds of thousands of readers. Still, their nationwide readership is small compared to their Soviet-era audience, which numbered in the tens of millions.

The share purchases by Oneksimbank were followed by changes in senior personnel at both newspapers. The longtime editor-in-chief of *Komsomol'skaya pravda* was replaced because he had favored selling shares in the newspaper to Gazprom rather than to Potanin's bank. In May 1997, *Izvestiya* journalists initially welcomed share purchases by Sidanko (an oil company then controlled by Oneksimbank). They anticipated that the bank would support the editorial staff in their clashes with managers of LUKoil, which already owned a major stake in the newspaper. (At the time, LUKoil was considered close to Prime Minister Viktor Chernomyrdin, whereas Potanin was an ally of First Deputy Prime Minister Anatolii Chubais, whom *Izvestiya* had long championed.) Instead, LUKoil and Oneksimbank used their majority on the newspaper's new board of directors to oust editor-in-chief Igor Golembiovskii. He and more than two dozen of his colleagues left *Izvestiya* in July 1997, and most stuck with Golembiovskii, who soon founded *Novye izvestiya*.[28]

In September 1997, Oneksimbank founded a new daily newspaper, *Russkii telegraf*. It was fully owned by the bank, and devoted particular attention to economic and business reporting.[29] Oneksimbank has owned a 34 percent stake in the business weekly *Ekspert* since that magazine began publication in 1996, and finances the news agency Prime, which concentrates on business news. The bank's other major holding in the print media is a 34 percent stake in the Segodnya Press publishing house. Segodnya Press and the French publishing group Hachette are involved in managing the radio station Radio Europe-Plus (Evropa-Plyus) and monthly magazines including *Elle, Parents,* and several regional Russian publications.

Stolichnyi Savings Bank–Agroprombank (SBS-Agro)

Stolichnyi Savings Bank, renamed SBS-Agro after it acquired the previously state-owned Agroprombank in late 1996, has kept a lower profile than other banks involved in the media business. It is a member of a four-bank consortium that owns a combined 38 percent of shares in ORT, the Channel 1 television network.[30] SBS-Agro does not own shares in any Russian publication but has provided financial support to several—most notably, it has extended credit to the Kommersant publishing house, which produces *Kommersant-Daily,* the weekly magazines *Kommersant-Vlast'* and *Kommersant-Den'gi,* and entertainment magazines *Domovoi* and *Avtopilot.* As of early 1998, Kommersant had reportedly repaid its loans from SBS-Agro.[31] SBS has provided some funding to the weekly newspaper *Novaya gazeta* and to *Sel'skaya zhizn',* a newspaper oriented toward rural readers, whose editorial policy was sympathetic to the Communist-allied Agrarian Party of Russia. SBS-Agro has also funded the obscure Moscow local radio station Radio NSN and its accompanying news agency, called the National Information Agency.

Menatep Group

The Menatep Bank, founded by Mikhail Khodorkovskii, has relatively few media holdings. It is one of four banks that collectively own 38 percent of ORT shares. Menatep also owns a 10 percent stake in the Dutch-based company Independent Media, publisher of the English-language daily *Moscow Times,* the English-language weekly *St. Petersburg Times,* the Russian-language business weekly *Kapital,* and Russian editions of various monthly magazines, including *Playboy* and *Cosmopolitan.* Menatep also owned a controlling stake in the weekly *Literaturnaya gazeta* until the Metropolis publishing house, which is linked to the Moscow city government, purchased that newspaper in the spring of 1998. In addition, Menatep provides subsidies to the advertising trade magazine *Reklamnyi mir.*

Khodorkovskii's Rosprom financial-industrial group, of which Menatep is a division, has had informal ties to the state-run news agency ITAR-TASS. Leonid Nevzlin, a former top executive at Rosprom, became deputy head of ITAR-TASS in September 1997. Nevzlin remained on the board of directors of Menatep and Rosprom after his appointment to the news agency and returned to work with the Rosprom group full-time in autumn 1998.

Alfa Bank

Mikhail Fridman and Petr Aven are the top executives at Alfa Bank, which owns no print media but has a wide-ranging and growing involvement in Russia's electronic media. Already a member of the banking consortium that owns a combined 38 percent of ORT, Alfa Bank created its own media holding company called Alfa-TV in July 1998. Its partners in the holding company are the U.S.-registered firm Story First and Sergei Lisovskii's advertising agency Premier SV. Story First owns a substantial stake in the Moscow local television station STS, which broadcasts mostly foreign-produced programs in Moscow and a number of other Russian cities. Premier SV obtained exclusive rights to sell advertising on ORT in 1995 and owns controlling stakes in a Moscow television station called

Channel 31, a number of regional television networks, and the entertainment music channel Muz TV. Outside the media world, Lisovskii is best known as one of the two Yeltsin campaign operatives who were caught carrying US$538,000 in cash out of the Russian government's headquarters in June 1996.[32]

Gazprom

The natural gas monopoly Gazprom controls one of Russia's most extensive media empires.[33] Although it has been involved in the media business since the early 1990s, Gazprom has recently placed new emphasis on this sector of its activities. In December 1997, the company created a new subsidiary, Gazprom-Media, to manage its media holdings. Viktor Ilyushin, a longtime, high-ranking Yeltsin aide who briefly held the post of first deputy prime minister, was the first president of Gazprom-Media. He described the holding company's purpose as "to legitimate [uzakonit'] our close relations with certain media."[34] The more experienced Sergei Zverev replaced Ilyushin in June 1998. Whereas Ilyushin had never worked in the media world before heading Gazprom-Media, Zverev had previously served as vice president at Media-Most.

Gazprom purchased a 30 percent stake in the private network NTV in 1996. Without the gas company's investment, the financing of NTV satellite networks would not have been possible. Gazprom has owned a 3 percent stake in ORT since that network took over Channel 1 broadcasting from Ostankino, but it has not exerted significant influence on ORT's editorial policy.

Gazprom is financing the Prometei television production project, which involves developing a corporate communication system dating from the Soviet period into a network of small, regional television stations.[35] In more than 20 cities, Gazprom has transformed broadcasting centers that were created to serve the oil and gas sector into technically well-equipped television stations that broadcast their own programming. Although the quality of the programming is poor and some of the stations serve areas with very small populations, the project could nonetheless enhance Gazprom's political weight, and might also affect local and regional elections in areas where the gas monopoly is a major employer. In the words of former Gazprom-Media president Ilyushin, Gazprom is "not indifferent as to who will govern the regions, who will pass legislation, and, in general, what kind of government we will have."[36]

Gazprom also has links to numerous print media. In 1997 the company purchased a controlling stake in the daily *Rabochaya tribuna,* the name of which was subsequently shortened to *Tribuna.* Gazprom also provides financial support to the daily newspaper *Trud.* The company's influence extends further, if one takes into account the Moscow-based weeklies that are partly owned by banks in which Gazprom is a major shareholder. Inkombank, which sold a 25 percent stake to Gazprom in 1998, owns a stake in *Vek.* The National Reserve Bank, also partly owned by Gazprom, owns a stake in the business publication *Kompaniya.* Bank Imperial, which is believed to have close ties to the gas monopoly, owns a stake in

Profil'.[37] Outside Moscow, Gazprom finances more than 100 publications that are based at gas sector facilities.

LUKoil

Russia's largest oil company, LUKoil, has several holdings in the television business. It financed the creation of the TSN television production company, which produces news programs for the Moscow-based private network TV-6. In addition, LUKoil owns a 75 percent stake in the private network REN-TV, which is also based in Moscow but is seeking to expand its broadcasting range. LUKoil is rumored to own the AST satellite television network, but that rumor could not be independently confirmed.

LUKoil's holdings in print media are limited to a minority stake in the newspaper *Izvestiya,* purchased in November 1996. The company's relationship with that newspaper's staff drew widespread attention within Russia and abroad in spring 1997, after *Izvestiya* reprinted an unsubstantiated article from *Le Monde* alleging that Prime Minister Chernomyrdin had amassed a US$5 billion fortune.[38] Senior LUKoil executives, including president Vagit Alekperov, complained that the report damaged the company's reputation. *Izvestiya* journalists protested against LUKoil's attempted interference in the paper's editorial policy, and sold a large stake in the newspaper to Oneksimbank. Apparently stung by the bad publicity from that episode, LUKoil remained a major shareholder in *Izvestiya* but took a back seat to Oneksimbank concerning the management of the newspaper.[39]

Media Outside the Main Empires

A few Moscow-based newspapers are owned by publishing houses that are relatively independent of Russia's major financial-industrial groups. Of these, the most influential are *Argumenty i fakty, Moskovskie novosti,* and *Kommersant-Daily. Argumenty i fakty,* a weekly that reportedly survives on revenues from advertising and sales, is one of the most widely read newspapers in Russia. Though its circulation has decreased since the Gorbachev era, when it totaled 30 million, *Argumenty i fakty*'s readers still number in the millions each week. The newspaper is widely available nationwide, and unlike other Russian weeklies, produces several regional editions, tailored to readers in different parts of the vast Russian Federation.

Moskovskie novosti is another weekly that reached its peak circulation during the Gorbachev era. In recent years it has received funding from businessman Aleksandr Vanshtein, who is chairman of the Moskovskie Novosti publishing company. But compared to the top Moscow newspapers, *Moskovskie novosti* receives less outside funding and pays its journalists lower salaries. The Moskovskie Novosti publishing company founded the daily newspaper *Vremya-MN* in May 1998. Its editor-in-chief, Vladimir Gurevich, was a longtime deputy editor at *Moskovskie novosti*. But although the new paper and the established weekly share the same building and publisher, they have separate editorial staffs and sources of financing. *Vremya-MN*, though formally independent of government or business interests, receives financial assistance indirectly through banks with close links to the Central Bank (including Sberbank and Vneshtorgbank) as well as the Moscow Interbank Currency Exchange.

Kommersant-Daily, the flagship publication of the Kommersant publishing company, has an influential audience in Russia's political and business communities. It is available in some cities outside the capital, and some of its articles are reprinted in a number of regional newspapers. A frequent beneficiary of leaks, *Kommersant-Daily* publishes many exclusive stories. It does not cover its costs through sales and advertising, but neither is it dependent on any one investor. *Kommersant-Daily* was previously funded through credit from SBS-Agro, but the newspaper's more recent sources of financing are unknown. During the first half of 1998, rumors linked the newspaper to Alfa Bank and Oneksimbank, among others. In June and July 1998, the newspaper ran a series of articles and interviews publicizing its plans to sell shares to a dozen investors, but the high-profile recruiting effort fell flat.

The Political Uses of the Media

Corporate media ownership is by no means a uniquely Russian phenomenon. Private media exist in nearly every Western country, and in the United States even public television and radio rely in part on corporate sponsorship. Nor is the relationship between corporate ownership and media bias a uniquely Russian concern. The study of how media owners can influence the tone and content of news coverage has spawned a vast scholarly literature.

However, in contrast to the media markets of Western countries, Russian corporate owners have been willing to subsidize loss-making media indefinitely, in the hope of securing political advantage. The media's financial constraints did not significantly influence journalists' behavior during the 1996 presidential campaign, because the business and journalistic communities concurred on the need to reelect Yeltsin. Moreover, staff at some outlets obtained formal assurances that investors would not interfere in the editorial process. The upheaval at *Izvestiya* in spring and summer 1997 (described above), following clashes with shareholders, signaled that financial constraints had caused a real erosion of journalists' autonomy; but the extent to which corporate-owned media would be used in disputes among business and political rivals became apparent only later.

Privatization Battles Spark Information War

Within a year of the presidential election, the grand coalition of businessmen who supported Yeltsin had fallen apart. When Oneksimbank was denied a chance to bid for a controlling stake in the oil company Sibneft in May 1997, a minor skirmish ensued in the press. The weekly *Ekspert*, partly owned by Oneksimbank, assailed the "scandalous" auction procedures, and newspapers linked to Security Council Deputy Secretary Boris Berezovskii *(Nezavisimaya gazeta)* and the bank SBS-Agro *(Kommersant-Daily)* defended the conduct of the auction and criticized Oneksimbank. Both Berezovskii and SBS-Agro head Aleksandr Smolenskii were associated with the company running the auction as well as the company that submitted the winning bid, which was lower than what Oneksimbank was willing to pay for the Sibneft stake.[40]

Sibneft was just one oil company, and not Russia's largest. The all-out information war between rival business groups did not break out until the government auctioned off a larger prize: 25 percent of the shares in the telecommunications monopoly holding company Svyazinvest. In late July 1997, a consortium led by Oneksimbank (and including George Soros's Quantum Fund) won the Svyazinvest auction. Berezovskii and Media-Most head Gusinskii were involved in the consortium that submitted the losing bid, and correspondents for ORT and *Nezavisimaya gazeta* (funded by LogoVAZ), as well as NTV, Ekho Moskvy, and *Segodnya* (owned by Media-Most), devoted unprecedented attention to the sale. First Deputy Prime Ministers Chubais and Nemtsov were the highest-ranking targets of the media criticism—Chubais, because of his influence over privatization policy, and Nemtsov, because he took the lead in defending the Svyazinvest sale and attacking those whom he accused of stirring up "media hysteria" surrounding the auction. The media criticism intensified after Oneksimbank won another controversial privatization auction, this one for the metals giant Norilsk Nickel.[41] Newspapers partly owned by Oneksimbank vigorously defended Chubais and Nemtsov and published attacks of their own, first against Berezovskii, and later against Prime Minister Chernomyrdin, who was considered close to Berezovskii.[42]

When the media criticism still had not died down six weeks later, Yeltsin summoned six businessmen to the Kremlin and urged them to "end their battle against Chubais, Nemtsov, and the government."[43] But the information war set off by the Svyazinvest sale never ended. Yeltsin's dismissal of Berezovskii from the Security Council in early November (either a loss of a tireless negotiator for peace in Chechnya or a victory over the "oligarchs," depending on which television network one watched) only raised the stakes. Within ten days, media linked to Berezovskii and Gusinskii were flogging new allegations against Chubais. Journalist Aleksandr Minkin revealed during an interview on Ekho Moskvy radio that Chubais and several associates each had received a $90,000 payment from a publishing company (for writing chapters for a book on privatization, which at the time had not yet been published) that had ties with Oneksimbank. The resultant scandal cost three high-ranking officials their jobs. Yeltsin also stripped Chubais of the finance portfolio, although he allowed him to retain the post of first deputy prime minister.

Periodic exchanges of fire continued through the winter, with state-owned Russian Television (RTR) and newspapers financed by Oneksimbank decrying attempts by the "oligarchs" to bend the government to their will (and conveniently failing to mention Chubais's role in creating the oligarchs' wealth and influence to begin with). The "young reformers" (code words for Chubais and Nemtsov) continued to receive mostly negative coverage in media outlets linked to Berezovskii and Gusinskii. For example, in December 1997, NTV, ORT, and *Nezavisimaya gazeta* devoted extensive attention to allegations that Chubais had leaked sensitive information to the International Monetary Fund and the World Bank.[44]

That politically slanted news coverage was now business as usual and not merely a consequence of one or two lightning rods in the government became clear after Yeltsin sacked both Chernomyrdin and Chubais in his sweeping March 1998 government reshuffle. Not surprisingly, criticism of the short-lived government of Prime Minister Sergei Kirienko, ousted after the August 1998 financial collapse, was most often found in the media that had previously targeted Chubais, whereas those outlets that had defended Chubais stood firmly behind the new government.

Biased reporting was by no means restricted to issues in which media owners had a direct financial stake. For instance, the coal miners' blockade of several major railroads in spring and summer 1998—the largest wave of social protest since 1991—evoked sympathetic coverage in some outlets, which depicted the blockades as proof of the government's incompetence and lack of political support.[45] But other newspapers argued that government policy was not to blame for the miners' problems; these papers pointed the finger at mismanagement and corruption within the coal industry. Some compared the railroad blockades to "terrorist" acts that would drag down other sectors of the economy, and suggested that unnamed political forces with their own agenda were egging on the miners.[46] In that vein, a prominent political commentator for *Russkii telegraf* accused NTV of broadcasting Soviet-style "propaganda" in its coverage of the miners' protests.[47] He was incensed by television reports in which would-be travelers at Moscow's Yaroslavl train station expressed support for the miners and called for changes in the composition of the government.

The biggest media firestorm during Kirienko's tenure occurred when government officials threatened to seize Gazprom's assets if the gas monopoly did not pay its taxes in full. Media linked financially to Gazprom, already critical of Kirienko's government, responded with a deluge of criticism.[48] NTV took the lead, comparing the government's threats toward Gazprom with Bolshevik methods of rule. The network's correspondents also played up the government's debts to Gazprom and portrayed the tax policy as inept and economically counterproductive—all without informing viewers that Gazprom owned a 30 percent stake in NTV.[49] Gazprom head Rem Vyakhirev received friendly treatment during a lengthy interview on NTV the day the story broke. When Kirienko appeared on NTV a few days later to defend the government's policy, the interviewer peppered him with hostile questions.

During the scandal surrounding Gazprom's tax payments, as in many domestic political controversies after mid-1997, 51 percent state-owned ORT and fully state-owned RTR were on opposite sides. This disparity suggests that the form of ownership of Russian media is less important than the degree of the media's financial dependence. Slanted news coverage tends to reflect the interests of those paying the bills, and for that reason, Berezovskii's viewpoint (as opposed to the official "state" position) came through most often on ORT's news and analytical programs. ORT and RTR provided similar coverage of some issues—for instance, both networks usually depicted the Communist Party and State Duma in an unflattering light. But whereas ORT reports often portrayed Chubais, Nemtsov, and Kirienko as political lightweights, RTR tirelessly defended the embattled ministers. The disparity was also striking in the networks' coverage of the Krasnoyarsk gubernatorial campaign in April and May 1998. Berezovskii supported Aleksandr Lebed's candidacy, presumably reasoning that if Lebed retained his political viability, he would eventually draw votes away from Moscow Mayor Luzhkov in a presidential election.[50] ORT's coverage of the Krasnoyarsk campaign favored Lebed, while reports on RTR were slanted toward the Kremlin-backed incumbent, Valerii Zubov.

Muckrakers or Hired Guns?

Among the most sensational media reports in any country are those implicating senior officials in personal corruption or criminal wrongdoing. In some countries, such allegations—if proven true—translate into acclaim and awards for the "watchdogs" who brought the stories to public attention. In contrast, Russian journalists who write exposés of public officials are often held in contempt by their colleagues, who assume they are hired guns. To understand why, it is worth examining the use of incriminating stories in the Russian media.

On a few occasions, the media have lent credibility to false accusations against prominent figures for the sake of political expediency. The smear campaign against Aleksandr Lebed shortly before and after he was sacked as Security Council secretary stands out in this regard.[51] Newspapers and television networks that just a few months earlier had given Lebed favorable exposure publicized unsubstantiated (and implausible) allegations that he was preparing a coup and his supporters were forming armed resistance units. Media campaigns of this type are neither good journalism nor healthy for the political discourse.

But evaluating reports that publicize true allegations is not so simple. Aleksandr Minkin, who has broken several major stories, has argued that the public has a right to know about high-level misconduct, no matter what ulterior motives cause evidence of misconduct to be leaked to journalists. Yet *kompromat* (incriminating information) has a way of appearing at remarkably convenient times. Minkin's story exposing corruption in the circle of former presidential bodyguard Aleksandr Korzhakov appeared shortly after Korzhakov's dismissal in the middle of the 1996 presidential election; presumably, those who had engineered

Korzhakov's dismissal feared that Yeltsin might hire back his longtime confidant.[52] Minkin's story revealing that First Deputy Prime Minister Nemtsov briefly held up the publication of a presidential decree for personal reasons appeared a week after the Svyazinvest auction, which Nemtsov had strongly supported.[53]

Above all, the media's treatment of allegations against Chubais raises doubts about what drives editorial policy at leading media outlets. As long as privatization spoils were being distributed amicably, most Russian media did not accuse Chubais of favoring well-connected banks or presiding over crooked privatization auctions (the main exceptions being communist and nationalist opposition newspapers, such as *Sovetskaya Rossiya*).[54] Minkin's revelation that Chubais and others took payoffs of $90,000 received enormous attention in November 1997, and few would argue that it was not in the public's interest to know about the apparent bribery.[55] Yet four months earlier (before the Svyazinvest controversy), few media outlets followed up on allegations that Chubais was the beneficiary of an interest-free $3 million loan from Stolichnyi Savings Bank, which eventually won control of a coveted state property, Agroprombank.[56]

Some targets of media attacks object to the political use of the media only when they are on the receiving end. Chubais complained bitterly about the oligarchs' campaign to discredit him, yet he was reportedly involved in spreading false stories about alleged Communist paramilitary units during the 1996 presidential campaign. Later that year, according to *Nezavisimaya gazeta* editor Tretyakov, Chubais urged newspaper editors to go along with the campaign to discredit Lebed.[57]

Viewing the glass as half full, one might argue that thanks to the information war, Russians who pay attention to a variety of news sources are well-informed about their leaders' activities. Without the sustained media attacks on Oneksimbank and Chubais, the public might never have learned (through a retaliatory article in an Oneksimbank-financed newspaper) that Chernomyrdin unlawfully issued government loan guarantees to a satellite television project involving Media-Most.[58]

But the selective nature of such journalism makes it hard to avoid the conclusion that the public learns about misconduct only if a particular media outlet or its owner has an ax to grind against the official in question. Journalist Leonid Krutakov, one of the authors of the *Izvestiya* article detailing Chubais's interest-free $3 million loan, left that newspaper soon after the story ran. He joined the staff of *Novye izvestiya* but was fired within months because he wrote an article for *Moskovskii komsomolets* that was highly critical of Berezovskii (a financial backer of *Novye izvestiya*). To complete the circle, Krutakov's dismissal was brought to public attention in an interview with *Komsomol'skaya pravda* (which was financed by Oneksimbank and therefore interested in discrediting Berezovskii).[59]

The experience of journalists like Krutakov fuels the cynical impression that media revelations serve primarily to score political points—especially since even the most damning media reports rarely lead to criminal investigations. It is not surprising that new bombshells are rarely hailed as courageous muckraking and usually give rise to the question of who stands to benefit.

Though the allegations contained in sensational reports are often newsworthy, the way such reports are used encourages ever more sophisticated attempts to manipulate media coverage. One of the most distasteful episodes involving the post-Soviet media was a fraudulent attempt to make political capital out of the death of journalist Andrei Fadin in a November 1997 car accident. Describing himself as a friend of Fadin's, journalist Sergei Mitrofanov tried to stir up suspicion surrounding the accident by claiming that the deceased had been working on an article containing damaging information about Berezovskii and Gusinskii. It turned out that the head of a think tank close to Chubais had given Mitrofanov a computer diskette with a copy of the alleged article (written on software used neither by Fadin nor his employer, *Obshchaya gazeta*).[60]

Journalists have not reached a consensus on what constitutes a legitimate use of the media to achieve political ends. Former ORT general director Sergei Blagovolin objected to his own network's negative coverage of Luzhkov and described ORT's weekly analytical program (home to some of Russia's most aggressive attack journalism) as "extremely destructive."[61] Lev Gushchin, former editor of the magazine *Ogonek,* accused Berezovskii of using the magazine to attack his political enemies. (Appropriately, he made that charge in a newspaper financed by Oneksimbank.[62]) Yet a few months later, in his new job as head of Metropolis, which manages various media financed by the Moscow city government, Gushchin acknowledged that one of his company's goals was to influence public opinion.[63]

Conclusion

The trends that shaped the Russian media in the mid- to late 1990s show no signs of abating. The economic crisis that began with the ruble collapse of August 1998 is likely to exacerbate the problems for media at the micro level. The advertising market has slumped, printing and production costs have risen further, and many citizens have seen their incomes decline, all of which will make self-sufficiency an unattainable goal for most media outlets. Yet even if the Russian economy remains unable to support truly independent media, the number of media outlets is unlikely to decrease to a level corresponding with consumer demand. Continuing economic problems may drive some publications out of business, and other media may be forced to find new sponsors, as established banks and corporations fall on hard times; but the media are simply too important a tool to be abandoned entirely to market forces.

Notes

1. For more on why Russian media are unable to support themselves financially, see Laura Belin, "The politicization and self-censorship of the Russian media," a paper pre-

sented at the annual conference of the American Association for the Advancement of Slavic Studies, at Seattle, Washington, in November 1997. The paper is available on line at www.rferl.org/nca/special/rumediapper/index.html.

2. For a detailed examination of the pervasive pro-Yeltsin and anti-Communist media coverage during the presidential campaign, see "Final report on the presidential election," published by the European Institute for the Media in 1996. Other aspects of the pro-Yeltsin media campaign are discussed in a series of Open Media Research Institute *Special Reports* on the presidential election, dated May–July 1996, available at www.omri.cz/Publications/RPE/Index.html, and in Laura Belin, "[Russia's] private media come full circle," *Transition,* vol. 2, no. 21, 18 October 1996, pp. 62–65.

3. The VTsIOM poll results were published in *Kommersant-Daily,* 29 August 1996, and *OMRI Daily Digest,* 25 September 1996.

4. J. A. Krosnick and L. A. Brannon, "The impact of the Gulf War on the ingredients of presidential evaluation: Multidimensional effects of political involvement," *American Political Science Review,* vol. 87, 1993, pp. 963–975; Krosnick and Brannon, "New evidence on news media priming: In 1992, it was the economy!" paper presented at the annual meeting of the American Association for Public Opinion Research, Chicago, 1995, cited in Joanne M. Miller and Jon A. Krosnick, "Anatomy of news media priming," in Shanto Iyengar and Richard Reeves, eds., *Do the Media Govern?* (Thousand Oaks, Calif.: Sage, 1997). Researchers have found evidence of agenda-setting by the media also during election campaigns in Japan and Spain: See Maxwell McCombs and George Estrada, "The news media and the pictures in our heads," in Iyengar and Reeves.

5. It was the recapture of Grozny by Chechen fighters, not pressure from journalists, that convinced key Russian officials that the war was unwinnable (Peter Rutland, "A fragile peace," *Transition,* vol. 2, no. 23, 15 November 1996, pp. 49–50).

6. See chapter 1 of Ellen Mickiewicz, *Changing Channels* (Oxford: Oxford University Press, 1997). A November 1997 TACIS survey in three Russian cities also found that nationwide television networks were the main source of news cited by respondents in Novgorod, Volgograd, and Rybinsk (Yaroslavl oblast). Stephen Whitefield of the University of Oxford directed the survey, and Vladimir Andreenkov conducted the fieldwork.

7. The editorial was signed by *Nezavisimaya gazeta* editor Vitalii Tretyakov and appeared on 10 July 1998.

8. Outside Moscow, the media market is quite diverse. In some regions of the Russian Federation, such as the republics of Bashkortostan, Kalmykiya, and Kabardino-Balkariya, the media are almost entirely under the political and financial control of the regional authorities. But many regions (e.g., Sverdlovsk, Novosibirsk, and Irkutsk oblasts) have thriving, privately owned media that present stiff competition to newspapers and television stations funded by the regional authorities. Information about the regional television market is available at the World Wide Web site of the nongovernmental organization Internews (www.internews.ru). For information about regional newspapers, see the September 1998 report by the Russian National Press Institute, available at www.nyu.edu/globalbeat/pubs/npi091698.html.

9. An earlier version of this section appeared as a special report by Floriana Fossato and Anna Kachkaeva, titled "Russian media empires IV," which was posted to the Radio Free Europe/Radio Liberty web site on 20 October 1998. It can be found at www.rferl.org/nca/special/rumedia4/index.html.

10. For information on the network's coverage during the early 1990s, see chapters 7 and 8 of Mickiewicz, *Changing Channels.* RTR's coverage of the 1995 parliamentary elections is described in chapter 6 of Laura Belin and Robert W. Orttung, *The Russian Parliamentary Elections of 1995: The Battle for the Duma* (Armonk, N.Y.: M.E. Sharpe, 1997).

11. The parliament had been without a newspaper since the government took over publication of *Rossiiskaya gazeta,* in the aftermath of the October 1993 shelling of the Supreme Soviet. During negotiations on the 1998 budget in late 1997, the government and Kremlin agreed to support the creation of *Parlamentskaya gazeta.*

12. *RFE/RL Newsline,* 18 February and 2 April 1998.

13. After Yeltsin fired him in December 1998, Komissar returned to Interfax.

14. After long denying that he harbored presidential ambitions, Luzhkov announced in October 1998 that he was prepared to seek the presidency in 2000 if no other suitable (in his view) candidate ran. He abandoned the idea after the party he created, Fatherland, did poorly in the December 1999 elections to the Duma.

15. In September 1998, thanks to a special resolution signed by Prime Minister Yevgenii Primakov, the Moscow government acquired control over one of Russia's largest presses, Moskovskaya Pravda. According to *Kommersant-Daily* (6 August 1998), the press services some 40 magazines and 128 newspapers. The paper said Luzhkov sought for six years to persuade the federal government to transfer control of the press to city authorities, but at several junctures Anatolii Chubais thwarted his efforts.

16. Interview by Anna Kachkaeva with Irina Lesnevskaya, chair and co-owner of REN-TV. According to Lesnevskaya, the loan was paid off in late 1997, when LUKoil purchased a 75 percent stake in the network.

17. *Kommersant-Daily,* 15 October 1997.

18. Anna Kachkaeva, "Ot Ostankino do ORT," special report for Radio Free Europe/Radio Liberty's Russian Service, broadcast on 5 August 1997. In November 1998, ORT general director Igor Shabdurasulov said that since the network's creation, private businesses had contributed some US$300 million toward its operating expenses, and state funding had been minimal.

19. *Kommersant-Daily,* 14 February 1998.

20. In September 1998, TV-6 introduced more prime-time political programming, fueling speculation that the network was gearing up for the 1999 and 2000 parliamentary and presidential campaigns.

21. See the commentaries by Tretyakov in *Nezavisimaya gazeta,* 19 December 1997 and 7 March 1998. Tretyakov vehemently denied that Berezovskii had any control over the content of articles published in the newspaper. In late summer 1998, Obedinennyi Bank's controlling stake in *Nezavisimaya gazeta* was transferred to the newly created NG Foundation, headed by Tretyakov.

22. A private communication with a former *Ogonek* journalist in summer 1998 suggested that Berezovskii had stopped funding that magazine, although that information could not be independently confirmed.

23. Mickiewicz analyzed NTV's Chechnya coverage in detail (see chapter 11 of *Changing Channels*). The impact of NTV's coverage of the early months of the war is discussed in *Zhurnalistika i voina,* published by the Russian-American Press and Information Center in Moscow in 1995.

24. The criminal investigations were closed without reaching trial (Belin, "[Russia's] private media come full circle").

25. The State Antimonopoly Committee sought to revoke that privilege in December 1997, but the following month Yeltsin signed a decree naming NTV as one of the nation-wide broadcasters entitled to pay government rates for transmission services. NTV also challenged the State Antimonopoly Committee's action in court; the Moscow Arbitration Court found in favor of the network in February 1998 (see *Kommersant-Daily,* 23 December 1997 and 22 January 1998, and ITAR-TASS, 11 February 1998).

26. Malashenko, interviewed by Anna Kachkaeva in September 1998.

27. Floriana Fossato and Anna Kachkaeva, "Russia: The origins of a media empire," feature for Radio Free Europe/Radio Liberty, 13 March 1998, available at www.rferl.org/nca/features/1998/03/F.RU.980313140126.html. In interviews following the devaluation of the ruble in August 1998, Malashenko said the economic crisis had placed great constraints on TNT, because the collapse of the advertising market left few re-sources available for developing the regional television network.

28. See Laura Belin, "Changes in editorial policy and ownership at *Izvestiya*," appendix to "Politicization and self-censorship in the Russian media," available on line at www.rferl.org/nca/special/rumediapaper/appendix2.html.

29. *Russkii telegraf* ceased to exist in September 1998, after the ruble devaluation, hav-ing been merged with *Izvestiya.* Although some employees of the defunct newspaper were able to stay on, their salaries were significantly reduced.

30. SBS-Agro was one of the first Russian banks to fail to meet its obligations in August 1998. It is not clear what happened subsequently to SBS-Agro's stake in ORT.

31. According to a senior editor at Kommersant publishing, in an interview with Floriana Fossato.

32. Lisovskii and his colleague, Arkadii Yevstafev, were transporting the money to Yeltsin's campaign headquarters. They never faced criminal charges, and an investigation into the incident was quietly closed in April 1997.

33. For a more detailed discussion of Gazprom's media assets, see Fossato and Kachkaeva, "Russia: The origins of a media empire."

34. Interview with Ilyushin, *Kommersant-Daily,* 13 January 1998.

35. LUKoil may also be involved in the Prometei project.

36. Interview with Ilyushin, *Kommersant-Daily,* 13 January 1998.

37. Since the Russian Central Bank revoked the licenses of Bank Imperial and Inkombank in the aftermath of the August 1998 economic crisis, the future of *Kompaniya* and *Profil'* is unclear.

38. The conflict surrounding *Izvestiya* is described in detail in Belin, "Politicization and self-censorship."

39. After *Izvestiya* merged with the year-old daily *Russkii telegraf* in September 1998, Mikhail Kozhokin became the editor-in-chief of the new *Izvestiya.* He was previously in charge of Oneksimbank's media strategies and chaired *Izvestiya*'s board of directors.

40. "Struggle over control of oil companies reviving," Foreign Broadcast Information Service analysis, 5 June 1997.

41. For example, Russian Public Television, *Vremya,* 26 July 1997; NTV, *Itogi,* 28 September 1997; *Nezavisimaya gazeta*, 29 July, 30 July, 13 September, 26 September, 27 September 1997; *Segodnya,* 28 July, 30 July, 7 August, 12 August, 13 August, 27 September 1997.

42. *Izvestiya,* 31 July, 11 September 1997; *Komsomol'skaya pravda,* 30 July, 1 August, 9 August, 20 August, 4 September, 2 October 1997.

43. See *RFE/RL Newsline,* 15 and 16 September 1997.

44. See *RFE/RL Newsline,* 23 December 1997.

45. For example, NTV, 20 and 21 May 1998; *Nezavisimaya gazeta,* 19 May, 21 May, and 14 July 1998; *Trud,* 21 May 1998; *Tribuna,* 8 July 1998.

46. See *Rossiiskaya gazeta,* 7 July 1998; *Izvestiya,* 20 May, 3 July, 10 July, and 15 July 1998; *Russkii telegraf,* 19 May and 21 May 1998.

47. Maksim Sokolov accused NTV of editing the segments in a misleading way, omitting the comments of travelers who were furious with the miners for causing delays (*Russkii telegraf,* 21 May 1998).

48. Prime Minister Chernomyrdin had headed Gazprom before joining the government and was viewed as the gas monopoly's protector during his five years as prime minister. From May through July 1997, the Gazprom-financed newspapers *Trud* and *Tribuna* printed more than a dozen articles attacking the Kirienko government's "anti-crisis program" and assailing the International Monetary Fund's role in Russia. The newspapers accused the government of following disastrous IMF prescriptions for Russia and of seeking to break up Gazprom, a charge government officials denied.

49. Near the beginning of a lengthy dispatch on the Gazprom controversy for the 5 July 1998 edition of *Itogi,* NTV correspondent Yevgenii Revenko blamed the conflict surrounding Gazprom for losses on the Russian stock market and the likely failure of an auction for a controlling stake in the Rosneft oil company. He added: "Deputy Prime Minister Boris Nemtsov announced that 'the government must be strong.' But here it should be added that the government does not have the right to be stupid."

50. Berezovskii explained his reasoning in an interview with NTV on 14 April 1998.

51. See David Hoffman, "Russia's evolving TV targeted Lebed; media barons launched on-air smear campaign to help Yeltsin," *Washington Post,* 19 October 1996; and Laura Belin, "Media campaign against Lebed intensifies," *OMRI Analytical Brief,* 18 October 1996.

52. Minkin's report appeared alongside an incriminating transcript of an interview with former National Sports Fund Chairman Boris Fedorov in *Novaya gazeta,* 8 July 1996.

53. That time, Minkin's article accompanied an incriminating transcript of a telephone conversation between Nemtsov and advertising executive Lisovskii (*Novaya gazeta,* 4 August 1997).

54. When Yeltsin named Chubais as his chief of staff soon after the presidential election, a *Nezavisimaya gazeta* headline called the appointment an "almost ingenious political move" by Yeltsin. NTV and many other Moscow-based media also gave Chubais glowing coverage during the months after the presidential election.

55. Chubais sued Minkin and Ekho Moskvy for alleging that the payments were bribes, but a court rejected his lawsuit, and a higher court rejected his subsequent appeal (*RFE/RL Newsline,* 29 April and 13 July 1998).

56. Those allegations were the subject of a lengthy article in *Izvestiya* on 1 July 1997.

57. *Nezavisimaya gazeta,* 7 March 1998. Tretyakov claimed that Chubais warned newspaper editors that if they did not go along with the campaign against Lebed, "bones would be broken."

58. *Komsomol'skaya pravda,* 2 October 1997.

59. *Komsomol'skaya pravda,* 29 October 1997.

60. In addition, Fadin's widow and colleagues said the article was not written in his style, and that having just returned to Moscow from abroad before his death, Fadin would

not have had time to write the article in question. See Tom Warner, "Russia loses a rarity," *Transitions,* January 1998, p. 7.

61. *OMRI Daily Digest,* 27 February 1997, and *RFE/RL Newsline,* 6 August 1997.

62. Gushchin interview, *Komsomol'skaya pravda,* 14 February 1998.

63. Interview with Gushchin, *Kommersant-Daily,* 12 August 1998.

CHAPTER 3

Moscow City Management:
A New Form of
Russian Capitalism?

Virginie Coulloudon

No city projects a more positive image than Moscow, both within and beyond the Russian Federation. The Russian capital, recently renovated and repainted, shows off its riches almost arrogantly. Ambitious building projects succeed one another. Following both Russian and Soviet traditions, Moscow is now a giant shop window, something that would have seemed impossible five years ago. In 1998 the city's projected budget was slightly in surplus, with a projected revenue of US$396 million, of which $25 million was expected to come from the city's most fashionable hotels.[1]

The Moscow municipal government offers several explanations for this outstanding achievement. According to one explanation, it was the product of a solid and coherent team. Moscow Mayor Yurii Luzhkov's aides are said to be perfect examples of devotion to their boss, in a solidarity that has earned Luzhkov the nickname of "clan leader."

However, a study of the biographies of this team reveals that most of them previously were closer to Russian President Boris Yeltsin than to Luzhkov. Vladimir Resin, Luzhkov's first deputy in charge of construction, had a privileged relationship with Yeltsin dating back to 1985–1987, when Yeltsin was still the first secretary of Moscow's Communist Party committee. The same was true of Petr Aksenov (prefect of the southwestern municipal district), Aleksei Ishchuk (prefect of the Zelenograd district), Yurii Korostelev (Moscow's finance minister), Yurii Roslyak (Luzhkov's deputy in charge of economics), and Luzhkov's first deputy Valerii Shantsev, formerly first secretary of the Perovo district's Party committee. Aleksandr Muzikantskii, prefect of Moscow's first district, was a member of Yeltsin's team during the 1989 legislative campaign. The prefect of the western district, Aleksei Bryachikhin, was selected by Yeltsin to head the Sevastopol district when the Russian president was still the Party boss in Moscow. In return, Bryachikhin set up supporting committees and organized demonstrations for Yeltsin during the 1991 presidential campaign. As for Luzhkov, he was tapped by Yeltsin and Moscow mayor Gavriil Popov to become the latter's deputy in 1991. Despite repeated attempts by the city parliament (Mossovet) to organize new elections and elect alternative candidates, Luzhkov was promoted to acting mayor by presidential decree after Popov resigned in June 1992.[2]

These links between Yeltsin and the Moscow team made sense in the tense political environment that followed the collapse of the Soviet regime. During these years of confrontation between the executive power and the Supreme Soviet, Yeltsin needed to avoid political and social instability in the federal capital. Predictably, he decided to co-opt the city leaders and offer the municipality unprecedented privileges in return for its wholehearted support.

This explains Moscow's subsequent economic well-being. It was precisely because it was granted a "special status" within the Russian Federation that Moscow was in a position to develop its own legislation and economic program, both of which sometimes contradict federal laws.[3] Such status gave Luzhkov full liberty to manage the capital's budget without any transparency, using secret funds, and to consolidate the municipality's control over the city's most profitable economic sectors.

This chapter is aimed at deciphering the Moscow city government's realpolitik. Through carefully crafted legislation and a huge municipal police force, Luzhkov transformed a territory into an industry during the first years of Yeltsin's regime and began using his financial power to influence political decision making. A potential contender on the eve of new presidential elections, Luzhkov needed to invest in profitable economic sectors in order to collect both money and votes. So far, his image among Moscow voters has been highly positive. But the industry he controls has inevitably the limits of his territory; and his management practices were challenged by a serious financial crisis even before the August 1998 crash.

Regulation Means Control

So far no one has managed to produce convincing evidence that Luzhkov has connections to Moscow's criminal elements. Mafia management of the city is still a myth. Neither Luzhkov nor any other key officials of the Moscow government appear to have acted illegally, if only because they write most of the relevant laws and get them approved by the local parliament. Whenever the mayor and his subordinates want the laws changed, they are changed. This legal flexibility has allowed the municipality to buy up the city's most lucrative businesses. By exerting administrative control over the "private" sector, the municipality is progressively turning Moscow's territory into a huge source of revenue, allowing in only investors who are willing to contribute to the municipality's enrichment.

Take the example of the death industry: Among the first economic sectors bought up by the municipality were funeral parlors. With a population of 9 million people and a monthly death rate of around 12,000, Moscow has a funeral market worth $1 million a month. On April 9, 1997, a "law on undertakers and funerals" passed its first reading in the Moscow parliament. This law, proposed by parliamentary deputy Anatolii Korotich, amounted to a death warrant for independent funeral homes in Moscow. It provided that the municipality's stake in private funeral homes' capital should not be less than 50 percent. When the law was adopted, Ritual Services (Ritualnye Uslugi) was the only company in conformity with the new legislation: One of its main shareholders was the municipal company Ritual, which owned 63 cemeteries and three crematoria.

It was no secret to its competitors that Ritual Services was seeking a monopoly of the funeral market in Moscow. As the weekly magazine *Kommersant* explained, in 1993 the company had tried to launch an advertising campaign in all the city hospitals, but the municipal health department objected. The company then decided to print death certificates with the addresses and phone numbers of its subsidiaries listed on the back. From 1994 to 1996, around 80 percent of the funeral market was in the hands of Ritual Services. The other companies fought back and regained 43 percent of the market, leaving Ritual Services only 8 percent.[4] The 1997 law adopted by the Moscow parliament allowed Ritual Services to take back some of this ground. Korotich did not even try to conceal the fact that the draft law was written with the help of the company's attorneys.[5]

In February 1997 the State Antimonopoly Committee opened an inquiry on Ritual Services, charging that it held an illegal monopoly of certain funerary services, particularly the registration of cremations. But the company managed to prove that it was authorized to offer such services by a city order issued on October 17, 1995. The Antimonopoly Committee then dropped its charges. Such methods of economic management are commonly used in the Russian capital. Since every transaction is carried out in compliance with local laws, it is impossible to accuse the Moscow municipality of illegal practices. But one should always keep in mind that the control exerted by the city government over the economy was made possible precisely because the local leaders benefited from tailor-made legislation that they themselves had written.

A Lack of Transparency in the Budget

It has generally been thought that Moscow's privatization program, which differs from the federal one, has been the city's main source of revenue. As Maxim Boycko showed in his study of Russia's privatization policy, the federal government planned in 1992 to transfer 25,000 medium and large enterprises to private ownership. Rather than individually negotiate the sale of these firms, however, the government decided to sell them at the lowest possible price in order to divest itself of them as quickly as possible and thus shed the burden of subsidizing them.[6] Concerned to educate a population new to a market economy, the federal government's program was also intended to multiply the number of shareholders by distributing privatization vouchers to Russian citizens, which they could use to bid for shares in firms.

The Moscow city government had very different priorities. It did not care about the education of its population and was confident that the first foreign investments in Russia would be made inside its territory, because it was the capital of the federation. Moscow officials were willing to wait for the market to yield high prices, which would help them finance both their social policy and the reconstruction of the city. Using the image of Moscow as Russia's shop window, as well as the capital's privileged status, they provoked a privatization war with the federal government in 1993, claiming ownership rights over some of the city's real estate. Luzhkov argued that one should not sell buildings and factories cheaply that would be worth ten times more once the "transition period" was over. Unlike the federal government, the Moscow city government restricted foreign investors' access and banned private ownership of land.[7] It also gave itself the legal prerogative of vetoing any privatization deal it did not like, allowing it essentially to select investors.

Systematic control over the privatization process was considered by the municipality as a legitimate way to exert control over the capital's economy. This control appeared first and foremost through the administrative management of the private sector. It is the municipality that decides to whom loans will be granted. And it is no secret that in Moscow, investors have to go through administrative procedures that do not exist in federal law. Among other things, they have to prove that the company in which they want to invest has been audited and that its potential market has been officially assessed. The justification given by the municipality is that commercial monopolies must be prevented from forming. Potential investors also have to submit an "ecological" survey of the company. Needless to say, the experts authorized to conduct ecological surveys are carefully chosen by the municipality. Such practices not only represent a significant source of revenue but they also allow the city to monitor the entire privatization process and to handpick the bidders.

The reformist team in the Yeltsin administration on occasion accused the mayor of Moscow of trying to make a personal fortune by selling municipal real estate at the highest possible price, and alleged corruption in Luzhkov's government. The municipality denied such charges, arguing that privatization was crucial for financing the city's budget and that consequently the selling price of real estate could not be lowered.[8]

Despite the municipality's claim, privatization was not the city's main source of revenue. Since the Moscow real estate market is overheated, Russian and foreign businessmen have only invested in the city's center, leaving other areas without enough income. Experts close to former acting prime minister Yegor Gaidar argue that Moscow's main source of income derived from the peculiarities of the city's budget, which was managed with the utmost secrecy. According to them, this secrecy has allowed the municipality to use secret, extrabudgetary, "charity funds."

The Moscow city government admits to around 150 such funds. Gaidar's team of economists, in contrast, has identified more than 300 of them and claims that most of these funds are in fact bank accounts set up within municipal departments.[9] The municipality distributes these charity funds and denies the federal government any control over them. Federal legislation requires that these sums, which may amount to US$400 million, should be properly spent as provided for in the initial statute on nonbudgetary funds, for education, culture, or employment. But the law is rarely observed.[10] The Federal Accounting Office reported in 1997 that the municipal employment fund had invested 8 million new rubles as founding capital in various private companies and banks, and that it had loaned nearly 190 million additional rubles to various enterprises that had yet to repay them.[11]

According to the city government, these charity funds are financed partly by the city budget (although federal laws forbid this) but mostly by private funds. What city officials call private donations are in reality a kind of tax paid by Russian and foreign enterprises to the local government in order to keep their businesses open.

Casinos are a perfect example of how the municipality channels money into its extrabudgetary funds. With an annual turnover of $250 million, the gambling market is lucrative enough to have caught the city government's attention. In this sector of the economy, widely known for its connection to the Mafia and notably used to launder money, Luzhkov does not mind behaving in an arbitrary way. On October 1, 1996, the Moscow mayor ordered the closure of 28 casinos, with no explanation. The remaining 30 gambling houses were forced by a municipal order to diversify their activities and to open entertainment rooms, bars, and restaurants.[12] The move came at a time when the city government was trying to raise funds to organize a celebration of Moscow's 850th anniversary. Whether they liked it or not, all of the capital's casinos thus became unofficial sponsors of these festivities. According to the Russian press, the casino directors were regularly asked by the municipality to contribute $20,000 a month to the reconstruction of the Church of Christ the Savior on the bank of the Moskva River.[13] The municipality is said to have collected as much as $1 million per month.[14]

Huge building projects, including those carried out for the city's jubilee in September 1997, regularly pour money into municipal coffers. In an interview with Russian television shortly after Yeltsin sacked Chernomyrdin, Gaidar accused Luzhkov of forgery and claimed that the budget for Moscow's giant construction projects had been inflated by an estimated 20–30 percent.

On September 9, 1997—although the original decision to build was taken in 1993—the city government gave its go-ahead to the construction of an entertainment center on Nagatinskaya Poima. For the Moscow municipality this project was no less important than the Church of Christ the Savior, the renovation of Manezh Square, or the construction of the "Moscow-City" business center. The

120-hectare Nagatinskaya Poima Amusement Park, designed by the Georgian sculptor Zurab Tsereteli, was to include several game areas, hotels, theaters, concert halls, and a track for Formula-One racing cars, at an estimated total cost of $4 billion. Construction would be finished by 2003.

In connection with this project, the Moscow city government planned to set up an investment trust known as Nagatino, in which, at least at first, it would be the only shareholder. The directors of the Moscow casinos offered the municipality $250 million in exchange for participation in the investment trust and authorization to open five casinos in downtown Moscow.[15] But city leaders clearly did not want to involve them in the project and freely acknowledged that they were negotiating with American consultants from Las Vegas.[16]

The Nagatinskaya Poima project is important for several reasons. First, its timing: Plans for the park would boost Luzhkov's popularity and enhance his chances of achieving higher office (e.g., the Russian presidency). He could now say that he had successfully fought organized crime by closing down the casinos in downtown Moscow. Secondly, as Gaidar alleged, the provisional budget of Nagatinskaya Poima was inflated by an estimated 20–30 percent, which would allow the Moscow city government to pour money into extrabudgetary funds and finance Luzhkov's presidential campaign.[17]

The Creation of Holdings: Sistema

Another municipal fund-raising method has been the creation of holding companies aimed at exerting control over profitable markets. Such companies were created between 1993 and 1995, when privatization was stalled. To keep its stake in sectors that the federal government was keen to include in its privatization program, the city government registered municipal companies as private joint-stock entities, thus avoiding their privatization. The Moscow government's holdings include hotels, restaurants, food processing plants, transport and trading companies, banks, and media.[18]

These holding companies were potentially so lucrative that the Moscow municipality decided to go further. In 1994, Vladimir Yevtushenkov had the idea of creating a financial holding company under the aegis of the Moscow Committee for Science and Technology, which he headed. The new company, known as Sistema, specialized in buying up small ventures, augmenting its portfolio without really managing the companies. As the main goal of the holding company was to acquire diverse investments, it is understandable why the Moscow government was so interested in participating. The financial weight of Sistema was considerable; it had capital of around $750 million by 1997.[19]

Sistema began by investing money everywhere possible. It acted sometimes as a central buying office, sometimes as a commercial bank investing in government bonds or shares with a 200–300 percent annual rate of return. It also managed to buy up a large number of enterprises during the initial stage of privatization, with a particular focus on industrial sectors that Russian and foreign investors were staying away from, such as electronics and telecommunications, because of political barriers and deficiencies in the regulatory framework.[20] Soon it became obvious that Sistema was in a position to invest because it had been authorized to manage municipal funds under cover of financing some of Moscow's military-industrial factories.[21] Although Sistema chairman Yevgenii Novitskii has claimed that his company is not linked to the municipality, he has admitted that the Moscow municipality holds shares in almost all of the 100 companies he owns, which include telecommunications, oil and gas, agriculture, marketing, construction, real estate, and tourism.[22]

Sistema allows the Moscow municipality to exert direct control over the capital's most promising industrial sectors. In February 1998 Sistema bought all of the shares floated by Guta-Bank for $577 million, consolidating the municipality's presence in the Moscow telecommunication operator MGTS, one of Guta-Bank's main partners.[23] It also controls the potentially very profitable Moscow gasoline market.

In the early 1990s Moscow's emerging fuel sector was in the hands of three enterprises: the Moscow oil refinery, the Mosnefteprodukt oil products distributor, and MPKA (the Moscow Auto Service Combine), a company that owned 240 gas stations and spare-parts shops. The Moscow refinery and Mosnefteprodukt were authorized by the city government to accept private investors, provided they kept a controlling share. In 1992, MPKA employees turned the company into a municipal enterprise and started "privatizing" its gas stations, leasing them in return for monthly rents totaling between 5 million and 10 million rubles. Statistics show that MPKA owned 196 gas stations in September 1997, 128 of which were leased to private investors.[24]

In the meantime, a hundred or so independent companies had already built a network of gas stations all over Moscow. By September 1997, the city had 640 stations selling an estimated 7,000 to 7,500 tons of gas daily, making the annual fuel market worth between $1 billion and $1.5 billion. Giant oil groups like LUKoil and Rosneft coveted this lucrative market, but they had no gas stations and were not the only companies supplying the Moscow refinery. Most of Moscow's gas stations were buying oil products from approximately 100 independent companies acting as middlemen.

In 1994 the Moscow government decided to set up its own Central Fuel Company (TsTK). But this decision took effect only after former Fuel and Energy Minister Yurii Shafranik was recruited by the city leaders in April 1997.[25] One of Shafranik's first moves was to reduce the number of supplying companies to three or four. Simultaneously, the Moscow refinery and Mosnefteprodukt came under the control of the Central Fuel Company. Until then, TsTK had confined itself to supplying the city's gas stations with fuel and was considering partnership with some of Russia's leading oil producers, such as the Tyumen Oil Company (TNK), Tatarstan's Tatneft, LUKoil, and Sibneft.[26]

Soon, however, the company started drawing up plans for its own network of gas stations. On June 9, 1997, Luzhkov granted TsTK tax and rent exemptions for 75 vacant lots. But the city prefects argued that the market was already saturated and that construction of new gas stations would not be profitable. The municipality then decided to take over the MPKA gas stations. Company employees protested the move, arguing that MPKA had been privatized in 1992 and that they were responsible for the management of the gas stations. Luzhkov counterattacked on July 1, 1997, ordering the seizure of the gas stations. The employees sued the municipality. The court ruled that Luzhkov's order was illegal and set a trial for August 20.[27] But on August 16, MPKA director Vladimir Monakhov was gunned down.

Monakhov's murder put an end to the dispute and left MPKA in disarray. Although the city administration was a regular customer, MPKA was getting paid quite irregularly. After Monakhov's death the company faced huge debts and had to place itself under the financial guarantee of the Moscow Privatization Committee (Moskomimushchestvo).[28] The holding company Sistema bought and now manages all of MPKA's gas stations, giving it a monopoly on the fuel market in Moscow. MPKA is now under the control of the municipality.

The Risk of Saturation and the Need for Development

By establishing holding companies in all the profitable sectors, the city government maintains absolute control over the capital's economy. But its territorial jurisdiction is, of course, limited, and Moscow may well be facing the risk of overexpansion.[29]

The first serious crisis came in the construction industry. The Moscow municipality claimed that in 1997 it had built 3.3 million square meters of new housing.[30] But after investigating this claim, journalists asserted that only half that amount had been built and that the costs had mysteriously doubled.[31] The municipality initially planned to sell the new buildings to the city's industrial enterprises, which in turn were supposed to give or sell them to their employees. Apartments were to be sold to people on the waiting list or to tenants living in Khrushchev-era buildings. But the new apartments were far too expensive for the targeted population. As a result, many were left unoccupied, and the municipality sustained a huge financial loss.

As this example demonstrates, Moscow has pushed its economic strategy to the limit and can go no further. Now that the municipality has taken control of the main industrial sectors, it must build a genuinely consumer-oriented market economy. Luzhkov recently has made efforts to boost light industrial production in the capital and other regions of the Russian Federation, but faces the same old obstacle: Moscow has not yet developed a sufficiently broadly based consumer class to guarantee a solid market demand. (If Luzhkov is as astute as he is rumored to be, he is certainly aware of this.[32]) The mayor has had little choice but to invest in other industrial sectors or regions. In the first half of 1998, the Moscow city government concluded investment agreements with several provincial municipalities, and the Association of Southern Russian Cities signed an agreement with the Moscow Interbank Currency Exchange to develop local stock markets.[33]

Luzhkov's restructuring of his team in 1997 and 1998 demonstrated his willingness to diversify his investments. Soon after the 1996 presidential elections, Luzhkov began to approach prominent industrial and military people, chosen for their connections in the automobile, aviation, and military industries.[34] As a result, the Moscow municipality attempted to reorganize the ZIL automotive plant in order to sell it to foreign investors, being aware that the financial picture was not sufficiently promising to attract them.[35] It also gained control over the Moskvich car plant soon after the reshuffling of the federal government in early 1998, and promised that significant funds would be disbursed to the company.[36] In the aviation sector, the city government was poised to acquire a 25 percent stake in the Atlant-Soyuz airline.[37]

The Moscow city government was also very interested in military-related industries. At the beginning of 1998 the municipality launched negotiations with the federal government to gain control over five federation-owned military-industrial enterprises located in the Russian capital, including the MiG aircraft manufacturer. Luzhkov hoped to gain a 50 percent stake in those enterprises, and in return was expecting the federal government to pay off its debt to Moscow. This proposal was discussed on March 18, 1998, at a meeting of the Moscow government with representatives of the five targeted enterprises.[38] Yakov Urinson, then minister of the economy, at first objected to the planned deal on the grounds that Moscow's leaders were insufficiently committed to the federal policy of economic reform. But lacking the cash with which to pay its debts, the federal government had no choice but to yield to the city's leaders.

In factories with a workforce of several thousand, the wage arrears problem is particularly acute. Taking control of Moscow's military plants would commit Luzhkov to paying salaries on time and avoiding layoffs, in a very difficult economic environment (the Russian military industry is not very competitive on the international market). This significant financial commitment was understood in the capital as an important step in Luzhkov's political campaign for national office.

Luzhkov's record does show a number of genuine achievements in the area of social policy. It makes no difference whether these achievements were made possible precisely because the Presidential Administration had chosen to turn a blind eye to legislative irregularities, the proliferation of secret funds, and the disappearance of businessmen opposed to the city's policies. Unlike many regional bosses in Russia, Luzhkov has managed to use the capital's coffers to defuse social instability and pay pensions on time, which makes him very popular among Moscow's residents.[39] Welfare spending, which includes payments to war veterans, pensioners, and unemployed persons, made up 41 percent of the city's budget for 1998.[40]

This raises the question of Moscow-style capitalism: Do these achievements justify the attempt to develop private business under state control? The Moscow government has generated popular support for its transformation into a large corporation by reinvesting profits in the city's social and economic sectors. As a "state capitalist," Luzhkov believes that the transition to a market economy should be conducted under the sole aegis of the government. But foreign investors have correctly noticed that state capitalism and free competition are antinomies. Luzhkov's ability to change laws by decree undermines the predictability of the legal environment, which intimidates some investors.[41] His authoritarian rule may well play against the interests of the municipality as soon as the support of the Kremlin ends.

Plainly, the seeming success of the city's economic policy was largely the result of collusion between Yeltsin and Luzhkov, neither of whom could probably have stayed in power long without the support of the other. Paradoxically, this collusion could well undermine Moscow's welfare in the future. After several years of laissez-faire, the federal authorities suddenly started to show concern about the Moscow city budget's lack of transparency. The very existence of secret funds was becoming a threat to the federal budget, since the Kremlin had found that subsidies to and tax transfers from regional budgets were hindering its ability to balance the federal budget. By hiding the real figures from the federal government, the Moscow municipality was trying to get more subsidies and pay less in taxes. If Moscow tolerated the spread of such practices on a similar scale to the entire federation, it would drive the federal budget into bankruptcy and drastically alter the relations between the center and the periphery. The federal government thus seems likely to enter into a new struggle with the Moscow city government now that President Yeltsin has left the political stage.

Notes

1. Annual expenses were set at US$396 million, including $11 million for the housing sector, $5 million for public transportation, $150 million for the construction of the Moscow city business center, and $14 million for the local TV-Tsentr news channel (*Kommersant,* 27 November 1997).

2. He kept this post until June 1996, when he was elected mayor by an overwhelming majority of voters.

3. This status was granted in 1992 by presidential decree.

4. The other enterprises were Gorbus (16 percent), Rekviem-94 (10 percent), Kedr (5 percent), Broniks (5 percent), Ritorg (4 percent), TB&K (2 percent), and Nekropol (1 percent). Ten percent of the market was controlled by several other small enterprises.

5. Aleksei Sinitskii and Aleksandr Malyutin, "Pokhoronnaya komanda: Meriya ili smert'!" [The funerary team: The mayoralty or bust!], *Kommersant Weekly,* no. 17, 6 May 1997.

6. Andrei Shleifer, Maxim Boycko, and Robert Vishny, *Privatizing Russia* (Cambridge: MIT Press, 1995), p. 71.

7. A similar ban was put on most real estate in the Russian capital. The land can only be rented, with a maximum 49-year lease.

8. *Nezavisimaya gazeta,* 25 January 1995.

9. *Kommersant Weekly,* no. 5, 17 February 1998.

10. The federal government has accused the Moscow municipality of having used "secret funds" worth 14.1 billion rubles in 1996.

11. *Kommersant Weekly,* no. 5, 17 February 1998.

12. Luzhkov later changed his mind and reinstated ten of the casinos' licenses.

13. *Kommersant Weekly,* no. 34, 23 September 1997.

14. In the same spirit, a year prior to the capital's 850th anniversary, the municipality threatened Western companies with fiscal investigations unless they agreed to take part in the rejuvenation of the city (for example, by repainting a building or repaving a road).

15. The cost estimate for the first stage of construction was $285 million.

16. Dmitrii Sokolov and Yelena Artemkina, "Ne v Poime—vor" [No thieves allowed in Poima], *Kommersant Weekly,* no. 34, 23 September 1997.

17. Interview with Yegor Gaidar, "Lyudi i den'gi," RTR, 28 March 1998.

18. See the interesting list of the city's assets in Astrid Wendlandt's unpublished paper, "Moscow's economic success: A Russian anomaly?" Harvard University, 23 January 1998. Wendlandt cited in her paper the example of the joint-stock company Moskva, which manages the city's hotel properties. Those properties include a 51 percent stake in the Moscow hotel Renaissance, a 50 percent stake in the Intourist, and a 30 percent stake in the Metropol (*Moscow Times,* 21 November 1995).

19. *Profil',* no. 26, 1997.

20. Olga Blinova and Aleksei Mukhin, *Imperii dvukh: Luzhkov i Gusinskii* [Two Empires: Luzhkov and Gusinskii] (Moscow, 1998), pp. 21–24.

21. *Profil',* no. 17, 1997.

22. Sistema holds a majority stake in 70 of these 100 enterprises (*Profil',* no. 26, 1997).

23. Of the shares in the telecommunication enterprise MGTS, 33 percent belonged to Sistema and 47 percent to Russia's telecommunications giant Svyazinvest. Svyazinvest had five representatives on MGTS's board of directors; Sistema, three; and Guta-Bank, one. Once they took control of Guta-Bank, Sistema and the Moscow government were clearly in a position to consolidate their presence inside the company.

24. At the time, Luzhkov argued that the municipality should fight against the "monopoly" MPKA had on the gas market.

25. TsTK's initial capital belonged to the Moscow Privatization Committee (82.3 percent) and the Moscow Property Fund (17.7 percent). The latter was created to manage Moscow's privatization policy.

26. Aleksandr Malyutin, "Bezopasnost' Moskvy pod ugrozoi" [The security of Moscow under threat], *Kommersant Weekly,* no. 32, 9 September 1997.

27. *Russkii telegraf,* 18 October 1997.

28. Anna Nogina, Tatyana Lysova, and Natalya Kalinichenko, "Koroli benzokolonok" [Gas station kings], *Ekspert,* no. 34, 8 September 1997.

29. Some Russian journalists began predicting the collapse of Moscow's financial pyramid in late 1997. See Aleksei Ulyukaev, "Moskovskaya osobaya" [Moscow special], *Ekspert,* 13 October 1997.

30. Interview with journalist Viktor Akimov, Moscow, 26 March 1998.

31. Aleksandr Kaminskii and Yurii Klubkov, "A bum—eto mnogo?" [A boom—is that a lot?], *Kompaniya,* 21 January 1998.

32. Luzhkov was generally viewed as both one of the most influential politicians and one of the most powerful businessmen in Russia. See the list of the most influential businessmen and politicians in *Ekspert,* 6 October 1997, and "Ekspert–50: Vliyatel'nost," *Ekspert,* 2 March 1998.

33. The municipalities involved included Krasnodar, Belgorod, Stavropol, Volgograd, and Pyatigorsk. In addition to these agreements, Moscow announced that it was ready to invest 600 million rubles (equivalent then to about US$100 million) in regional projects in 1998. The funds were to be allocated to joint investment projects with Omsk, Rostov-on-Don, Saratov, Yaroslavl, and Kaluga (A. Yevplanov, "Several agreements signed in Krasnodar," *Finansovye izvestiya,* 2 May 1998).

34. The former minister of defense Igor Rodionov, General Andrei Nikolaev, the former director of arms sales monopoly Rosvooruzhenie Aleksandr Kotelkin, and the former chairman of the Kamaz automobile plant Nikolai Bekh were among Luzhkov's new advisers. See *Nezavisimaya gazeta,* 16 April 1998; Blinova and Mukhin, *Imperii dvukh: Luzhkov i Gusinskii,* pp. 42–44.

35. Dmitrii Sokolov and Yelena Artemkina, "Flyuger perestroiki" [Weathervane of perestroika], *Kommersant,* 9 September 1997.

36. *Nezavisimaya gazeta,* 4 April 1998; also, Interfax, quoted by *Russkii telegraf,* 27 May 1998.

37. Interfax, quoted by *Russkii telegraf,* 19 May 1998.

38. *Ekspert,* 23 March 1998; Yekaterina Titova, "Moskva gotovitsya k eksperimentu po vyvodu oboronnykh predpriyatii iz krizisa" [Moscow prepares for experiment to ease crisis in defense plants], *Finansovye izvestiya,* 26 March 1998.

39. Luzhkov won the municipal elections in June 1996 with an overwhelming majority.

40. ITAR-TASS, 11 December 1997, quoted in Wendlandt, "Moscow's economic success: A Russian anomaly?"

41. *Kommersant-Daily,* 16 March 1995.

CHAPTER 4

The Political Economy of Russian Oil

David Lane

By 1998 the major steps in the transformation of the Russian economy from state ownership and administrative control to private ownership and market relations were completed. Although the structures and process of state socialism still leave an imprint, the principal political contest has been between groups with different interests about the type of market economy being constructed in Russia and the relative role of different political and economic institutions—the state, investors, management, and financial interests (including foreign ones). The Russian oil industry has to be analyzed in the context of international, regional, and sectoral interests that seek to influence the government. This chapter considers the ways in which the oil industry has relatively successfully adapted to a world market economy, examining divisions within the industry between management and financial interests, and disagreements within the ruling political apparatus about the extent and type of regulation and control. It then outlines the main forms of interest articulation. Lastly, it arrives at several generalizations about the Russian model of capitalism.

Compared to other Russian industries, oil has made a relatively successful transition to a market economy. However, it is confronted with serious internal problems of price and investment policy with respect to the wider economy. Also there are significant differences of interest between management, financial, and political interests; between local and central political authorities; and between different sectors of government and their constituent interests. The elites running the industry lack cohesion, and the industry faces a particularly hostile parliamentary elite. The tendency of free market capitalism toward fragmentation is amplified under Russian conditions, which results in what can be characterized as "chaotic capitalism." It is hypothesized that an alternative form of coordination and cohesion may be achieved through corporate cooperative capitalism.

From State Socialism to Radical Reform

Unlike many other industries, Russia's oil and gas interests have been well placed to benefit from the transition to world market conditions. They were an important

101

industrial asset of the Soviet economy under Leonid Brezhnev: By the 1970s, centralized state control of industry and pricing led to the profits and rents from energy exports being utilized to maintain economic growth and consumer satisfaction. Oil and gas had become the main sources of foreign currency earnings for the country—earnings that were used to increase imports of machinery, equipment, and consumer goods. Within the USSR, prices of fuel and power were as little as 5 percent of world prices, and thus its COMECON partners in Eastern Europe were able to import Soviet energy at prices considerably below the prevailing world level. This low energy price policy had the effect of subsidizing manufacturing industry as well as domestic consumers, and its imprint is still important to the Russian economy. It was (and still is) a crucial component in maintaining political and social stability.

With the move to a market economy, the fuel and power complex remains a key sector. In 1997, its companies (in terms of capitalization) dominated the top ten slots in the Russian economy. Gazprom was first, followed by United Energy System (EES), LUKoil, Yukos, Surgutneftegaz, Sidanko, Surgutneftegaz (subsidiary), Sibneft, and Slavneft. (In 1998, the merger of Yukos and Sibneft into Yuksi put this company just ahead of LUKoil.) Compared to Western companies, in terms of output, Gazprom is the largest single energy company, three times larger than Royal Dutch Shell. Yuksi and LUKoil, however, are smaller than Shell, Exxon, Mobil, BP (British Petroleum), Chevron, and Amoco.[1] In terms of earnings, of the top 20 Russian companies, 13 are in the oil/gas complex, including five of the top six.[2] The sector accounts for 25 percent of Russia's industrial output, 38 percent of federal budget revenues, and more than 50 percent of the overall value of exports. It absorbs more than one-fifth of the total internal investments. As a major provider of basic industrial inputs, the fuel and power complex influences production costs of other sectors of the economy, and energy prices are an important component in determining the level of inflation.[3] Western oil companies and financial institutions seek to profit from Russia's abundant reserves of oil, and Western governments also have a strategic interest in the price and supply of this major source of energy. However, since the move to a market economy and the privatization of the oil industry in 1993, production of oil has declined. Crude oil production fell from 11.3 million barrels per day in 1986 to 7.12 million barrels in 1993, and to 5.04 in 1996, and recovered to 5.99 million b/d in 1997. Refinery output fell from 3.58 million b/d to 2.62 million b/d between 1993 and 1996.[4] Net oil exports, however, rose from 3.14 million b/d to 3.43 million b/d in the same time span.[5]

These facts illustrate the export-driven character of the oil and gas industry, which has adapted to and profited from exposure to the international market. Manufacturing industries and agriculture, however, due to the contraction of the domestic market, have experienced a considerable fall in production, and have no compensatory advantages from exports. Imports have undermined their share of the domestic market, due to the policy of trade liberalization advocated in 1992 by Prime Minister Yegor Gaidar. The share of the military-industrial complex in GDP fell from 25 percent in Soviet times to 5 percent in 1997, and arms exports earn only one-tenth the income of energy exports.[6] The actual (or potential) ability to compete under world market conditions distinguishes the adaptability of different economic sectors. This ability in turn affects the ideological and political sympathies of elites representing not only the newly formed companies but also regional political interests. What lies behind the political claims for the free market advocated by the companies of the oil and gas sector, and for greater government intervention and protection on the part of manufacturing and agriculture, is that oil and gas are able to profit from international free trade, whereas the latter suffer from it. Due to its ability to earn considerable economic rents, Russian oil is a site of perpetual contest. At the international level, Russia's tremendous oil and gas resources also make foreigners important actors in the country, as investors and purchasers of energy; Russia has the second-largest proven oil reserves in the world, after Saudi Arabia.

To some extent, the industry's political interests have their roots in structures and values inherited from state socialism. The evolution of the contemporary Russian oil industry has been, in current political science terms, "path dependent." But the industry has moved beyond that legacy, as market and international forces have brought their influence to bear on the formation of the Russian economy.

Many accounts of state socialism have assumed a monolithic, centrally administered economy, but in the oil industry there was no single controlling hub in Soviet times. Rather the industry was horizontally organized, with extraction, production, refining, and distribution of oil products coming under different ministries.[7] Under state socialism, one might picture the industrial structure of the oil industry as a heterogeneous set of units, each with its own economic (and political) interests. The remote geographical situation of extraction facilities provided the oil and gas management with operational independence from the center as well as a social identity. The oil executives were spatially separate from the Moscow elites, and they had a strong sense of identity as well as considerable administrative control over production at the enterprise level. Their political outlook was narrow—bounded by their engineering background and their orientation toward meeting production targets whatever the costs. As the president of LUKoil, Vagit Alekperov (a former general director of an oil extraction complex), has put it: "When the Soviet Union and the all-Union industrial ministries existed, . . . after having delivered the oil, we were merely given funds for equipment, and our main goal was to get out more foreign and Russian equipment in order to develop new oil fields. We had no export or import policies of our own, independent of the global politics of the state."[8]

The opportunity to enhance their position came with Mikhail Gorbachev's reforms. By the end of the 1980s, the leaders of enterprises were given unprecedented prerogatives: their rights over production were extended to finance and marketing. In the latter Gorbachev period, enterprises sought to maximize short-term profit, and investment was neglected. The domestic prices for oil and oil derivatives between 1990 and 1992 were approximately 5 percent of world prices. Many extraction units, refineries, and commercial intermediaries bought products at domestic prices, and also received export quotas and licenses to sell on the foreign market. The difference between the state-fixed prices for oil and oil derivatives and the prices in the free market led to enormous fortunes being made, legally and illegally.

The managerial personnel in the oil industry became economic and financial benefactors of Gorbachev's reform policy. But their view of the effectiveness of the oil industry was not as negative as the Gorbachev leadership's view of the Soviet economy: Hence they were followers, rather than leaders, of the radical reforms. On the basis of interviews conducted with oil executives having the status of director, deputy director, president, or vice president, I found that over half of the respondents believed that the oil industry in the former Soviet system was effective, 8 percent considered there was no need for change, and 43 percent believed that reforms could have been carried out within the system of state socialism.[9] At the other end of the scale, 23 percent believed that the industry was completely ineffective, compared to 40 percent of the members of the previous Gorbachev political elite, who when asked about their views of the Soviet economic system, answered that it was completely ineffective and impossible to reform.

The Transition: The Structure of the Oil Industry

With the collapse of the Soviet ministries in 1990–1991 and the shift of control from the USSR to the republics and regions, a spontaneous process of privatization began. Enterprises and organs of local administration together began to form independent companies. The management of the local companies, as well as leaders of the local administrations, took over assets in the oil industry. The new political structures, however, were weak, and management, being in control of productive assets, was strongly positioned to act in its own interests with regard to extraction, production, refining, and sales. In 1991, the all-Union ministries of the USSR were liquidated and a single Ministry of Fuel and Power of the Russian Federation was formed (i.e., Mintopenergo, or Ministerstvo topliva i energetiki RF). But its activity was confined to the legal and general regulation of the fuel and power complex, and it had no direct control over production activities. It became a channel between government and industry. Perhaps even more important is the fact that institutional reforms were not imposed from the top but developed with the participation of oil industry executives, including those heading the enterprises that would be affected.

The destruction of the command-administrative system and the subsequent period of chaos were followed by a gradual shift to a market system, begun in 1992 by the Gaidar government. For the oil industry, the Gaidar reforms may be summarized as follows. The first step was to bring domestic prices for oil and oil derivatives gradually into line with world ones; the second, to move from fixed governmental prices to regulated ones; and the last, to free prices. During a two- to three-year transition period, export controls would be established[10] in order to prevent an unregulated flow of fuel and raw materials abroad: As domestic prices approached world ones, both the tax and tax-free export barriers would be ended, and enterprises would begin to finance their own investments and current expenses. In the last stage, the enterprises would be privatized, forming vertically integrated oil companies.

To maintain state control, the government of the Russian Federation planned to form several holding companies from parts of the oil complex. Here the intention was to reorganize the oil companies on a vertically integrated basis, on the model of the leading Western oil companies, with which the leading Russian oil directors were well acquainted.[11] By the middle of 1992, it was proposed to organize the oil industry into 10 to 12 large, vertically integrated companies able to compete, it was thought, on Russian and world markets. Unlike Middle Eastern governments, which in the post–World War II era sought control through nationalization (or at least the threat of nationalization), the Russian government for reasons of political legitimacy had to privatize the companies and adopt a market strategy. However, the industry was crucial to the well-being of the economy, and it was conceded that some form of government control was essential.

The plan was to form two types of company: holding companies and subsidiaries. There are some similarities here with the form of nationalization pursued under Carlos Perez, in Venezuela, where the government, when considering nationalization plans, also was confronted with a strong indigenous management structure. In the end it set up a state holding company (Petroleos de Venezuela) and three or four integrated oil companies based on previous units, on the premise that competition between them would enhance efficiency. The holding company would ensure that rents and taxes accrued to the state. The government of the Russian Federation also was to retain from 45 to 51 percent of the shares in the holding companies for a period of at least three years. In theory, this would not only ensure a flow of earned profits to the central treasury but also would secure the new companies under the jurisdiction of the federal government, safeguarding its right to taxation revenues.

In the postcommunist settlement in Russia, the central government asserted its rights to the tax income from this major export industry, which also had major international implications. This right is questioned by many of the regional republics and is arguably a central cause of the secessionist movement in Chechnya. (In Chechnya, the material interest is in royalties from the pipeline running through its territory as well as a small amount of extraction and refining.)

Privatization and the Role of the Government

"Official" privatization of the oil industry occurred from 1993 to 1997. This process involved the redistribution of assets of the production enterprises that had undergone "spontaneous" privatization along the lines described earlier, and the concurrent organization of vertically integrated holding companies. In some cases, the holding company has a strong position, with financial and managerial control over the subsidiaries; in others, the "subsidiaries" maintain effective control over physical assets. Divisions within and between holding and subsidiary companies reflect differences in the ownership and control of assets. The principal actors are the government of the Russian Federation, the governments of regions and localities, financial institutions (such as the banks), and managerial executives working in the industry. The forms of political contestation for control resembled those in the postwar period among the governments of the states that were members of OPEC (the Organization of Petroleum Exporting Countries), Western governments, and the oil companies—except that Western oil companies were major, established powers, whereas the Russian ones were (and still are) in formation. In the Russian case, moreover, the government was faced with an entrenched management that had control of production.

This settlement in the Russian oil industry was a consequence of discussions between the management of the oil industry; the first head of Mintopenergo, Vladimir Lopukhin; and the management of Goskomimushchestvo (GKI) (the State Committee for the Management of State Property), which was headed between 1991 and 1995 by Anatolii Chubais. There were, however, divisions of opinion within the political elite about the course of privatization. The radical reformers (particularly, interests around Chubais and GKI) wanted to ensure greater competition and believed that privatization in the industries of the fuel and power complex should be done quickly and according to the rules common to all industries. But the management of the oil units was sufficiently well organized politically to resist the general plans of privatization drawn up by the reformers. Oil and gas as strategic industries were not subject to the open privatization procedures of other industries, and their prices were still regulated after the price liberalization introduced on January 1, 1992. The "oil generals" supported Mintopenergo's scheme for restructuring the industry, which envisaged the restriction of privatization and the retention of a controlling packet of shares of the newly established companies in state hands for three years. Ownership rights of the government were also a contested terrain within the political apparatuses. The industrial ministries (and committees) shared the view of Mintopenergo that state ownership was and should remain an important instrument of control over the oil companies.

The general laws on privatization of the oil complex were laid down by presidential decree in November 1992. This decree supported the position of Mintopenergo. Crucially, the government would have majority ownership rights in the holding companies, which in turn would have a majority interest in the subsidiaries. The government's intention was to privatize the assets and form competing companies while giving the state a significant level of control over the privatized companies. The problem here, for the market reformers, was that if the subsidiaries were controlled by the holding companies, which operated in local markets, then local monopolies on the supply of fuel would develop.

The decree envisaged the division of assets between subsidiaries and holding companies in the following way. The subsidiaries' stock was divided into two parts: the smaller part (25 percent) comprised preference (nonvoting) shares. These were to be distributed free of charge among the employees (management and workers) of the enterprises. The remainder, the ordinary voting shares, were to be divided as follows: 38 percent of shares were to be placed with an oil holding company, or in some cases, transferred for temporary management to the state enterprise, Rosneft—the objective being to give a controlling stake of 50.7 percent of voting shares to the holding company; 10 percent were to be put on sale at advantageous terms to the enterprise's workers, and another 5 percent, to the enterprise's management; 3.75 percent were to be sold at auction, in exchange for privatization vouchers, to the members of ethnic minorities in the Russian Far North (where most of the oil and gas are produced) and to employees of the joint-stock companies (JSCs) of oil pipeline enterprises; and 18.25 percent of shares were to be auctioned for vouchers and/or cash to other (local and foreign) buyers. A limit of 15 percent of total assets was imposed on ownership by foreign investors.

Given the strategic importance of oil and gas, privatization in the fuel and power complex was slower and more cautious than in other sectors. Initially, as a major stakeholder, the government appointed representatives who became directors of oil companies. As privatization progressed, these government-appointed directors were replaced by others. By 1997, there were usually two or three nominees from ministries and other government bodies on (privatized) oil companies' boards. However, in companies that were totally privatized, with no government stake, there might not have been any representative of the government.

The strictest governmental control was in the sphere of transportation of oil and oil products: Fifty-one percent of share capital in the companies Transneft and Transnefteprodukt would remain federal property for the foreseeable future, and the other 49 percent, for three years. The aim of this measure was to regulate the activity of monopolists in the transport of fuel and also to maintain an additional lever of governmental influence over the oil companies. This control, it was contended, would ensure that the fuel companies continued to function without interruption during the transition to the free market. Another argument in favor of more gradual privatization was financial: The market value of assets of the Russian oil industry was estimated at more than US$200 billion. Neither Russian citizens nor private financial institutes could raise such a sum, and even potential Western investors would find it difficult. Rapid privatization in this context would lead to the undervaluation of state assets.

The Rise of Finance Capital

The initial intentions of the administration of President Boris Yeltsin to maintain significant state ownership in the oil industry, however, did not materialize; in the mid-1990s, the government began to shed its ownership rights. An unmistakable shift in policy toward greater company autonomy occurred through the 1995 "loans-for-shares" scheme devised by Vladimir Potanin, the president of Oneksimbank. This scheme involved investors (banks or financial institutions) lending the government money in return for state share packages in partially privatized companies as collateral. In the event of the loans not being paid back, ownership and rights of control (including sale) would remain with the banks. Mintopenergo actively opposed the loans-for-shares auctions, fearing that they might separate several companies from direct government control, but the policy of the reformers in the government apparatus prevailed.

Within the government and presidential apparatus, the interests favoring continued state ownership of domestic industries were opposed by liberal reformers in the ministries of economics and finance and GKI, who advocated a minimal role for the state and whose views coincided for the most part with those of the IMF, which was urging a more rapid and rigorous privatization policy. Anatolii Chubais and GKI supported the extension of privatization to the oil and gas industry and favored the loans-for-shares deals. What tipped the scales in favor of the liberal reformers around Chubais was the Russian government's precarious financial position on the eve of parliamentary and presidential elections. This situation allowed Yeltsin to authorize shares to be "swapped" for loans, which could be used to plug gaps in the federal budget.

Table 4.1 shows the significant shift in ownership to the private sector, in which the banks and financial companies, often working through intermediaries, secured control. In 1997, the government relinquished its ownership rights in a large number of companies. Pipeline operator Transneft and Rosneft were privatized through an offering of 25 percent of their stock to present and former employees and another 25 percent offering to the investment market. Despite political pressure from the State Duma and from regional authorities, President Yeltsin—confronted with serious budget deficits—lifted restrictions on the sale of oil assets in 1997. Since then, destatization has continued at an unprecedented rate.

The major private stakeholders in oil are Russian banks, particularly Alfa Bank (which owns 40 percent of Tyumen Oil); Oneksimbank (85 percent of Sidanko); Menatep (85 percent of Yukos); and SBS/Berezovskii (99 percent of Sibneft) acting through intermediaries such as Laguna, Interros Oil, Sins, Rifainoil, Monblan, and Finansovaya neftyanaya korporatsiya (FNK).[12] Imperial Bank (owned by LUKoil and Gazprom) purchased 5 percent of LUKoil shares. The merger of Yukos and Sibneft in 1998 was a consequence of both of them having banks as controlling shareholders—FNK with respect to Sibneft, and Menatep (through Rosprom) in the case of Yukos. The merger was intended to strengthen the companies' capacity to bid for Rosneft, Onako, and Slavneft when the latter were privatized, and to achieve better access to international capital markets.[13] The merger subsequently failed, however, in the wake of the August 1998 financial crash.

TABLE 4.1   The Government's Share in Russian Oil Companies, 1994–1997 (as percent of total shares)

	1994	1995	1996	1997
Sidanko	100	85*	51*	0
Vostsibneftegaz	100	85	38	0
Sibneft+	–	100*	51*	0
Yukos+	86	53*	0.1	0.1
Surgutneftegaz	–	40.1	40.1*	40.1*0
Komitek	100	100	92	0-22
LUKoil	42.1	26*	16.6*	6.6
NorsiOil	–	100	85.4	45
Tatneft	46.6	46.6	35.1	20-25
Transneft	100	100	75	51
Rosneft	–	100	100	51
Tyumen oil	–	100	91	51
Sibur	100	85	85	51
Vostochnaya oil	100	85	85	51
Slavneft	93.5	92	90.1	56–68
Onako	100	85	85	85

*Wholly or partly in the hands of a "pledgeholder."

+In January 1998, these two companies merged to form Yuksi, the largest Russian oil company in terms of oil and gas output. The merger failed in the wake of the August 1998 crash.

SOURCE: Eugene M. Khartukov, *Oil and Gas Journal*, 18 August 1997, p. 38.

Due to the uncertain legal status of capital, the difficulty of repatriating profits, the extent of crime and corruption, and the hostility of sections of the government, the oil industry, and the Russian parliament, foreign direct investment in the oil industry has been small. In 1996, joint ventures accounted for just 7 percent of oil production and 12.5 percent of exports, though these proportions rose slightly in 1997 (to about 8 and 15 percent, respectively).[14] Shareholdings of foreigners in oil companies were limited by law, and foreign shareholders were effectively excluded from the boards of companies, as they had fewer shares than necessary to qualify for election. In 1997, however, President Yeltsin revoked federally mandated limitations on the proportion of shares that could be owned by foreigners—although companies themselves could fix a legal ceiling.

In practice, foreign investors still do not enjoy the same rights as Russian ones, and laws do not govern the terms under which investments take place (contracts, for example, may under certain circumstances be amended retrospectively). The Law on Production Sharing, giving rights to foreign investors to export income, was signed in June 1997, but the parliament approved its application only to seven sites. Despite these problems, external actors (e.g., foreign funds and companies) may become more important as the entrenched oil management seeks alliances and capital to strengthen its position. Joint ventures like those between

Shell and Gazprom, Sidanko and British Petroleum, LUKoil and ARCO (Atlantic Richfield), and Yukos and Amoco also may become more significant. In 1998, however, Western companies were somewhat hesitant to form strategic alliances with Russian oil companies.

Managerial Control?

Ownership is an important aspect of the organization of companies, but one cannot assume that it necessarily affects control of the company. Owners are confronted by managerial and technocratic personnel who themselves may be exercising ownership in their own right. Possessing knowledge about the organization of the company and also being masters of production, they are able to exert influence over company strategic plans. As the decisionmaking process is often secret and internal to the "inner circle" of company directors, it is usually very difficult to discover who controls companies and to determine to what extent ownership rights translate into control. Western industrial sociology has a vast literature on the subject. Ideally, one would like to conduct a number of case studies of decisionmaking in various oil companies to determine the extent of control of different interests. However, such studies are not possible even in Western countries, let alone in Russia. Two other methods are open to political scientists and sociologists: first, to consider the background of the executives in the companies; and second, to interview directors and management about who controls strategic decisions. These methods were used in gathering material for this chapter.

Initially, the executives and managers in control of production enterprises in the Soviet oil industry benefited greatly from the dissolution of the ministerial system. During the period of reforms, despite the disagreements and problems that arose, the oil and gas managerial strata (in contrast with the leaders of most other industries) seldom directly criticized the main direction of President Yeltsin's policies. Unlike in other industries, there have been virtually no large-scale strikes or mass antigovernment demonstrations in the oil and gas industry. As the chief of LUKoil, Vagit Alekperov, put it: "The direction of economic reforms carried out by the president generally suits us."[15]

But the process of consolidation into vertically integrated companies weakened the power of the management of the subsidiary enterprises, and the management of the holding companies had to break the resistance of the directors of extracting production units and refineries. There is also competition among the holding companies for the most promising enterprises and markets, access to new fields, and state-established quotas for transportation of oil along export pipelines.

The business environment is also changing, and many oil executives have moved their headquarters from Siberia to Moscow to facilitate communications with Western businessmen and Russian bankers. The former corporate unity of the oil elite has been weakened somewhat by the appearance in the top administrative echelons of people from outside—experts with special skills and knowledge in the areas of financial management and marketing. In 1995, the boards of directors of vertically integrated oil companies still consisted wholly of "oil generals" and ministry officials. In 1996, in a number of companies (particularly Yukos, Sidanko, and Sibneft), bankers and financiers were recruited onto the boards of directors. Representatives of other businesses also appeared among the vice presidents of these companies (e.g., Zia Bazhaev at Sidanko, and Mukharbek Aushev at LUKoil). In 1998, the merger of Yukos and Sibneft was engineered by two financiers with major interests in the company: Mikhail Khodorkovskii (Menatep Bank and Yukos chairman) and Boris Berezovskii (a major shareholder in Sibneft, with other significant stakes in LogoVAZ and other companies). The upshot of the settlement is that considerable political divisions remain among the different interests within the oil industry and between the industry's leaders and people on the outside. The ascendant ruling group is the banking and financial services sector.

Social and Political Origins

It is quite clear that the leaders of banking and finance came from different backgrounds, and it seems likely that they may have different attitudes toward the industry. To determine the occupational background of members of the oil and banking elites, the proportion of time was calculated that they spent in different statuses in the seven years (from August 1981 to December 1988) prior to the collapse of the USSR. It was from these positions that the elite moved in the postcommunist period.

Table 4.2 reveals the different career paths of the oil and banking elites.[16] For the oil elite, by far the most common activity was that of industrial executive (posts in production enterprises accounted for 54 percent of the career time of the elite in this time period), followed by positions in the professions. Party and other government executive positions were relatively low in proportion. In the banking/financial services elite, however, the largest group came from positions in the Soviet economic administration (e.g., Gosbank). Work in such organizations accounted for 24 percent of the aggregate career time of the banking elite; in other government institutions, 10 percent; and in a variety of other professional environments, 14 percent. Many more had been students during that period—hence the generally held impression that the new business elite is "young." In sum, my research shows that executive capital was by far the most important asset transferred from banking/finance to the oil industry during this period.

The other important elite sector of the Soviet political system was the government apparatus. Therefore I performed an analysis of all positions held by the oil/gas and banking/finance elites in the previous Soviet government apparatus before July 1, 1990. Those in the oil elite who had previously occupied positions in the economic administration (members of Gosplan or of the state bank) numbered

TABLE 4.2   The Oil and Banking/Financial Services Elites: Soviet-Era Occupational
Experience (by sector; positions held between August 1981 and December 1988*)

Occupation	Oil	Bank/Financial
Industrial executive office (chief engineer, factory director)	54	11
Profession (e.g., doctor, lawyer, lecturer)	9	14
Higher education (student)	7	14
Soviet economic organization (e.g., Gosbank)	4	21
Research	0	9
Enterprise	7	5
Government	8	10
Party or Komsomol apparat	6	8
Central Committee of the Communist Party of the Soviet Union	0	1

*Columns sum to 100; figures refer to percentage of time all members of elite spent in
each occupational category.

SOURCE: Author's compilation based on original survey data.

16 (29 percent), whereas the figure was 66 among the bankers (56 percent). The
two elites also had different social and educational backgrounds. Unlike the members of the new banking/financial services elite, 37 percent of whom were born in
Moscow or Leningrad, all of the oil leaders were born in the provinces of the
USSR. With regard to higher education, 79 percent of those in the oil elite had
graduated from faculties of applied science and engineering (compared to only 34
percent of those in banking and financial services); and only 11 percent had graduated with degrees in economics (the corresponding proportion in banking and financial services was 53 percent). Just 3 percent of the banking group had attended
a higher Party school, and none of the oil elite had done so.

Those who benefited from the policy of transformation were mainly middle-
aged male managers and technocrats in the oil industry: On January 1, 1997, 49
percent of the sample were more than 50 years old and 89 percent were more than
40. (In banking the figures were lower: 34 percent were over 50, and 73 percent,
over 40.) The first conclusion is that the power and benefits of economic leadership in contemporary Russia accrue to relatively middle-aged men. Very few in
the top business elite were women: Only seven women were in the sample of
bankers and financial services managers, and out of the sample of 55 members of
the oil elite, none were women.

As far as previous Communist Party attachment is concerned, the banking elite
had a far greater linkage to the former Party apparat. I used the following method
for determining the average political "saturation" of the two groups: Positions in
the Party apparatus were weighted by rank in the hierarchy (a weight of 10 was
assigned to the post of secretary of the Central Committee of the Communist
Party of the Soviet Union, and pro rata, down to 1 for the post of local Party sec-

retary), and this figure was multiplied by the number of years in the post. (The length of time as a mere member of the Communist Party was ignored.) This gave an average Party/Komsomol index of 8 per person for the bankers and 4 for the oil executives—showing a much greater salience of previous political capital for the bankers than the oil elite. A second conclusion we might draw is that the oil elite is more technocratic, less economically oriented, and more steeped in the culture and mores of the oil industry.

Attitudes Toward Decisionmaking

It is one thing to show that the oil elite is composed of oil executives from the Soviet period, or bankers from the old command system; it is a very different matter to determine who has influence over the strategic decisionmaking of the oil companies and whether they have brought their orientations from the Soviet period with them. Therefore a sample of executives in the oil industry, defined above, were asked their opinions as to which of the following interests on the board of the company were important in the making of "strategic decisions" in the company: management, financial institutions, other companies, the labor collective, large personal shareholders, foreign shareholders, and government representatives. The respondents were asked to rank the items on a five-point scale (from "of no importance" to "very important").

Those ranked highest in importance were the representatives of management; government delegates; and financial interests. Labor collectives can clearly be ruled out as an important interest, and individual shareholders also seem to have very little significance.

The respondents were asked also to consider the role of external interests not on the board of directors. These included: the Russian government, federal Russian institutions, regional powers, other Russian oil companies, and foreign oil companies. Of these, the political groups—the Russian government, and federal and regional powers—were of greatest importance, and foreign and other oil companies were considered to play a minor role over strategic decisionmaking within the companies. However, the proportion that described the former groups as "very important" was much lower than that reporting on the importance of groups internal to the company.

Although the government has sold off assets in oil companies, we cannot conclude that the government has an insignificant influence on the economy or on the oil industry. Quite clearly, however, the ascendant interests are to be found in the financial sector. The limits to their power may be located in the absence of a well-defined stock market enabling hostile takeovers to occur. Merger by consent is the most likely form by which existing "management-controlled" companies will be taken over. The 1998 merger of Yukos and Sibneft was an exception because these companies had a very high penetration of finance capital.

Securing the Oil Industry's Political Interests

We have discussed the outcomes of the "political settlement" with respect to the ownership and structure of the oil industry and also considered the influences pertaining to its decisionmaking. Let us now consider how the elites of the oil industry relate to politics, how they turn economic power into political influence and political decisions in their favor. We will analyze the promotion of the oil industry's interests in two areas: within the complex of government (which is the most important), and through parliamentary and extraparliamentary pressure groups (parties and associations).

There are ten major areas of influence that might influence decisionmaking on the oil industry. Five are internal to the state apparatus, and five are external. First, within the government apparatus, is the Ministry of Fuel and Power (Mintopenergo); second are the processing and manufacturing groupings and consumers of energy, consisting of industrial ministers and often one of the first deputy prime ministers. The third is the "macroeconomic bloc": the liberal reform ministries and committees that are steering the economy toward the market—principally, the ministries of Economics and Finance, GKI, and the State Antimonopoly Committee (GKAP, Gosudarstvennyi komitet po antimonopol'noi politike). Fourth are the ministries whose policies are affected by issues of energy: Particularly important in this regard are the ministries of foreign affairs and defense. Fifth, the president and his apparat play a key role in interest aggregation.

Constituencies external to the formal governing apparatus include: first, committees of the state administration and leaders of the Russian Federation's republics and regions (presidents and governors); second, the State Duma, the lower house of parliament; third, financial and economic interests; fourth, international financial institutions and companies, particularly the IMF; and fifth, other Russian companies and political parties. The policy of the state in relation to the energy complex is formed as a result of the interaction of these political forces.

To ascertain which of these institutions were regarded as important influences over the control of the economy, two groups of interviewees were asked to appraise their relative importance. Questions were posed to the oil executives previously mentioned and to 30 politicians having an interest in the energy field.[17] There was considerable agreement on the part of both oil executives and politicians that the government of the Russian Federation, followed by the president, have the most influence over the economy, and that the Russian parliament and state enterprises are at the other end of the scale. However, some important differences of opinion emerged. The politicians ranked external influences much more highly than did the oil executives; the IMF figured highly in their view, but foreign oil companies were ranked considerably higher. The oil executives considered regional Russian powers to have significant authority. These findings point to the importance of "within-system" interests in Russia—the government and the president—and to the external influence of the IMF. Let us now consider how the interests in the oil industry seek to exert influence on political institutions.

Within-System Interest Articulation

There are three main clusters of institutions that articulate interests with respect to the energy sector: the governmental administration; the Ministry of Fuel and Power (Mintopenergo); and other ministries and committees.

The government of Viktor Chernomyrdin (who was prime minister from December 1992 to March 1998) has often been called "the government of the energy complex," implying that Chernomyrdin's industrial background and sympathies (some have said "pecuniary interests") gave the oil/gas network unlimited opportunities for interest representation. Chernomyrdin entered the government in May 1992 as a deputy prime minister in charge of the fuel and power industries. As founder and head of Gazprom, the natural gas monopoly, he brought with him, and was able to effect, a vision of a single, vertically integrated gas industry working within a market society. During his six months in office as deputy prime minister, Chernomyrdin obtained a large credit for the oil industry and some important privileges for Gazprom. After he became the head of the government in December 1992, he was able to protect Gazprom from efforts to divide it into several independent companies.

But his influence went both ways. In 1994 and 1995, he used his office to persuade oil and gas industrialists to freeze their prices on oil and oil derivatives for six months, and to resume supply to their debtors. Gazprom cleared some of its tax arrears, which enabled wages in the state sector to be paid. In the first half of 1996, on the eve of the presidential election, Russian gas consumers ceased to pay Gazprom, but despite the loss of billions of dollars, supply was not stopped. Obviously, this noncommercial behavior on the part of industrialists strengthened economic, social, and political stability in the country.

At the beginning of 1995, due to pressure from the radical reform wing of the government and the IMF, the government increased pressure on the oil/gas complex to pay its tax arrears, to help reduce the acute problems associated with the budget deficit. The oil industry lost most of its concessions for export, and the excise taxes for raw oil and petrol were repeatedly raised.[18] It is, therefore, an oversimplification to describe the government of Chernomyrdin as an appendage of the oil/gas complex.

The Ministry of Fuel and Power performs two roles: that of an organ of state supervision, and that of advocate for the oil/gas complex's interests. At different stages of Mintopenergo's existence, the ratio of these two roles has varied. The advocacy role, however, has often overshadowed the supervisory one. Mintopenergo's first head, Vladimir Lopukhin, during the government of Yegor Gaidar, acted more as an advocate of the government's reform strategy. An economist by education and a supporter of radical reforms in the oil/gas industry, he nonetheless failed to convert the oil sector to his policy preferences. In January 1993, Yurii Shafranik became the head of Mintopenergo. Unlike Lopukhin's, Shafranik's entire career was tied to the oil industry. In the 1980s, he was general director of the Langepasneftegaz oil company, then chairman of the Tyumen oblast council and head of Tyumen oblast. In the first two years of his leadership, Shafranik and the office led by him acted in the interests of the fuel and power complex—especially of the oil industry. It was largely due to Shafranik's efforts that almost all of the Russian oil companies in 1993 and 1994 received considerable advantages for oil exports. Shafranik became an active supporter of reduction of the tax burden on the complex. He consistently defended the peculiarities of restructuring and privatization in the fuel and power industries against attacks by GKI and GKAP. Yet the ministry had its own agenda—to maintain its own supervisory functions—and should not be considered simply a conduit for the oil and gas companies.

Shafranik, however, came into conflict with other influential members of the government: the macroeconomic bloc, which was more inclined toward radical reforms. When Chubais was restored to power after Yeltsin's election to the presidency in 1996, Shafranik was dismissed. The post of the head of Mintopenergo was filled by Petr Rodionov, a gas industrialist who had been the head of the enterprise Lentrangaz and in spring 1996 had become a member of Gazprom's board of directors.

Unlike Shafranik, who had supported the lessening of the tax burden on the complex, Rodionov was expected to concentrate on the collection of taxes and to uphold state interests. The oil companies in 1996 had debts to the federal budget of 5 trillion rubles (about US$1 billion). This was a consequence of the rapid fall in the GDP of the Russian Republic—by approximately 40 percent between 1991 and 1997—resulting in massive debts to the fuel and power sector. In 1997, oil and gas companies made up eight of the top 10 debtors to the Russian government. However, Rodionov followed a political line similar to Shafranik's, emphasizing the importance of a reduction of the tax burden on the fuel and power companies. He also followed his predecessor's example in trying to increase the supervisory role of Mintopenergo over the fuel and power industries, but failed to convince the government to transfer its shares to the ministry.

One might generalize that the policy of Mintopenergo is to maximize output of oil and to seek greater control for itself over prices, investors, and investments. It has also sought to maintain a greater share of state ownership—here it comes into conflict with other parts of the government and the president's apparatus. It distances itself from the oil companies over free market pricing and is prone to support policies that it sees as being in the general interest of the economy—that is, subsidies for other industries, and penalties for nonpayment of taxes by oil producers. The role of the oil companies in using Mintopenergo to express their views depends on the issue and has changed over time. As privatization matures and the companies become stronger, the trend is for them to become more independent: They conduct business with financial interests and foreign companies, and they influence public policy directly through contact with the president's office or indirectly through political groups.

Because the fuel and power sector is a major source of tax income and a primary factor determining the cost of living and manufacture, many government departments and ministries have an interest in this sector: There is a powerful Fuel Administration within the Ministry of the Economy. The Ministry of Industry has oversight of the development of all industrial sectors; with regard to oil and gas, it deals mostly with the processing industry, especially chemical engineering and the manufacture of equipment. Financial issues affecting industries are dealt with in special sections of the Industrial Department of the Ministry of Finance. A number of departments within the Ministry of Science are dedicated to coordinating scientific and technological progress.[19]

The ministries of finance and of the economy, GKI, and GKAP seek a free market policy. Generally, these interests support an anti-inflationary monetary policy, and their views usually coincide with those of the IMF: They support a minimal state role in the economy, open market pricing, priority to financial stabilization, competition and privatization of assets, free movement of capital, and Western involvement. Some of these policies coincide with the interests of the oil elites, but others do not. These ministries, in comparison with the industrial ones, are considerably more influential.

On the other side, seeking protection for particular interests (consumers of fuel) are ministries and committees associated with production and consumers. Ministries associated with the military-industrial complex are important here, as are those concerned with social welfare. These ministries seek low fuel prices to keep down costs in their sectors. The foreign and defense ministries also are concerned with the strategic aspects of fuel. Here, price levels; the enforcement or nonenforcement of debts against foreign countries (most notably, Belarus and Ukraine); and the threat to national security posed by foreign ownership, company alliances, and financial dependence on foreign capital probably are the main reasons why these ministries support protectionism and oppose a free market policy. Apparatuses concerned with state security also have an interest with respect to financial dependency and crime—particularly money laundering, illicit sales of products and assets, and the private policing (Mafia) of such processes.[20] The energy complex itself needs investment in order to function and develop, and therefore favors a high price policy and foreign investment.

The president is a crucial determinant in the aggregation of interests. His task is to reconcile a number of contradictory policies: to balance the interests of the energy-producing and the consuming industries; to provide tax income from the energy sector to the budget sufficient to finance the public sector; to hold levels of inflation; to stimulate competition through the market; and to utilize oil as a strategic resource in foreign policy. Yeltsin was often inconsistent, but generally he sided with the liberal reformers and conformed to the free market policy of the

IMF. The president is also confronted constantly by other political interests in society, particularly in the Duma.

External Interests: Parties and Pressure Groups

The political strategy of the oil companies and Gazprom has been to utilize direct contacts with the government and to gain access to it through Mintopenergo. They are not as active in lobbying through parliament or political parties. Members of the oil and gas elite typically claim that they have no partisan political allegiance.[21] There are a number of professional and trade associations that not only bring together leading industrialists but also act as pressure groups on their behalf. The best known are the Union of Information and Collaboration in the Fuel and Power Complex (SISTEK), the Union of Oil and Gas Industrialists (Soyuz neftegazopromyshlennikov, or SNGP), the Union of Oil Exporters (Soyuz eksportov nefti, or Sonek), the Union of Energy Exporters, and the House of Oil (Neftyanoi dom).

There is a significant difference between the oil companies and other industries that have played a more positive and prominent political role. The agricultural interests, for example, have supported the long-established Agrarian Party and its fraction in the Duma, and allied themselves with the Communists in their opposition to many aspects of marketization. The interests of the military-industrial complex and other manufacturing industries have been represented at various times by the Civic Union (Grazhdanskii soyuz); the Congress of Russian Communities (Kongress russkikh obshchin); and the Russian Union of Industrialists and Entrepreneurs (Rossiiskii soyuz promyshlennikov i predprinimatelei, or RSPP), which has taken an active role in politics.

In the Duma, Deputy Vladimir Medvedev emerged as a significant supporter of oil interests. Medvedev was elected from Tyumen oblast and heads the small Russian Regions parliamentary fraction, which consists of deputies like himself, elected from single-mandate constituencies and not from national party lists. In fall 1996, in the course of debates in the Duma about budget planning, Medvedev made several suggestions for relieving the tax burden on the oil industry.

Perhaps the most significant role has been played by the movement Our Home Is Russia (Nash dom—Rossiya, or NDR), led by Chernomyrdin. This movement's tendencies with regard to the oil and gas industry are signaled by the fact that among Russian political pundits it was derisively labeled "Our Home Is Gazprom" (Nash dom—Gazprom). However, given Chernomyrdin's status within the government, he could not easily champion Gazprom or the oil companies at the expense of other interests. He (as prime minister) and NDR in general were supported by a wide spectrum of industrial and regional elites, which they could ignore only at their peril. Most of the NDR members in the Duma (especially those elected from the single-mandate territories) represent the interests of their own regions, which are linked directly to various industrial interests.

TABLE 4.3   The Effectiveness of Political Reforms Since 1992 (as percent of total responses)

	Oil Executives (N=65)	Politicians (N=30)
Effective, and almost no need for change	4.5	0
Effective but needing some reforms	27.7	10.0
In general not effective, but significant reforms could be carried out under present system	52.3	40.0
Completely ineffective, and complete change is necessary	13.8	50.0
No response	1.5	0

Chi-square = .003. Difference between the responses of the two sets of respondents is statistically significant. Responses were elicited by the question "As a result of the political and economic reforms that have taken place since 1993, is the present political system…?"

SOURCE: Author's compilation based on original survey data.

Most parties and parliamentary fractions, however, are critical of the interests of the oil and gas industry. The liberal wing in the Duma (e.g., deputies from Yabloko, the party of Grigorii Yavlinskii) supports measures to increase the tax pressure on the complex. They have criticized Chernomyrdin and his government for their support of oil industrialists and Gazprom.

Most communist and nationalist members of the Duma do not share the attitude toward economic reform and policy that is adopted by the higher management of most of the oil and gas industry. I have attempted to gauge these differences of opinion by interviewing a number of oil executives and politicians.

Divisions Between Oil Elites and Elite Politicians

The oil executives and politicians surveyed above were asked their opinions about the effectiveness of the political reforms since 1992 and the current economic system. The responses are shown in Tables 4.3 and 4.4. Attitudes toward the political system were divided, with a majority of the oil elite advocating considerable change, and half of the politicians calling for complete systemic change. This is obvious evidence of considerable doubt among the politicians and a substantial concern among oil executives about the effectiveness of the present regime. As to the economic system, there is a striking difference between the politicians and the oil executives: Of the former, 50 percent called for a complete change; of the latter, about 8 percent said that a complete change was unnecessary, but more than half believed that the system was ineffective. It seems clear from these responses that a critical mass, even among the oil executives, had lost confidence in prevailing policies. They sought reforms but were prepared to work

TABLE 4.4   The Effectiveness of the Current Economic System (as a percent of total responses)

	Oil Executives (N=65)	Politicians (N=30)
Effective, and almost no need for change	1.5	0
Effective but needing some reforms	32.3	10.0
In general not effective, but reforms could be carried out under present system	53.8	36.7
Completely ineffective, and complete change is necessary	7.7	50.0
No response	4.6	3.3

Chi-square = .00011. Difference between the responses of the two groups of respondents is statistically significant. Responses were elicited by the question "As a result of the political and economic reforms that have taken place since 1993, is the present economic system...?"

SOURCE: Author's compilation based on original survey data.

within existing structures to achieve change. Far greater disillusionment, however, was expressed by the politicians.

A lack of confidence is also indicated by the very large numbers of respondents believing that corruption and lawlessness is widespread. Over three-quarters of the oil executives and politicians agreed that corruption was widespread (see Table 4.5), and 41 percent of the oil executives and 83 percent of the politicians thought that lawlessness characterized economic life (see Table 4.6). The politicians had a significantly more negative view of the extent of corruption than the oil executives. These views are indicative of the attitudes of most deputies in the Duma, who support a considerable strengthening of state control of the oil and gas sector; a massive redistribution of resources from these industries to those unable to withstand competition (the consumer and manufacturing industries and agriculture); and increased support for social welfare. Their agenda includes the restoration of the state monopoly for the export of oil, gas, and oil derivatives, and the maintenance of state property through government ownership of shares in the energy complex. In the past, the left opposition opposed privatization and insisted on annulling the loan-for-shares auctions. But after 1996, there was no active campaigning for the renationalization of the oil companies and Gazprom—even by the Communists.

The nationalist-communist-agrarian faction in the Duma advocates the regulation of prices for energy and their maintenance at levels much lower than world price levels. It supports the transfer of the tax burden to the energy complex, and the use of rents and profits from the oil/gas industries to support other domestic industries. It seeks to limit the access of foreign investors to the strategic sectors

TABLE 4.5   The Extent of Corruption

	Oil Executives (N=65)	Politicians (N=30)	(percent responding positively)
Completely agree	76.6	83.3	
Agree, with reservations	20.3	16.7	
Do not agree, with reservations	1.6	0	
Completely disagree	1.6	0	
No response	1.5	0	

Responses were elicited to the statement "Today in Russian society there is widespread prevalence of corruption."

Source: Author's compilation based on original survey data.

TABLE 4.6   The Extent of Economic Criminalization

	Oil Executives (N=65)	Politicians (N=30)	(percent responding positively)
response: "Lawbreaking occurs..."			
From time to time	1.7	0	
Often, but economy in general is healthy	57.6	16.7	
Economic life has in general a criminal character	40.7	83.3	
No response	9.2	0	

Responses were elicited by the question "How do you evaluate the level of criminalization in economic life?"

Source: Author's compilation based on original survey data.

of the economy, particularly in the energy sector (the left opposition blocked the introduction and then the implementation of the 1995 production-sharing law). This type of opposition helps explain why the oil/gas elite unequivocally supported Yeltsin and his administration.

As to the upper house of the Russian parliament, the Federation Council, in which sit representatives of the regions, here the interests of the fuel and power complex again are in the minority. Most of the Russian regions lack energy resources, and their enterprises and communal services as a rule are unable to pay the rising prices of fuel and power. They therefore support regulation of fuel prices.

One can point, however, to the formation (beginning in 1994) of an interest group in support of the oil and gas lobby: a bloc of representatives of the oil/gas territories of Russia, calling itself the Association of Economic Inter-Relationships, whose main goal was to represent the interests of these regions.

Among the members were representatives of the Tyumen, Tomsk, Orenburg, and Sakhalin regions; Khanty-Mansi and Yamalo-Nenets autonomous okrugs; and the republics of Bashkortostan, Tatarstan, and Komi. The association has not been very active in supporting the oil and gas companies, but one can expect it to support regional interests against those of the center.

We may safely conclude that the oil and gas companies do not enjoy much support in parliament. The hostility of many members of the Duma is potentially a significant problem for the oil elite, as the Duma may block or significantly influence legislation affecting their well-being. The industry therefore may find it necessary to intensify pressure on deputies in the Duma. On the eve of the election in 1995, for instance, some leaders of the industry tried to organize their own pre-election campaign, in which a leading role was to be played by the association SISTEK (Union of Information and Collaboration in the Fuel and Power Complex), which was to finance 94 regional newspapers, through which election-eering (propaganda in support of particular candidates) would be carried out. It was also proposed that when the new parliament was formed, their supporters would try "to persuade" nonaligned deputies to support the lobby. [22] This proposal was also supported by the management of SNGP, led by Vladimir Medvedev. However, the oil and gas elites did not formally support it, and in the election, they instead backed the NDR movement.

The prevailing policy of "within-system" interest articulation had its limits, and one can expect the oil companies in future to take a more positive public role. One important step was their buying into the national media industry: Gazprom owns a large share in the television company NTV as well as in regional newspapers. LUKoil bought *Izvestiya,* then lost control to Oneksimbank. As banks and financial services increase control over the oil companies, they may use their media control (for example, Most-Bank controls NTV and the papers *Segodnya* and *Moskovskii komsomolets*) to influence public opinion. If the Duma becomes a more significant obstacle to the president's powers, it may be necessary to create there a more favorable climate toward the energy sector's interests. Also, the policy of the presidential administration as well as the advisory role of external agencies (the IMF and the World Bank) may work against the present interests of the industry. This was the case under Yeltsin, with respect to the collection of taxes from the energy sector, resulting in a call for support by the president of Gazprom, Rem Vyakhirev, to the deputies of the State Duma.

Conclusions: From "Chaotic" to Corporative Capitalism?

From this analysis of the oil industry one can draw a number of generalizations concerning the type of capitalism that is developing in Russia. My hypothesis is that we are witnessing an extreme type of "disorganized" capitalism, which may be called "chaotic capitalism."

Advocates of markets insist that they not only secure the coordination of economic activity but also enhance the efficiency and effectiveness of modern enterprise. The market promotes coordination and coherence: The forces of demand and supply embedded in a competitive market with a free price system lead to the rational and optimal allocation of resources. The market approach is also adopted in political and social life, in a democratic form of competition between groups and a pluralistic, multifactorial analysis of society. In both the economic and the political spheres the market was recommended as a model for the postcommunist states by influential Western economic advisers, and it has formed the policy background of the radical reforms which have taken place.

But the operation of "free markets" has been increasingly criticized in market economies on the grounds that competition leads to disorganized capitalism, with its attendant tendencies toward recession, inflation, unemployment, and a fragmented political structure and civil society.[23] The relationships among economy, state, and society under developed capitalism, critics contend, are asymmetric. These same asymmetric tendencies also have characterized Russian society during the transition, but in a more extreme way than in other societies, and what prevails in Russia therefore might be termed *chaotic capitalism*. Chaotic capitalism is a social and economic system that lacks coordination: goals, laws, governing institutions, and economic life lack cohesiveness. Its prevalent characteristics are elite disunity; the absence of a mediating class system; criminalization and corruption; inadequate political interest articulation; and an economy characterized by decline, inflation, and unemployment.

In postcommunist Russia, industries vary greatly in their capacity to adapt to market conditions, particularly when exposure to global competition is taken into account. As a consequence of marketization, the industries of energy and raw materials (metals), on the whole, have adapted to the world market, whereas manufacturing and agriculture have not. The adoption of a free market policy by the oil and gas industries—for instance, by raising internal prices to the world level—would be detrimental (at least in the short run) to such industries, and would severely depress domestic production of consumer goods. Russia is not Kuwait; the country is a major world power, it has a comprehensive industrial economy, a major military capacity, and a highly educated and urban population. The weakness of the Russian economy directly affects the politics of Russian oil, which—should the industry adopt internally a fully free market policy—would have unacceptable political and social costs.

The free market approach has been challenged—first, by sociologists and elite theorists, and second, by advocates of "institutional capitalism." Coordination under conditions of Western market capitalism, these critics assert, can never be achieved solely through market competition. A dominant ruling class and state, bound together through amorphous social and political networks, must provide cohesion, countering the tendency toward disorganization entailed in market operations.[24] In Russia, however, there is no ruling class supportive of a property-owning democracy and its attendant forms of civil society. Study of the Russian oil industry illustrates that its economic and political elites are fragmented and divided, and contribute to the development of chaotic capitalism. Networks of power and social cohesion have not been formed.

The state has provided another framework for coordination, expressed in theories of monopoly capitalism, corporatism,[25] and—in an extreme form—state socialism. However, in capitalist countries a downturn in profits and upsurge in state fiscal problems have led to a decline of the state's coordinating and regulatory role.[26] The power of the state has weakened, and it has become less concerned with welfare and more with the provision of an environment in which capitalism can flourish. Similar developments occurred in the former USSR and continue in postcommunist Russia. The movements for market reform were inspired by the economic thinking of the New Right in Western countries. Emergent capitalism in Russia, legitimated by a market philosophy, predates the role of the IMF, and has eroded the strong role previously played by the state in the USSR. The serious fiscal problems of the state and the fragmented and weak state apparatus promote chaotic capitalism.

The early settlement for the oil and gas industry led in the direction of the state providing a shell of coordination-giving cohesion to the system. The intention of the early Yeltsin government, in support of the fuel and power ministry, was to maintain a large stake of property in its ownership, which might have provided the basis for an evolving system of state capitalism. This would have involved competition among partly privatized companies in a market economy. Gazprom is a model in this respect.

By 1998, however, state assets in the oil industry had been sold, and the industry was largely privatized. There are numerous reasons for a move to a still more privatized market economy: Radical reformers in the government and presidential apparatus are ideologically committed to it; and outside interests such as Western governments, financial services, and the IMF strongly support it. The oil companies themselves profit from it, and in attempting to strengthen their market position they have sought further capital investment not only from Russian banks and financial institutions but also from foreigners. Oil executives as a whole appear to accept the movement toward a company-owned oil industry operating on market principles. The deep national budget deficits, themselves a consequence of state attempts to counter disorganization of the economy, have been a further factor leading to the sale of government assets.

Ironically, perhaps, the feudal sheikdoms of Kuwait, the Muslim traditionalists of Iran, and the military dictatorship of Iraq provide a stronger political shell for the preservation of their respective national oil industries than does Russia's fragmented and weak government. But the governing apparatuses are not in agreement, and the legislative chambers in general do not support a free market policy. Politicians are more sympathetic to supporting other Russian industries through subsidies to keep oil prices low, and they support greater state involvement and control. This is a major point of conflict in the regulation of the oil industry. In this context, external international agencies, such as the IMF, play an important role in restructuring the economy. Under present conditions, external involvement can only lead to strengthening the market and weakening the role of the government. The contradictory interests of the oil and gas industry, the dominant factions in the parliament, the market-oriented coordinating apparatuses, and the fragmented governmental ministries and departments all point to the weakness of the state as a means of coordinating capitalism. All of these factors have contributed to chaotic capitalism.

What, then, are the possibilities in Russia of coordination being based on a model of cooperative capitalism rather than competitive capitalism—in other words, on the German or French model? There are many developments in the oil industry and elsewhere that would point in this direction. First is the role of financial institutions and the interlocking ownership of holding and subsidiary companies. Russian banks and financial institutions, between 1994 and 1997, clearly became the leading institutional owners, with the government maintaining only residual holdings. Second is the power of management in controlling the companies. Management not only owns considerable numbers of shares but is strategically positioned in companies to provide leadership. The management interest, inherited from the state socialist system, is far more confident in pursuing a hegemonic role than that usually found in the oil industry in the West—though a similar situation has occurred in Venezuela. Third, one must consider the political factor. The orientation inherited from state socialism is a corporate one.

These developments point to a model of cooperative capitalism, with financial institutions and other companies having considerable stakes in the holding companies, and management having power over strategic decisions. The state, moreover, may play a greater role in coordination. It is not a homogeneous body with a unitary, free market ideology and interest. This position is taken by the ministries of finance and of the economy, GKI, and GKAP. However, other ministries—particularly those associated with manufactures (the ministries of industry, agriculture, science, defense, and possibly foreign affairs)—as well as regional political authorities may well adopt a more corporatist and interventionist approach, in support of various domestic constituencies favoring state ownership. The state is still a significant owner of assets in the economy.

The political context of potential state control and the crucial role played by the energy industries in the economic development of the country could significantly limit the power of the banking and financial interests as well as the narrow interests of the oil companies. Hence the German model of "cooperative capitalism" needs to be adapted to provide a greater role to political actors (as is the case in France). At the macro level, to maintain coordination and coherence of the economy, political leaders in control of ministries and the economy—particularly the president—have much more potential in Russia than they have in the West. The Yeltsin leadership used its power to strengthen market elements and in so doing created a structure of disorganized or chaotic capitalism. This trend could be reversed by a new presidential administration.

To conclude, the present Russian polity and economy may be defined as chaotic capitalism. There is no clear compact between the elites concerning the extent of state regulation and market competition. But the wider context of political and economic interests may yet see a revival and strengthening of the state. Even a deregulated, privatized oil industry is subject to political intervention—as the history of the Middle East bears witness. It seems unlikely that the Russian federal government will retake a controlling interest in the major oil companies. Not only is the state divided between federal and regional bodies, but external interests—other Western governments and international agencies—are likely to be influential players, and at least in the foreseeable future, will demand a privatized and open economy. A possible constellation of political interests is that of the dominant groups in the Duma allied with industries and their ministries operating principally for the domestic market. In opposition are currently relatively successful export industries, such as oil, which are associated with radical market reformers and external powers, such as the IMF. There is an affinity here between the doctrine of free markets and economic interest. The free market policy, which has predominated, has not led to stability but neither has it led to breakdown; it has led to chaos. In this context, the political becomes a major determinant of economic change. A key factor is the presidency; Russia's new president could well turn the country in the direction of corporate, cooperative capitalism.

Notes

The research for this chapter was supported by a grant from the British Economic and Social Research Council. I also acknowledge the research work of Iskander Seifulmulukov, which contributed to the chapter.

1. Each had approximately a quarter of the output of Shell (*Economist,* 24 January 1998, p. 68).

2. *Ekspert,* no. 38, 6 October 1997.

3. *Sotsial'no-ekonomicheskoe polozhenie Rossii,* no. 12 (Moscow: Goskomstat RF, 1995).

4. There was a rise of 1.5 percent in oil (and condensate) production between 1996 and 1997.

5. World Energy Analysis and Forecasting Group, cited by Eugene M. Khartukov, *Oil and Gas Journal,* 18 August 1997, p. 39.

6. *Izvestiya,* 31 July 1997, p. 2. Cited by Peter Rutland, *Lost Opportunities: Energy and Politics in Russia* (Washington, D.C.: National Bureau of Asian Research, 1997), p. 12.

7. Extraction came under the Ministry of the Petroleum Industry (Minnefteprom), refineries under the Ministry of the Petrochemical Industry (Minneftekhimprom), and distribution under the State Supplies Committee (Gossnab); and export was controlled by Soyuznefteksport, a division of the Ministry of Foreign Economic Relations. Exploration and exploitation of mineral resources came under three ministries (Geology, Minnefteprom, and Mingazprom [the Ministry of the Natural Gas Industry]). Also linked

to the oil and gas complex were ministries of oil and gas equipment and building. Refineries were independent from oil production associations and were subordinate to Minneftekhimprom. The domestic oil products distribution network was organized on a regional basis and included oil storage facilities and filling stations. In the early 1980s, a Bureau for Fuel and Power was formed within the Soviet government, which coordinated the policy of the various ministries. At the level of oil production, moreover, production associations were formed, into which were brought extraction units and related production plants, such as oil exploration and transport.

8. *Ekspert,* no. 22, 10 June 1996, p. 4.

9. Most of the interviews were organized by the polling agency VTsIOM in summer 1997. Forty respondents worked in Moscow, 5 in Bashkortostan, and 5 in Tatarstan. Fifteen supplementary interviews on a limited range of questions were carried out with other oil executives in Moscow. This gave a total of 65 interviews. Of these executives, 24 were employed by holding companies, 3 by subsidiaries, 28 by independents, and 9 by government companies.

10. For example, export quotas, registered exporters, and foreign currency exchange controls.

11. In 1990 and 1991, before setting up the LUKoil concern, Vagit Alekperov had visited the headquarters of several large Western oil corporations, and he was well aware of their structure and organization.

12. Eugene M. Khartukov, *Oil and Gas Journal,* 18 August 1997, p. 38.

13. Yukos, Sibneft press statement, 21 January 1998.

14. *Finansovye izvestiya,* 27 March 1997, p. 1. Cited in Rutland, *Lost Opportunities,* p. 23.

15. *Kommersant-Daily,* 6 February 1996.

16. The oil elite was initially defined as members of the boards of directors of holding companies in 1995–1996: 55 biographies were analyzed to give a composite picture of the contemporary leaders of the oil industry. By way of comparison, 118 leading people in banking and financial services also were considered. These individuals were selected on the basis of published studies of the top hundred "most influential" entrepreneurs and bankers (chosen by a panel of Russian finance experts in 1996), and some were selected from among the leading entrepreneurs listed in business directories published in Moscow in 1996 and 1997.

17. The politicians' group included 8 members of the government of the Russian Federation and 22 members of the Russian Duma, selected from committees or areas with an interest in energy. They included representatives from Tyumen, Komi, Orenburg, Krasnodar, Khanty-Mansiysk, Bashkortostan, Samara, Irkutsk, Ivanovo, Perm, Yakutiya, Krasnoyarsk, Irkutsk, and the Koryak autonomous district. (Others were directly elected on party lists.)

18. The government raised excise taxes for natural gas twice in the course of 1995, and Gazprom's special "stabilization fund" was liquidated. From September 1, 1995 until April 1, 1996, the government virtually froze natural gas prices; on April 1, 1996, the export tax for gas was abolished, but this did not outweigh the harm to Gazprom revenues.

19. The development of contacts with the countries of the CIS is the responsibility of the Ministry of Foreign Economic Relations (MVES). The collection and use of geological information and the granting of licenses for deep extraction are within the purview of the Ministry of Natural Resources.

20. Capital flight has been estimated at between $10 billion and $15 billion per annum (*Finansovye izvestiya,* 22 April 1997). Cited by Rutland, *Lost Opportunities,* p. 18.

21. See, for example, the interview with Sergei Muravlenko in *Kommersant-Daily,* 27 April 1995.

22. *Kommersant-Daily,* 16 August 1995.

23. For a discussion of liberal, organized, and disorganized capitalism, see Scott Lash and J. Urry, *The End of Organised Capitalism* (London: Polity Press, 1989).

24. M. Useem, *The Inner Circle: Large Corporations and the Rise of Business Political Activity in the US and UK* (Oxford: Oxford University Press, 1984); John Scott, *Corporations, Classes and Capitalism* (London: Hutchinson, 1985), p. 246.

25. P. C. Schmitter, "Still the century of corporatism?" in P. C. Schmitter and G. Lehmbruch, eds., *Trends Toward Corporatist Intermediation* (London: Sage, 1979); R. E. Pahl and J. T. Winkler, "Corporatism in Britain," in *The Corporate State: Reality or Myth?* (London: Centre for Studies in Social Policy, 1976).

26. James O'Connor, *The Fiscal Crisis of the State* (New York: St. Martin's, 1973); *Accumulation Crisis* (New York: Basil Blackwell, 1984); Michael Keating, *The Politics of Modern Europe* (London: Edward Elgar, 1993), p. 4.

CHAPTER 5

Between a Rock and a Hard Place: Russia's Troubled Coal Industry

Stephen Crowley

Russia's coal industry is in dire straits. The industry is poised to become one of the clear losers of market reform. Long a proud symbol of Soviet industrialization, the industry is far too large given the country's present and likely future demand for coal. The Russian government, backed by the World Bank, has responded by cutting subsidies and closing coal mines at a rate that the industry cannot absorb. The lead organization of the coal industry—the Russian coal company, or Rosugol—has been dismantled. On top of all this, Russia's coal miners are confronting a rise in catastrophic accidents; they lead the country in wage arrears; and they are responding with increasingly desperate measures.

The case of the Russian coal industry raises some interesting questions: How can this huge industry so needed at one stage of industrial development be downsized to fit current needs? How quickly should such reductions be carried out, and who should bear the burden? How can an appropriate balance be struck between what is economically compelling and what is politically feasible? Finally, what influence do institutions such as the World Bank have over such structural reforms in a country like Russia? On this last question, some have argued, the World Bank and the International Monetary Fund (IMF) can be quite influential, and even sinister. Others have argued that the influence of the Bank's conditionality has been overrated, and that when it is effective, it is relatively benign.[1] The reality in this particular case is more complex than either characterization.

The players in this drama extend beyond the arenas of business and state, along a continuum from the international to the local. They include the World Bank; the Russian government; the coal industry (which is made up of Rosugol; twenty or so coal associations, each controlling roughly twenty mines; and individual mine managers); and lastly, the miners and their trade unions. The interests of these actors, particularly concerning the rate of change and the number of jobs lost, also follow this continuum.

Although it is an industry in trouble, the coal sector has had high visibility within Russia. Since it is heavily concentrated in certain regions, and as Russia's miners have repeatedly demonstrated they are the most militant segment of Russia's labor force, coal's influence extends beyond its economic importance. In the words of a study commissioned by the World Bank, the reform of the coal industry is "one of the key issues that influence the balance of politics in Russia."[2]

Russia holds one-fourth of the world's estimated reserves of coal, and its industry is currently the fourth-largest coal producer in the world. As recently as 1992, the industry employed 900,000 people, though the current number of coal industry employees is probably less than half that amount. Production has also been cut almost in half: In 1988, production of coal in Russia peaked at over 400 million tons; in 1997, Russia produced only 225 million tons.[3] About 80 percent of all underground and open-cut mines need immediate modernization and new equipment.[4] Only one basin meets world standards in terms of coal quality and extraction costs—the Kuzbass, in West Siberia; but unfortunately, the basin is thousands of kilometers from the nearest point of export. The World Bank argues that although under market conditions the Russian coal industry will remain one of the largest in world, the future "viable core" of that industry will probably be about two-thirds the size it was in 1994, and total employment could be less than half.

The reshaping of the Russian coal industry is part of the larger process of integrating Russia into the world capitalist economy. For the industrialized countries of the capitalist world, high rates of growth in production and consumption of raw materials and fuels such as coal were an essential part of industrialization many years ago. Over time, these rates slowed, stabilized, and in some cases, declined. As industrialized countries capitalized on their comparative advantage in processed and manufactured goods, investment capital was drawn to these industries rather than to the extractive industries such as coal, which were accordingly downsized.

In the case of coal, this downsizing accelerated with the arrival of cheap, imported oil in the early 1960s. As a result, in the past four decades or so, the "coal industry world-wide has been through a long and painful restructuring."[5] During this period, the number of jobs in the industry was cut by 75 percent in Belgium, France, Germany, and the United Kingdom, and by more than 50 percent in the United States. In Russia this process has barely begun.[6]

Even though Western experience uniformly points in the direction of cutting back on coal mining, there are significant differences among Western countries in how this was carried out. In the United Kingdom, coal industry employment was reduced from 490,000 in 1960 to 30,000 in 1993. Many of the layoffs occurred between 1981 and 1993—recall the wave of strikes in 1983 and 1984, under Margaret Thatcher, when 181 out of 211 mines were shut down and 255,000 of 281,000 workers were let go.[7] In contrast, West Germany reduced its coal industry from 400,000 to 90,000 employees over 30 years—on average, a 4 percent annual reduction in employment over the three decades. This slower approach, too, was not without costs: Germany continues to subsidize coal jobs. This means that for political and social reasons Germany decided to spread the costs of coal industry reduction to consumers and other industries as well as miners. Roughly speaking, the World Bank and liberals in the Russian government want Russia to take the Thatcher route, whereas Russian coal miners and industry officials prefer the German approach.

The next sections of this chapter examine Russia's coal industry in the late 1990s, then focus on the interests and actions of various actors. Here we will look particularly at the main industrial body—Rosugol—and the World Bank's successful attempt to do away with it. Finally, we will focus on the miners—the last, formidable obstacle to the rapid contraction of Russia's coal industry.

From Plan to Market

Russia's coal problems began as far back as the late 1950s, when "a brake was applied to the development of the coal industry" as planners in Moscow decided to place greater emphasis on oil and gas. As a result, the coal mines lacked funds for necessary reconstruction.[8]

The problems in the Soviet coal industry only deepened with the first attempts at economic reform under Gorbachev, years later. One important step was the introduction of full *khozraschet,* or self-financing, which was intended to increase management's concern with profits and losses. Yet because this step was not accompanied by a commensurate reform in pricing, it had a perverse effect, particularly in the coal industry. The price a mine received for one ton of coal extracted (the official, wholesale price) was roughly one-half the cost of extraction. The wholesale price was arbitrarily fixed and in no way reflected the real level of demand. This situation made coal the only "planned-loss" industry in the country. Since the wholesale price of coal was administratively set at such a low level, it was nearly impossible to disentangle the exact costs of extraction and the amount of subsidies, or to calculate profits should the price of coal be raised to reflect its market value.

This resulting economic squeeze was one cause of the 1989 miners' strike, which marked the entrance of coal miners onto Russia's political stage. Beginning in a single mine in the Kuzbass, the strike soon spread throughout the Soviet Union. The impact of this strike is hard to overestimate: As Mikhail Gorbachev himself conceded, "The rapid destruction of the social order that existed for 70 years began with the miners' [strike] wave."[9] As surprising as it seems now (and for reasons I have sought to explain elsewhere), the miners began to argue that their salvation lay in the creation of the market.[10] This trend was especially evident in the Kuzbass—Russia's largest coal basin, and the former Soviet Union's only source of world market–quality coal.

This push for the market was driven in no small part by the very low state purchase price for coal relative to the world market price. The miners argued that if they were allowed to retain their above-plan coal and sell it on the world market, they would have a better standard of living. With this understanding, they joined a growing alliance of liberal reformers around Boris Yeltsin, and backed him in spring 1991, in a two-month strike that helped bring about the end of the Soviet Union.

Although Yeltsin had promised coal miners the market as their salvation, as the president of independent Russia he paid off the miners with greater subsidies to the industry—initially, in return for their political loyalty, and later, because of their increasing militancy. When the Russian government led by Prime Minister Yegor Gaidar embarked on a policy of "shock therapy," leading to sharply rising prices and falling real wages, the "only serious challenge to the Gaidar measures came in the coal mining regions."[11] The miners' strike threats and actual work stoppages "met little resistance from the government." One strike by the miners ended with the tripling of miners' average wages to 7,000 rubles, when the national average was 900 rubles.[12]

Given a nearly twentyfold rise in the general price level in 1992 and corresponding further wage increases, the government was hard pressed, trying to print enough money to keep up with wage payments; thus began Russia's wage arrears problem.[13] The high wages paid to miners, combined with the still artificially low prices for coal, meant that by May 1993, subsidies to the coal industry alone were absorbing 20 percent of revenues to the Russian state budget.[14] (Coal subsidies have since remained second only to those of agriculture.) The sharp increase in subsidies helped expand a ballooning budget deficit, amid fears that the Russian economy might reach hyperinflation and spin out of control.

It was at this point, and for this reason, that the World Bank decided to intervene—not to improve the efficiency of the Russian coal industry per se but to reduce the burden that coal placed on the government budget and on the economy generally.

Despite Russian miners' earlier avowed support for the market, when the Yeltsin government proposed "freeing" coal prices as a means of cutting subsidies and the budget deficit, the proposal met with strong opposition. Yeltsin's decree on liberalizing coal prices as of July 1, 1993 led to protests from miners, since they justifiably feared that market prices would not cover their losses and might lead to the closure of half of Russia's mines.[15]

Coal prices before the decree had approximated 4 percent of world market prices; after it, they quickly shot up by a factor of nine, forcing the price of domestically produced steel above world prices.[16] The resulting protests, both from miners and from large coal consumers such as the steel industry, resulted in a considerable softening of the decree and in continued subsidies, reversing most of the decree's intended effects on the budget and on inflation.[17]

Soon after gaining wage increases and promises of continued subsidies, the mining regions were hit with proposed pit closures. Within weeks of the announced liberalization of coal prices, miners in Vorkuta staged a warning strike over a proposal to close mines, stating that guarantees needed to be in place to provide new jobs for any miners let go.[18] The proposal to close mines was also softened, so that in October 1993 the plan was to shut down 42 mines by the year 2000.[19] (Yet, further strikes were called over the government's failure to provide any social guarantees for unemployed miners in the event of layoffs.) Russia's plan for limited closures was announced the same month as the World Bank's draft proposal calling for between 30 and 40 mine closures, or the layoff of 50,000–100,000 redundant coal workers, per year.[20]

After that, the coal industry's troubles only deepened. Coal was especially hard hit by nonpayments and wage arrears: The industry led the country in wage arrears, with average delays of seven months, giving rise to considerable labor conflict.[21] Inter-enterprise debt was also high.

Another central reason for the coal industry's debt crisis was that it was being squeezed by three of Russia's most powerful monopolies: electricity, gas, and railroads. Most coal goes to electric power plants; and Unified Energy System (EES) holds more than one-half of all coal debts. Gazprom also exerts a weighty influence; in Russia as elsewhere, natural gas is coal's main competitor. Domestic prices have strongly favored natural gas: In 1994, when Russian coal prices were two and one-half times lower than world prices for coal, domestic gas prices were more than five times below world gas prices. And whereas coal was subsidized, oil and gas enjoyed considerable tax breaks. According to one source, more than half of the coal subsidies are recovered in taxes (or would be, at least, if taxes were paid more often in Russia).[22]

The third monopoly squeezing coal is the rail industry. As mentioned earlier, Russia's one world-class coal basin is thousands of kilometers from places of export. When the Kuzbass miners demanded market reforms, they were counting on market prices for coal but not on market prices for rail freight. In addition, since the Russian rail industry is a natural monopoly, true market prices for rail freight are not easily determined. From 1991 to 1995, rail freight prices increased three times more than prices for industrial goods.[23] This further damaged the coal industry relative to gas, since gas transport costs remained constant.

The combined effects of these disadvantages led to some rather absurd outcomes. In the Kuzbass, of all places, energy users began switching from coal to gas.[24] A further, bitter blow to the Kuzbass miners who had pushed for entrance to the market was the World Bank's plan, under which "the most difficult situation will be in the Kuzbass, where total employment could fall from about 300,000 to 70,000–80,000 workers at the end of the restructuring period"—ideally, within three to five years.[25]

The World Bank to the Rescue?

Let us now turn to the World Bank's Russian coal project in some detail. The Bank's role has been central, since, unlike oil and gas, the coal industry in Russia has dim prospects of becoming profitable, and private capital in the form of domestic financial-industrial giants or multinational corporations has not been clambering to gain control. In these conditions, public funds can have considerable leverage.

A loan for substantially reducing Russia's coal industry also looked appealing to the World Bank, because, besides pushing Russia toward fiscal order, the loan appears "green": Less coal use can mean cleaner air, and air quality has been a major problem in Russia. This effect would enable the Bank to defend itself against environmentalists, who have long accused it of pursuing projects harmful to the environment.[26]

The Bank could also claim, as we shall see, that much of its funding would be aimed at creating a social safety net for coal communities. This would be an important factor in launching the program, which had caused some internal as well as external controversy in that regard. As a World Bank consultant on a similar World Bank coal project for Ukraine explained to me (though not for attribution), the Bank's legal department had raised objections over the program because of a clause in the Bank's charter stating that it must never knowingly cause poverty.

The coal loan was the first sectoral adjustment loan (or SECAL, in Bank language) financed by the Bank in Russia. This made the coal restructuring project a visible one, with high stakes for both the Russian government and the World Bank. As one source put it: "The coal loan is in a class by itself.... The World Bank is especially concerned about the likely failure of this project in Russia."[27]

The Bank's report stated that the current situation in the Russian coal industry was catastrophic. The demand for coal was falling, and yet employment levels were largely unchanged. Subsidies were larger than the total wage bill for the industry—leading the Bank to note that it would be cheaper to pay miners not to mine than to continue subsidizing the industry. The longer the restructuring was drawn out, the report contended, the greater would be the burden on government budget. Hence the recommendation that the bulk of restructuring be carried out within three to five years.

The Bank report urged the government to decentralize its restructuring strategy. In this regard, much of the Bank's concern was focused on the national coal company Rosugol. Price controls on coal had been removed, but Rosugol continued to exert a strong influence on coal prices through its distribution of subsidies. Rosugol, the bank charged, was cross-subsidizing (supporting weak producers at the expense of the strong), and hence creating perverse incentives. The Bank called for shifting government support from subsidizing production to funding social services and providing temporary support for laid-off miners.

The first draft of the coal report was given to the Russian government in November 1993, just weeks before the parliamentary elections of that year. In those elections the reform parties were unexpectedly drubbed and the top party vote was taken by the Liberal Democratic Party of Russia, led by radical nationalist Vladimir Zhirinovsky. In consequence, the tone of the report was softened considerably. When the official report was released in December 1994, the references to 40 mine closures and 100,000 layoffs per year had been dropped. But the impact was the same: The report called for "zeroing out" all coal subsidies within four years. In order for this goal to be reached, there would have to be even more closures per year than the earlier report had anticipated.[28]

Some of the Bank's advice was ludicrous, suggesting the degree to which the international lending agency was removed from Russian reality. For instance, the draft report recommended that entrepreneurial training for laid-off miners be run by the mining communities' "chambers of commerce." (There were no such organizations.) Other palliatives were so trivial as to seem condescending, such as the "'Golden Rules' of Restructuring," the first of which states, "Restructuring means change, which is never easy." But more central and more problematic was the proposal that employment be cut in half within three to five years.[29] Surprisingly, given that this proposal was aimed at the single most militant labor force in Russia, there was practically no mention of strikes in the two-volume report.

This proposal would not have been so influential had it not found sympathetic ears in the Russian government. Given the miners' militancy, the government's responsibility for the coal industry was a political noose around its neck. From the perspective of liberal reformers, a nonsubsidized, privatized, and substantially smaller and therefore less influential coal industry would be a worthy goal indeed—if it could be achieved.

But the state's position was divided. Rosugol was also a government entity, and its perspective, as one would imagine, was quite different from that of the liberal reformers. Rosugol responded to the Bank's proposal by claiming that its own forecast of the demand for coal was much higher, and therefore the number of mine closures should be that much lower. In contrast to the Bank's call for zero subsidies, Rosugol pointed to the considerable state support for the coal industry in most of world. It argued that closures were permissible only if funding was available to pay the costs, which included replacement jobs for miners, and where necessary, relocation of displaced miners. (Given Russia's housing shortage, this meant new housing and social infrastructure.) Hence, the pace of mine closures would not only be determined by future demand, itself under dispute, but also by the costs of downsizing; and as a result, the process would take much longer than three to five years.

No doubt high on the list of Rosugol's concerns was the Bank's proposal to do away with Rosugol. The Russian coal company was a strange, truly post-Soviet entity—a hybrid of state planning and the market. It was a state enterprise, set up by presidential decree in 1993. As such, it was fully owned by the state, and was responsible for distributing state subsidies to the various coal associations. Yet Rosugol was also a profit-making entity.

Headed by Yurii Malyshev, Rosugol had considerable clout.[30] Its powers included deciding on mine closures, purchasing major equipment, setting production targets, establishing consumer linkages, overseeing employment policy, and negotiating wage agreements.[31] It had control over substantial state funds in the form of subsidies, and the de facto ability to appoint coal managers, which in turn gave it the backing of the coal "generals" in the regions. Because it employed the top coal specialists in the country, it had a virtual monopoly on information about the industry. Even top government officials such as Anatolii Chubais and Yeltsin were said to depend on Malyshev; in cases such as the Primorye energy crisis and coal strikes, he alone was said to be able to get coal moving with a single phone call.[32] Critics alleged that Malyshev and other coal bosses instigated at least some of the coal strikes in the mid- to late 1990s.

In the words of *Segodnya:* "[Rosugol] for all practical purposes is the ruler of the coal mining regions. Its representatives often have a greater say than the local administrations in all local decisionmaking, from providing jobs and paying wages and salaries to turning on the heat in apartment buildings."[33] In short, Rosugol was a monopoly, although it did not enjoy the enviable market position of Gazprom.

This distributor of state subsidies was also engaged in various profit-making ventures, including banking, insurance, coal export, equipment import, and investments in transportation and communication. It obtained a copper concession and sought gold and diamond concessions. According to Rosugol, the coal company was merely diversifying and preparing to provide employment for laid-off miners. According to the World Bank, it was implicated in conflicts of interest, selling services to and making profits from the same enterprises to which it provided subsidies. Rosugol, the Bank argued, should confine itself to organizing mine closures. Instead, being engaged in "commercial activity," it took money earmarked for closures and transferred it to profitable mines, and even used it to finance the construction of new mines.[34]

A central condition of the World Bank funds became the de-monopolization of Rosugol. In essence, the national coal company was being asked to liquidate its position as the monopoly owner of property and distributor of resources. Not surprisingly, Rosugol put up a fight during negotiations between the Russian government and the World Bank regarding the coal industry loan.

A nationwide coal strike took place in February 1996, lasting two days and involving as many as 80 percent of the country's coal mines. The strike "brought the government to its knees," and "it satisfied all the miners' demands."[35] Some claimed the strike had been instigated by Rosugol. According to *Izvestiya,* "It was made rather clear to the government that if any document [on coal restructuring] is not to the liking of the coal lobby ... the authorities will be in big trouble with the politically united miners' movement." The commentator continued, "In effect, the position of the coal industry—both the trade unions and Rosugol—boils down to the following: Rosugol should continue to parcel out state subsidies.... and maintain control over state shares in mines." Until the World Bank came along, *Izvestiya* argued, "The only opponent of the powerful coal lobby was the Ministry of the Economy."[36]

The strike ended with a decree stating that Rosugol, initially a state enterprise, was to become an open-type joint-stock company, with Malyshev as president. Contrary to what *Izvestiya* claimed, the "coal lobby" was not united: The main miners' trade union, Rosugleprof, called for Rosugol to become a ministry again instead of a joint-stock company.[37] Thus, while Rosugol was seeking greater profits and the World Bank was trying to break it up, the miners' representatives were trying to re-tie their industry to the state.

An agreement on the first coal loan was signed by the Bank and the Russian government in May 1996, and the first tranche of US$250 million (then equivalent to 1.4 trillion rubles) was disbursed by the Bank in July. However, not long afterward it became clear that not all of the money was being spent as promised. The State Duma Audit Office charged Rosugol with doing an unsatisfactory job of closing mines: Less than one-half of the amount allocated for closures was spent on that purpose. The government subsequently announced that some 30 percent of government funds for the coal industry had been misappropriated.[38]

Such misspending made the coal loan a bone of contention in relations between Russia and the World Bank. Although Rosugol took the blame, much of the blame resting on it was misplaced: Of the first tranche, only 300 million rubles had been allotted to the coal industry, "while the rest was used for emergency measures to plug holes in the budget."[39] When the coal money did reach the coal regions, it was diverted again by local governments on the grounds that teachers and doctors were as much in need of their back wages as were miners.[40]

Given this dismal record, the prospects for receiving the second tranche of the coal loan did not seem bright. Indeed, the second tranche was linked to a new loan in 1997, of $800 million. The Bank's conditions for the second tranche included the transfer of 1.8 trillion (old) rubles for social services from mining enterprises to local governments; audits of six coal companies, including Rosugol; and the de-monopolization of the industry (the effective liquidation of Rosugol).[41] Not surprisingly, Rosugol became the focus of negotiations. For his part, Malyshev argued that those encroaching on Rosugol would bear the responsibility for mounting "social and political tension in the coal regions."[42]

Another nationwide coal strike took place in December 1996, with about 400,000 miners walking off the job. The strike was again said to have been instigated by Rosugol, sending the message, the newspaper *Segodnya* claimed, that "without the company's controlling hand, things will get worse."[43] But the government also knew that keeping Rosugol would mean saying good-bye to the second tranche of $250 million and the proposed second loan of $500 million (later, $800 million), both of which were already written into the government's budget. In fact, what seems to have set off this major strike was not Rosugol but the delay in receiving this second tranche, which the government had counted on to meet its coal expenditures for the end of the year.[44]

Within days after the end of the strike, First Deputy Prime Minister Vladimir Potanin announced that state-owned shares in five coal associations accounting for one-quarter of Russia's output were to be sold by competitive bidding, as part of the Bank's terms.[45] As Potanin noted, "There is one highly delicate aspect: the World Bank is insisting that Rosugol not participate in the bidding." Since the Bank's board would be deciding on the second tranche in a matter of days, "concessions are unavoidable here, since the government hasn't fully met the World Bank's requirements for the first tranche." He added, "As for the tough terms the World Bank has set for the credit, they are of course inconvenient, but they are doing a good job of mobilizing us."[46]

Bank president James Wolfensohn appeared to draw another line in the sand when he stated, "Russia will receive the second tranche of the coal loan after the structural reform of Rosugol."[47] The Bank later relented, releasing the second tranche with Rosugol largely intact, but it made clear that the second loan would be conditional on the dismantlement of Rosugol.

In July 1997, Rosugol and the energy ministry proposed that 51 percent of the coal company's shares remain state-owned and controlled by Rosugol "until the end of the restructuring of the branch." This announcement implied that the industry could be restructured successfully without the World Bank's second loan. The loan was described as a "bone in the throat" of Rosugol, but its loss would threaten the government with "great unpleasantness" in the form of restive miners.[48]

The following month, the Bank halted negotiations on the second coal loan, blaming Rosugol. The government had planned to use the Bank's money "to soften the deep cutbacks in state aid" to the coal industry. Said one government official, "We had all our hopes pinned on that Washington loan."[49] According to *Segodnya*, Chubais was having little success in convincing the Bank that "Russia's coal industry is in a unique predicament, which made it impossible to spend the loan in the way the bank prescribed," and that "the industry cannot get by without a second loan," since the government would likely face a "fall explosion" of coal strikes.[50] Chubais's political reputation was said to be in jeopardy, since the proposal to do without the bank loan "would amount to an admission that serious reform of the industry is impossible and the capitulation of the Chubais team to Rosugol." Furthermore, "At stake is the success of [Russia's] first major industrial modernization project, a project that will make it clear how capable the government is of carrying out reform in general."[51]

One month later, in September 1997, Chubais traveled to the annual meeting of the IMF and the World Bank in Hong Kong to plead with Bank president Wolfensohn over the coal loan. As a result, Russia received the $800 million. Overall, Chubais said the talks between Russia and the Bank over the coal loan were "the most complicated negotiations over the period of bilateral cooperation."[52]

The World Bank argued that it had achieved several positive results from the first loan. The government's coal subsidy had been reduced from 1.4 percent of

GDP in 1993 to about 0.2 percent in 1997, with the subsidy in 1997 nearly halved in real terms relative to 1996. Moreover, 58 mines had been closed, and preparation had been made to privatize four coal associations. But "the elimination of Rosugol ... was the main condition for obtaining the loan from the World Bank." The Russian national coal company was indeed dismantled at the last minute—just as the World Bank managing director boarded the plane for Moscow.[53]

Thus, at the cost of a total of $1.2 billion in promised loans, the World Bank defeated Rosugol. In the end, the coal company had lost a number of its potential allies. Just before the government's decision, Rosugol was criticized by the governors of various coal regions at a meeting of the Interdepartmental Commission charged with overseeing the industry. Some were explicit: Vladivostok mayor Viktor Cherepkov called the coal company a "soap bubble," and Kemerovo (Kuzbass) Governor Aman Tuleev said that "three girls" could take the place of Rosugol. Instead of the 300 billion rubles promised the Kuzbass at the last commission meeting, he complained, only 70 billion had arrived. When the national coal company was abolished, there was little reaction from the Kuzbass miners or the local government.[54]

Political leaders in the coal regions might have been expected to support the World Bank's call for decentralization of the coal industry. However, it remains far from clear that the problems associated with Rosugol could have been solved by giving more power to regional elites as opposed to entities controlled (at least, theoretically) by the state. For example, take Tuleev: Having been chastised by many of his local supporters for serving in the Yeltsin government in Moscow, Tuleev would have had every incentive to return to his old populist game and distance himself from Yeltsin politically by demanding more financial support from the center (without Rosugol as intermediary) and backing up this demand with threats of mass action.[55]

The Shape of Things to Come

The Bank's plan to privatize the coal associations as independent joint-stock companies does not seem particularly promising as a solution to the industry's problems. According to a social assessment of the coal project commissioned by the World Bank: "The management structures of almost all local coal associations seem unprepared to deal with the consequences of restructuring. Managers appear unaware of the fragile economic outlook for coal in the medium to long term and do not appreciate the need to reduce employment."[56] These same local coal managers have been charged with a variety of misdeeds including the misallocation of state subsidies and World Bank funds; the setting up of shadow firms to siphon off coal profits; collaboration with criminal gangs; and the deliberate withholding of wages.[57] Nor has this sort of behavior changed when mines are privatized: In one now infamous case, the Kuznetskaya mine—privatized in 1991 as a joint-stock company with an Austrian firm—had not paid its workers for two years, before miners and their wives locked the mine's top managers in their office and held them hostage.[58]

Indeed, it is the coal miners, not the managers or Rosugol, who present the biggest obstacle to planned cutbacks in the Russian coal industry. Russia's miners have a proven tendency to intervene at crucial points in national politics. This tendency has been reinforced as their well-timed strikes or strike threats have in the past led to considerable concessions and side-payments. The Bank's proposal challenged the miners in at least three crucial ways. First, the Bank called for abolishing the national "tariff agreement" on wages that the miners' unions had long sought. The Bank's report rather baldly states that when the national agreement was abolished, wages would fall, making the industry a less attractive place to work; this step was "crucial to the success of the employment reduction program."[59] Ironically, although the Bank envisioned this step as a move toward an American-style, flexible labor market, the tariff agreement, first demanded by the miners back in 1990, was part of an effort by the Independent Miners' Union (NPG) to become more like Western unions. Apparently the miners' original proposed tariff agreement was taken almost verbatim from a national contract of the United Auto Workers, with only minor changes in wording to reflect the differences in the industries.[60] The abrogation of the tariff agreement would not only mean lower wages for coal miners but would significantly weaken if not break the national unions, which unlike almost all other unions in Russia, had proven themselves to their members by obtaining these national wage agreements. According to Aleksandr Sergeev, head of the NPG, destroying the agreements would "ultimately threaten the process of reform and democratic change in Russia."[61]

The second crucial challenge to miners was the transfer of social assets and services to local mining communities. In theory, this seems a very reasonable proposal. The coal companies would get out of the business of providing housing and social services, and concentrate instead on their core mission—mining coal. Social assets and services such as day care and housing would become the responsibility of local governments, which would accordingly receive the state subsidies for social services. Much of this has taken place already, at least on paper. In 1992, there were more than 900,000 employees working in the coal industry, but well over one-third of these would, in a market economy, have been employed by contractors or local authorities. A significant portion of the reduction of coal industry employees has occurred by transferring such jobs out of the industry.

Yet, according to the Bank-sponsored social assessment, instead of increasing efficiency, "the transfer of services such as housing, health, and education to financially pressed local governments has meant either that these services were no longer available or that the quality of the service deteriorated." More specifically, in some mining regions, "social support services such as hospitals and kindergartens have either closed or are unable to fulfill their functions."[62] This of course is hardly surprising: In the Soviet Union, where state funding was concerned, he who shouted loudest got the most. Although coal may be weak relative to other industries, coal generals can shout much more loudly than, say, the mayor of a mining town in Siberia. This is especially problematic, given the ongoing crisis of nonpayments and the inability of the Russian government to meet its obligations.

As the winter of 1997–1998 approached in the Kuzbass, there was major concern over this issue. Heating stations had been transferred from the mines to the cities, but the money to pay for them had not arrived. The local administrations openly stated that they did not welcome the additional responsibility of caring for such social assets and were not opposed to returning ownership either to Rosugol (when that was an option) or to the coal enterprises. When this issue was raised at the miners' congress, Chubais responded, "Anything like that, however, will mean saying good-bye to the coal loan from the World Bank."[63]

The most central challenge to the miners from the Bank's proposal came in the closure of mines and elimination of jobs. By 1998, at least 58 mines had been closed since the start of the industry's restructuring, and a significant number of jobs had been eliminated.[64] A large portion of the latter were eliminated through the transfer of services as well as the reduction of working pensioners. (Since coal miners are eligible for pensions at age 55, with the rise in the cost of basic goods and services, many continue to work while receiving their industry pension.[65]) Even so, unemployment in mining regions is already higher than the Russian average and is certain to grow.[66]

The closure of coal mines—which in many cases means the abandonment of entire communities—is painful in the best of circumstances; but under Russian conditions, it has been disastrous.[67] Among the problems: Mines have been shut down without the proper forewarning required by law. Furthermore, according to the Bank's social impact assessment, the funding allotted for closures and to pay miners' severance packages in many cases never arrives—an outcome that is hardly surprising in a country plagued by nonpayments and wage arrears. The closures and resulting unemployment are further compounded by the often highly concentrated nature of coal mining. In Kemerovo oblast, close to 20 percent of the population is directly employed in the coal industry, with many more employed in related industries; and in such regions as Vorkuta in the Far North, the percentage is much higher.

Although many coal miners have come to see the loss of mining jobs as inevitable, they have high expectations that the state will provide new jobs for those who are laid off. Such expectations form part of a moral economy in Russian coal communities.[68] But the expectation of new jobs is especially difficult to fulfill given the increasingly depressed state of the various coal fields, to say nothing of the general malaise in the Russian economy, where unemployment levels are expected to grow. The American option—of picking up and relocating to a region with a more vibrant economy—is effectively blocked by the continuing housing shortage in Russia and the lack of a functioning housing market. The situation is more problematic in Vorkuta, located above the Arctic Circle, where the mining industry initially drew its labor from Stalin's prison camps, and later attracted workers with high wages to compensate for the harsh conditions. Miners and their families routinely put away part of their wages so as to retire in relative comfort someday in the south of Russia. Their plans were crushed when price liberalization and the resulting inflation wiped out their savings. Vorkuta miners demand and expect to be resettled free of charge elsewhere in Russia. Such expectations, given the inability of the government to meet its most basic obligations, might seem to border on the absurd; but they have been encouraged by no fewer than four separate presidential decrees promising the relocation of Vorkuta mining families.[69]

In its official response to the World Bank proposal for the coal industry, the main coal union Rosugleprof accused the Bank of "market bolshevism" and conspiring to cripple Russia's heavy industry. The plan would create refugees from mining regions, the union argued. It was designed by foreign experts who did not understand that Russia suffered from a housing shortage and was already unable to house its relocated military personnel and refugees from former Soviet republics. It described the proposal as a "plan for the organized impoverishment of miners," and said it was based on "inhuman principles." The plan "would bring the country to the brink of economic collapse and would mean the suicide of the current government." The proposed pace of the closures was said to be "extremely dangerous in our conditions: it may cause a social explosion of unprecedented force among miners, who will be supported by workers in other sectors. If that is what the [Bank] is after, then it has fulfilled its task well."[70]

Even with such rhetoric, it would be misleading to say that Russia's miners do not understand the need for change, even for radical change. In December 1997, 67 miners were killed in a single explosion in a Novokuznetsk mine; a month later, 27 more were killed in a mine accident in Vorkuta. With coal customers failing to pay for delivered coal, many mines simply do not have the money for safety equipment. Miners constantly risk their lives at work—and without pay, they often do so on empty stomachs. The level of pay in the industry has dropped: Coal miners, once the highest paid of industrial workers, are now in seventh place, and often they are not even receiving that meager wage. Miners argue that it is not some love of the trade that keeps them mining coal, but that there are few clean and safe jobs in coal regions waiting to be filled by laid-off miners.

Nevertheless, in the wake of the accident at Novokuznetsk, Russia's economic minister, Yakov Urinson, announced plans to shut down 86 of some 200 coal mines in 1998. Urinson appeared to be using the disaster to push for as many closures as possible before the World Bank money was used up in early 1999.[71]

Explaining the Outcome

The outcome of the Russian government's efforts to restructure and substantially reduce the size of Russia's coal industry is not yet clear. When it was officially announced in 1994, the World Bank's proposal for eliminating all coal subsidies in four to five years seemed as utopian as Stalin's call to fulfill the five-year plan in four years. And yet, Russia is apparently on track to do just that. The Bank's proposal was radical, and radically different from the Russian government's plan for the industry before the Bank loan. Among other outcomes, the Bank succeeded in disbanding "the powerful coal lobby" in the form of Rosugol.

Why was the World Bank seemingly so successful in reshaping the Russian coal industry? Political economist Barbara Stallings has suggested a useful framework for understanding and analyzing the power of international lending agencies by employing the concepts of markets, leverage, and linkage.[72] The market concept in this particular case is straightforward: Coal prices have been declining worldwide, and Russian export prospects are minimal in even the best scenario. In short, the market position of the Russian coal industry is almost the direct opposite of that of oil and gas. The leverage concept refers to the amount of money being offered by the international lending agency, and how badly it is needed. The Russian government was clearly in a difficult fiscal position, having allocated the loans even before the Bank had agreed to release them; clearly the leverage provided by the money was significant. But by itself it was not sufficient to radically alter Russia's plans for its coal industry. Stallings's third concept of linkage is an important element: the presence of like-minded individuals in positions of power and influence. In proposing the radical restructuring of the coal industry, the Bank was pushing the government in a direction in which many top officials wanted it to go.[73]

And yet the leverage—the $1.2 billion—was critical. It was so because the loans substituted for a domestic coalition for reforming the coal industry. There are benefits to be had from a restructured and downsized coal industry, such as reduced government spending, cleaner air, and eventually lower prices for energy consumers; but these benefits are diffuse, spread out across the population and over time. In other words, other than, say, officials in the Ministry of the Economy, there was no constituency to push through these difficult changes, especially when the costs were not diffuse but were felt painfully and immediately by Rosugol, by coal miners, and by coal-producing regions. In other words, the Bank succeeded in getting Russia to adopt a course of action that would not have occurred through domestic politics alone.[74]

Stallings argues that although this framework is useful for explaining a government's *adoption* of a structural adjustment program, successful *implementation* is another matter. In the case of Russia's coal industry, implementation will likely be determined by the one significant obstacle remaining: the coal miners.

From the miners' perspective, structural adjustment is something of a shell game: The pea of financial support for the coal industry was at first being moved around under the shell of state subsidies, and now it is being moved around under the shell of World Bank loans. When that shell is lifted and the pea has vanished, it is not likely that Russia's coal miners will walk away quietly, grumbling to themselves. The Bank may succeed in its ambitious plan to "zero-out" coal subsidies by the time the last installment of coal loans is handed out in early 1999; but more probably, the Russian government will be left with restive miners who will extract further subsidies—meaning that the government will be left paying subsidies and repaying the Bank loan.[75]

Russia's miners have consistently said, even before the collapse of the Soviet Union, that they would accept significant restructuring. As one miner put it after the recent accidents, "Does Russia need coal that is stained with blood?" But they have also consistently demanded new jobs; as I have argued, such a demand forms part of the moral economy of Russia's coal communities. If the demand goes unfulfilled, Russia's miners will surely make their dissatisfaction known. The question is not whether miners will protest the proposed closures and eliminations of subsidies, but whether they will do so in a way that is politically effective.[76]

One could argue that the restructuring of the coal industry, including the liquidation of Rosugol and the proposed privatization and further decentralization of the industry, will have the effect of isolating the miners' protests. There is little evidence that Rosugol instigated miners' strikes; however, it might have fulfilled a coordinating function for nationwide strikes. And state support for the industry generally acted as a lightning rod for protests aimed not at management but at Moscow. Yet, even in the absence of Rosugol and with the elimination of coal subsidies, the miners' dissatisfaction is likely to be expressed—whether through desperate protests or by voting for extremist politicians—in ways that prove costly.

In recent years miners have engaged in hunger strikes and in numerous small, wildcat strikes as well as in nationwide, organized strikes; they have occupied underground shafts and refused to surface; they have blockaded the Trans-Siberian railway and other transport routes, and have seized trains and taken their crews hostage; and they have taken mine managers and local government officials hostage. They have waved Communist flags at their demonstrations, they have courted Zhirinovsky, and they have burned Yeltsin and other government figures in effigy. They have even called on the soldiers of the Siberian military district to join them and to bring their guns. Perhaps most troubling for the government, in January 1998, miners' strikes for the first time spilled over into other industries.[77]

Given this record, a final comment is warranted concerning the World Bank's program for the Russian coal industry. The Bank proposal, in describing Western experiences with coal restructuring, cites a time-frame of 20 to 30 years. In France, the proposal notes, the "goal is to stop coal mining as soon as socially and politically feasible." It says of the German approach, "While slow and expensive, the process did improve productivity significantly without social or political disturbances."[78] Yet for Russia the Bank has counseled urgency and the elimination of all subsidies within three to five years.

Why such divergence from world experience? The World Bank would likely argue that given Russia's economic difficulties, the government cannot afford to delay cutbacks in the coal industry. Equally persuasive is the argument that given Russia's precarious political stability, the government cannot afford to move too quickly.

Notes

1. For two strongly contrasting views on the World Bank, compare Robert Ayres, *Banking on the Poor* (Cambridge: MIT Press, 1984) and Michel Chussodovsky, *The Globalization of Poverty: Impacts of IMF and World Bank Reforms* (London: Zed Books, 1997).

2. Ayse Kudat and Vadim Borisov, "Russian Coal Sector Restructuring: Social Assessment," World Bank, ECA Country Department III, mimeograph, undated, p. ii.

3. "Russian Federation: Restructuring the Coal Industry: Putting People First," World Bank Report No. 13187-RU, 12 December 1994, vol. 2, annex A, p. 13; *Mining Journal,* 2 January 1998.

4. *Nezavisimaya gazeta,* 10 December 1996.

5. "Russian Federation: Restructuring the Coal Industry," World Bank Report No. 13187-RU, 12 December 1994, vol. 1, p. 6.

6. Ibid., vol. 1, p. 18; this is also the source of the figures cited below.

7. On the British miners' strike, see Peter Gibbon, "Analyzing the British miners' strike," *Economy and Society* (May 1988); Peggy Kahn, "Union politics and the restructuring of the British coal industry," in Miriam Golden and Jonas Pontusson, *Bargaining for Change* (Ithaca, N.Y.: Cornell University Press, 1993); Huw Beynon, ed., *Digging Deeper: Issues in the Miners' Strike* (London: Verso, 1987).

8. "Travma," *Ekonomicheskaya gazeta,* 1989, no. 7, p. 17.

9. Gorbachev subsequently argued that the strike marked the beginning of the end of the USSR (Mikhail Gorbachev, *Zhizn'i reformy* [Life and Reforms] [Moscow: Novosti, 1995], p. 460).

10. See Stephen Crowley, *Hot Coal, Cold Steel: Russian and Ukrainian Workers from the End of the Soviet Union to the Post-Communist Transformations* (Ann Arbor: University of Michigan Press, 1997); "Coal miners, cultural frameworks, and the transformation of the Soviet political economy," *Post-Soviet Affairs,* vol. 13, no. 2 (April–June 1997).

11. Peter Rutland, *Business Elites and Russian Economic Policy* (London: Royal Institute of International Affairs, 1992), pp. 41–42.

12. Ibid.; Leonid N. Lopatin, ed., *Rabochee dvizheniya Kuzbassa* [The Kuzbass Workers' Movement] (Kemerovo: Kemerovo izdatel'stvo, 1993), pp. 550–558, 565.

13. *Megapolis-Ekspress,* 24 February 1993, p. 15.

14. *Izvestiya,* 8 May 1993, cited in *Radio Free Europe/Radio Liberty (RFE/RL) Daily Report,* 11 May 1993.

15. *RFE/RL Daily Report,* 22 June, 23 June, and 24 June 1993. As one Russian newspaper warned in its headline, "Coal prices are let go: So are miners" (*Megapolis-Ekspress,* 30 June 1993).

16. *Kommersant,* no. 25, 21–27 June 1993, as translated in *Current Digest of the Post-Soviet Press,* vol. 45, no. 26, 1993.

17. *RFE/RL Daily Report,* 24 June 1993.

18. Ibid., 20 July and 29 July 1993.

19. Ibid., 29 October 1993 and 15 November 1993.

20. The draft, labeled "Confidential," was entitled "Russian Federation: Restructuring the Coal Industry," [World Bank] Draft Working Group, 18 October 1993.

21.. *Moscow Times,* 16 December 1997.

22. Annette Robertson, "The experience of the coal industry: Russia and the World Bank" (unpublished manuscript).

23. *Izvestiya,* 6 February 1997.

24. *Moscow Times,* 16 December 1997.

25. "Russian Federation: Restructuring the Coal Industry," World Bank Report, vol. 1, p. 13.

26. Although Russia's economy has shrunk considerably, its emissions of carbon dioxide rank third in world, mainly due to inefficient energy use. On the environmental problems stemming from high rates of coal use in former Communist countries, see the special section on global warming in the *New York Times,* 1 December 1997.

27. *Segodnya,* 10 November 1996.

28. This point is well made in Simon Clarke, ed., *Labour Relations in Transition* (Cheltenham, U.K.: Edward Elgar, 1996).

29. The Bank proposal rather disingenuously described its three-to–five-year plan as a "phased approach," positioned "between two extremes, which we describe as business-as-usual and privatize-or-close," in which all subsidies would cease immediately. Neither of these options, especially the latter, were under consideration by the Russian government, and the Bank language can only be explained as part of its negotiating strategy. But what then should we think of the objectivity of the rest of the report, such as the Bank's seemingly careful calculations of future coal demand in Russia, which are so crucial for determining how quickly and deeply to cut the Russian coal industry? ("Restructuring the Coal Industry," World Bank Report, vol. 1, pp. 88–89.)

30. The politically ambitious Malyshev ran for the Federal Assembly in December 1993, as a candidate from the Kuzbass. Had he been elected, it would have added fuel to the charges of conflicts of interest, since he would have been a top economic official distributing coal subsidies and other benefits throughout Russia, and at the same time a local political official responding to the needs of a single, albeit major, coal region. Despite the benefits that such an arrangement might have brought to their region, Kuzbass voters solidly rejected Malyshev's candidacy. See Stephen Crowley, "The Kuzbass: Liberals, populists and labor," in Timothy Colton and Jerry Hough, eds., *Growing Pains: The Russian Elections of 1993* (Washington, D.C.: Brookings Institution Press, 1998).

31. "Restructuring the Coal Industry," [World Bank] Draft Working Group, 3.2–3.5.

32. On the crisis in Primorye and the resulting miners' strikes, see *Segodnya,* 2 August and 3 August 1996; *Izvestiya,* 6 August 1996; *Segodnya,* 8 August and 12 August 1998.

33. *Segodnya,* 21 August 1997.

34. Some of the criticisms of Rosugol were contradictory. On the one hand it was accused of cross-subsidizing—taking profits from efficient mines to prop up loss-making mines. On the other hand, it was accused of transferring subsidies earmarked for loss-making mines and investing them in more profitable ones.

35. The government was said to be trying to buy the miners' loyalty in the June presidential elections. *Kommersant,* 6 February 1996.

36. *Izvestiya,* 13 February 1996.

37. According to Anton Kobyakov, chair of the Miners of Russia sociopolitical movement, the government "for a long time shut its eyes to the fact that the main employer (Rosugol) was robbing the coal miners" (*Moskovskie novosti,* no. 44, 3–10 November 1996).

38. *Transition: The Newsletter About Reforming Economies* (Washington, D.C.: World Bank), December 1997, p. 29; *Moskovskie novosti,* no. 36, September 1997.

39. *Segodnya,* 1 October 1996.

40. According to *Moskovskie novosti,* "Particularly at fault for unauthorized expenditures were the local administrations, to whom control was assigned … for the use of loan funds" (*Moskovskie novosti,* no. 36, September 1997).

41. *Segodnya,* 10 November 1996. Coal companies were said to be preventing the auditors, Coopers and Lybrand, from completing their audits (*Izvestiya,* 12 November 1996).

42. *Segodnya,* 21 November 1996.

43. *Segodnya,* 5 December 1996. Much of the reportage in mainstream newspapers, such as *Segodnya* and *Kommersant,* was so openly critical of Rosugol and the mining industry that the industry's management said newspaper accounts were "provoking an exacerbation of the social crisis in the coal-mining regions" (Ibid.). Most mainstream newspaper reports were no more sympathetic to the coal miners.

44. Other strikes were clearly spontaneous, even beyond the control of the miners' trade unions (*Izvestiya,* 30 July 1996).

45. It is unclear why these particular coal associations were chosen for privatization; but the fact that they are all isolated and probably the least militant coal regions suggests the possibility that the path of least resistance had been chosen for demonstrating commitment to the privatization of the industry.

46. *Segodnya,* 15 December 1996. Potanin's remarks suggest rather clearly that the Bank's leverage was aiding liberals in their struggle with Rosugol.

47. *Kommersant,* 15 April 1997.

48. *Segodnya,* 22 July 1997.

49. Ibid., 15 August 1997.

50. Ibid., 21 August 1997; 15 August 1997.

51. Ibid., 21 August 1997.

52. ITAR-TASS, 18 December 1997.

53. *Kommersant,* 21 November 1997; *Segodnya,* 22 November 1997.

54. *Segodnya,* 28 November and 21 August 1997; *Kommersant,* 21 August 1997.

55. On Tuleev's past as regional leader in the Kuzbass, see Crowley, "The Kuzbass: Liberals, populists and labor."

56. Kudat and Borisov, "Russian Coal Sector Restructuring: Social Assessment," p. 2. Given Russia's experience with privatization to date, it is unrealistic to assume that management will change when mines are privatized, particularly in such an unprofitable industry.

57. *Ogonek,* no. 7, February 1996; *Segodnya,* 3 July 1997.

58. *Nezavisimaya gazeta,* 29 January 1998; *Financial Times,* 1 April 1998. Even profitable mines were not paying workers on time: Kuzbassrazrezugol, whose shares were actively traded on the Russian stock exchange, was still delaying the payment of wages by two and a half months. Such cases gave credence to the charge that managers were taking advantage of the wage crisis to increase profits (*Segodnya,* 3 July 1997).

59. "Putting People First," World Bank, vol. 1, p. 93. In their response to the Bank's draft proposal, the main coal union Rosugleprof notes that the English version of the Bank's draft states that one of the plan's basic aims is "to cut employment in the coal mining regions," whereas the Russian translation states that the goal is to "cut down the level of *unemployment* in the coal mining regions." Clarke suggests that the Russian translator was simply unable to believe the goal was actually to cut the level of employment.

60. Anna Temkina, personal communication.

61. "Putting People First," World Bank, vol. II, annex H, p. 51. The NPG, it should be recalled, played a significant role in bringing Yeltsin to power.

62. Kudat and Borisov, "Russian Coal Sector Restructuring: Social Assessment," p. 6, v. Where the services were available, charges had increased, and miners owed months of back pay often could not afford them (Ibid., p. 6). An indication of the difficulty, both socially and politically, of transferring these social assets out of the coal industry was the fact that Yeltsin's decree in June 1994 mandating the transfer of enterprise assets was delayed for the coal industry until December 1994 (Robertson, "The Experience of the Coal Industry: Russia and the World Bank").

63. *Segodnya,* 22 March 1997.

64. Because of different ways of defining the coal labor force, as well as statistics that are simply wrong, it is difficult to determine just how many coal workers there are at present and how much of a reduction has taken place. For instance, *Segodnya* said there were 359,000 "working in coal-producing enterprises" at the end of 1997, and 383,000 at the beginning of 1997; *Nezavisimaya gazeta* said there were 567,000 workers "throughout the coal industry" at the beginning of 1997; and the *Financial Times* claimed, mistakenly, that there were more than 800,000 miners at the end of 1997 (*Segodnya,* 2 December 1997; *Nezavisimaya gazeta,* 13 February 1997; *Financial Times,* 21 November 1997).

65. In 1993, Rosugol estimated that as many as 27 percent of its employees were of pension age. The World Bank proposal targeted working pensioners as a seemingly painless way to achieve job reductions. Yet many miners saw the early pension as an entitlement, given their difficult and dangerous work—the more so since, according to one source the life expectancy of Soviet miners was 47 years of age! (*RFE/RL Report on the USSR,* vol. 2, no. 32, 10 August 1990, p. 11). The safety record has since gotten worse, not better.

66. Between 1994 and 1998, at least 17 Kuzbass mines were shut down, but the funding received to pay for the closures was only 20 percent of the amount approved by the government. Almost 17,000 miners had lost their jobs, of which only 7 percent had found new employment; and nearly 35,000 more had lost jobs at auxiliary enterprises. Not surprisingly, the social situation in Kuzbass mining towns was said to be "extremely tense" in late 1997 (*Nezavisimaya gazeta,* 3 December 1997).

67. For two studies of the effects of such changes on Russian coal communities, see Robertson, "The Experience of the Coal Industry: Russia and the World Bank"; and Sarah Ashwin, "'There's no joy any more': The experience of reform in a Kuzbass mining settlement," *Europe-Asia Studies,* vol. 47, no. 8, 1995, pp. 1367–1381.

68. James Scott, *The Moral Economy of the Peasant* (New Haven: Yale University Press, 1976); E. P. Thompson, "The moral economy of the English crowd in the eighteenth century," *Past and Present* (February 1971). The moral economy argument is applied to workers in Soviet-type societies in Jeffrey Kopstein, "Chipping away at the state," *World Politics* vol. 48, no. 3, pp. 391–423 (January 1996).

69. Kudat and Borisov, "Social Assessment," p. 41. These promises were typically made to end strikes.

70. "Putting People First," World Bank, vol. II, annex H, pp. 84–91, 53.

71. *Segodnya*, 2 December 1997.

72. Barbara Stallings, "International influence on economic policy: Debt, stabilization, and structural reform," in Stephan Haggard and Robert R. Kaufman, eds., *The Politics of Economic Adjustment: International Constraints, Distributive Conflicts, and the State* (Princeton: Princeton University Press, 1992).

73. In 1993, before the World Bank was officially negotiating with the Russian government, the *RFE/RL Daily Report* cited an AFP story, which claimed: "In private ... members of the Russian government are saying that, in the new year, the Yeltsin leadership will have to follow the example of Thatcherite Britain and face down a challenge from organized labor. They say that the only industries in which independent unions are strong enough to mount a sustained strike are coal mining and defense production and that the government could defeat a strike in either. This is because coal stocks are high following the general fall in production" (Elizabeth Teague, "Gaidar warns insolvent firms," *RFE/RL Daily Report*, 15 November 1993). Such plans were evidently put aside when the government parties were defeated in the polls.

74. The destruction of Rosugol could turn out to be a mixed blessing for the goal of radically restructuring the coal industry: It simply returned responsibility for the coal industry to the Coal Department of the Ministry of Energy and Fuels. It may prove more difficult to push through painful changes without a national coal body, on which West European countries, including the United Kingdom, have relied. The obstacle that Rosugol posed was not caused by rent-seeking bureaucrats (the explanation relied on in many models of postcommunist politics). Rather, Rosugol's problem from the perspective of further marketizing the industry was caused, ironically, by earlier moves to marketize Rosugol, giving it independence and making it a profit-seeking entity. In short, the problem with Rosugol was not rent-seeking but profit-seeking.

75. This is especially so since a significant portion of the Bank's coal loans appear to have been used to pay off restive miners.

76. According to Kobyakov of the Miners of Russia movement, "Hunger, cold, and the feeling that they have no rights have transformed the inhabitants of mining regions into a supercombustible material that could ignite at any moment" (*Moskovskie novosti*, 3–10 November 1996, no. 44).

77. Vadim Borisov, "The strike as a form of worker activism in the period of economic reform," in Clarke, ed., *Labour Relations in Transition*. In Primorye, electric workers, military-industry workers, and municipal employees joined miners in their protests, and participated in blocking the Trans-Siberian rail line (*Kommersant*, 28 January 1998; *RFE/RL Daily Report*, 28 January 1998).

78. "Putting People First," World Bank, annex C, pp. 17, 13. According to *Nezavisimaya gazeta:* "In Japan, the elimination of a coal basin with 200,000 miners was stretched out over 20 years and accompanied by the construction of plants for the production of electronics. In our country, the number of people working in the coal sector has decreased by 250,000 in three years, yet the authorities are pretending there are no problems" (10 December 1996).

CHAPTER 6

Trade Unions, Management, and the State in Contemporary Russia

Linda J. Cook

Russian trade unions are no longer "transmission belts" of the state, which was the way Vladimir Lenin had characterized their role in the Soviet Union. During reform they have become independent organizations and gained legal rights to organize, bargain collectively, and strike. However, the economic and social position of their members has been seriously damaged by reform policies and continues to deteriorate. Real wages have fallen by more than 30 percent, social protections have decreased, unemployment has increased, and since 1995 large numbers of workers have simply not been paid for weeks and months at a time. How have unions sought to defend the position of labor in this transitional economy? Do they address their grievances primarily to managers as in a typical market economy, putting their efforts into organizing and bargaining? Or do unions line up with managers, as in the pre-reform system, pressing the state for resources to resolve their problems? And, given their well-known weakness, do Russia's unions carry any weight? Does it matter what they do?

The central argument of this chapter is that unions, for the most part, line up with management to pressure the state. Leaders of the main national trade union organization, the Federation of Independent Trade Unions of Russia (FNPR), blame state policies for the collapse of production and the nonpayments crisis. They have collaborated with managers and their organizations, both at the enterprise level and in national politics, to demand changes in these policies and to lobby for exceptions. The FNPR directs its national protests almost exclusively against the government; and at regional and local levels as well, governmental authorities are more often the object of workers' demands than are enterprise managers. Union-led protests also are often supported by both managers and political authorities, in a kind of regional lobbying to press the federal government for funds. There are direct labor-management conflicts in Russia, but they are much fewer in number and smaller in scope than protests directed at government.

I have borrowed from a recent work by Peter Rutland to define the "managerial agenda"—a list of what business elites want from the government:[1]

- subsidies and investment from the state budget;
- industrial development policies;
- tax exemptions, and tax and debt relief;
- import quotas and tariffs to protect domestic production;
- cheap energy, and price regulation for products of natural monopolies;
- elimination of governmental payment arrears; and
- access to stock in privatizing firms.

Clearly, this agenda does not reflect the interests of all business or managerial elites. It is heavily weighted toward the old industrial sectors, where both managers' organizations and unions are concentrated, and even here there are divergent positions on these issues. Nor does this list capture the interests of the booming financial sector, which has its own complex ties to government and is almost completely nonunionized. It does, however, resonate strongly with the positions of Arkadii Volskii's Russian Union of Industrialists and Entrepreneurs (RSPP); Yurii Skokov's Congress of Russian Commodity Producers; Rosugol; the agrarian lobby; and managerial groups in the defense, machine-building, and other industrial sectors.[2]

The FNPR subscribes to most of this agenda. In his major speech to the Federation's Third Congress in December 1996, for example, Chairman Mikhail Shmakov highlighted union demands for a program of state investments and direct subsidies for industry. He called for decreases in taxes on production and a large increase in taxes on imports of finished goods, with part of the income to be invested in corresponding domestic production. And he argued that high imports and tight monetary controls were major sources of industry's decline, and that excessive taxes undermined the profitability of Russian enterprises.[3] Elsewhere the Federation has called for price regulation, particularly of energy, and targeted the government's late payments to industry and the public sector as major causes of mutual nonpayments and of wage arrears.[4] In other words, in the view of Russia's dominant trade union, government policies are mainly to blame for the failure of managers to operate enterprises profitably and for the rapid increase in the numbers of loss-makers (see Table 6.1). By implication, then, most managers cannot be expected to deliver more in the present circumstances. Rather, managers and workers share an interest in pressing for policy changes that will "restore production" in the medium term, and in getting subsidies, loans, overdue payments, state orders, tax relief, or anything else that will allow the enterprise to survive, and pay its workers something, in the shorter term.

Why has this predominant pattern of labor-management cooperation against the state emerged? I will argue below that it is a product of three legacies of the Soviet period.

First and most important are structural legacies of the state-built economy, which have left the state deeply enmeshed in economic relations despite its efforts to extricate itself. Although much of Russian industry has been privatized,

TABLE 6.1   Loss-Making Enterprises and Real Profits in Russian Industry

	1994	1996
Loss-making enterprises (%)	23	43
Real profits (1994=100)	100	50

SOURCE: *OECD Economic Surveys: Russian Federation, 1997* (Paris: OECD [Organization for Economic Cooperation and Development], 1997), p. 114.

state ownership or dependence remains significant in the coal, defense, and agricultural sectors. The huge public sector created in the Soviet period—teachers, doctors, municipal workers, and others—is also fully dependent on government budgets. There is in addition a residue of government subsidies, price controls, and regulations throughout the economy, and an overlay of international restructuring aid that flows through governmental channels. All tend to focus the struggle for resources on government.

Second is the legacy of unions' close, subordinate relationship to management in the Soviet period. This history has produced a union leadership that remains far more comfortable with elite-level alliances than with rank-and-file organizing, that looks to industrial managers for political leadership, and that has much to lose at the enterprise level from genuine confrontation with them.[5]

Third is a legacy of expectations that the state remains responsible for the economic and social well-being of Russia's population. Surveys of Russians show that substantial majorities consider the state responsible for providing a minimum income and full employment.[6] In the working class such expectations are complemented by a history of dependence on managers who helped workers get social goods from the state and who controlled workers' access to those same benefits. These factors combine to explain a labor politics that tends to direct demands at government rather than at economic actors.

The Unions' Strengths and Weaknesses

Communist-era unions formed the subordinate part of a party-management-union troika in enterprises. During the first major strikes of the reform period, in 1989, activist workers repudiated these unions as an arm of the state and threatened to replace them "from below" with new labor leadership. The unions responded by separating themselves from the state and the collapsing Communist Party, but not from management. Both unions and managers took a critical attitude toward reform policies. When the Communist Party was banned from workplaces by Russian Federation President Boris Yeltsin after the August 1991 coup attempt, the unions stayed, retaining their organization, membership, property, and distributive functions. In 1992 they claimed 60 million of Russia's 73-million-member labor force, organized into a Federation-wide system of committees

TABLE 6.2   The FNPR's Largest Branch Unions

Branch	Members (in millions)
Workers of the agroindustrial complex	9.6
National education and science	4.8
Health care	3.5
Local industry and communal services	2.7
State institutions and social services	2.0

SOURCE: "III S"ezd Federatsii nezavisimykh profsoiuzov Rossii," in *Profsoiuzy*, no. 1, 1997, p. 2.

that extended from Moscow to virtually every enterprise and institution. They administered a broad range of benefits, including sickness and maternity payments, pensions, housing, and vacations. And they owned property, including office buildings, hotels, sanatoria, children's camps, and resorts.

The FNPR, the Russian successor to the Soviet-era state union organization, has used its inherited resources to secure the dominant position as labor's representative throughout the Russian Federation. It remains the only union in the vast majority of workplaces, and it continues to control the distribution of some benefits. It dominates labor's side of the Tripartite Commission for the Regulation of Social and Labor Issues, in which the government formally recognizes this union as the bargaining agent for most workers in Russia. It leads semiannual, nationwide demonstrations and brief work stoppages to protest labor's deteriorating conditions, and coordinates smaller but longer strikes in some sectors. Union-led activism is particularly strong in coal mining and in the public sector, where several of the FNPR's largest unions are concentrated (see Table 6.2). Union leaders negotiate legally binding collective contracts for their members. And the FNPR is rich, deriving most of its income (as much as 95 percent, according to one informed estimate) from the commercial use of its properties, with the residual 5 percent coming from membership dues.[7]

Still, the FNPR is in comparative terms a weak and circumscribed union. Most rank-and-file members neither trust it nor believe that it has any influence. In a representative 1995 survey of workers, for example, only 16 percent trusted national officials to look after their interests, and only 27 percent trusted officials at their place of work. Unions were seen as having almost no influence on how the firm was run.[8] The FNPR has lost millions of members because of such disaffection as well as the splitting-off of branch affiliates, the departure of workers to join new, independent unions, and movement of labor into the nonunionized private sector. Of its original 60 million members, the FNPR now claims 45 million—a decline of 25 percent in 5 years—and some experts put present membership below 40 million.[9] Many who stay on as members do so to receive the shrinking package of benefits that is distributed by the union. Turnout for national protests is always disappointing, and the overall level of strikes is comparatively low. A nationwide survey conducted by the All-Russian Center for the Study of Public Opinion (VTsIOM) found that only 6 percent of the workforce participated in strikes between May 1997 and May 1998.[10] According to one close observer, "Except for coal miners and teachers, the FNPR is not seen for the most part as sticking up for workers."[11] The union is also riven by internal divisions. Territorial unions will neither forward dues nor follow the center's political leadership. Despite these problems and the deteriorating position of its members, the FNPR has experienced no turnover among its leaders and little among the rank and file. Mikhail Shmakov, chair since 1993, ran unchallenged for reelection at the FNPR's Third Congress in December 1996, and large majorities of FNPR officials have been reelected in territorial and branch organizations.[12]

Since the beginning of reform, most enterprise-level unions have pursued a strategy of cooperation with managers. During the major privatization campaign of 1992–1994, unions and managers saw a common interest in protecting their enterprises against takeovers by outsiders, and collaborated—successfully, in most cases—to keep majority share ownership in the hands of the "labor collective." During this period managers needed a temporary alliance with unions and workers in order to secure "insider" privatization, and they generally continued paternalistic policies. In the aftermath of privatization, though, managers have gained control of most enterprises, whereas the unions have failed almost completely to translate workers' shareholding into influence. The authors of a large study of post-privatization enterprises in Russia concluded: "Theoretically, groups of workers and their trade unions [as large shareholders in their own right] could have meaningful independent power on those company boards.... Yet we have not recorded one case in which they did so."[13] Thus, managers have much less need for the unions' cooperation, and union cooperation has paid diminishing dividends for union organizations and their members.

Managers, under both financial and political pressure, are gradually shedding the infrastructure of housing, day care facilities, and other social benefits that the unions need in order to attract and hold members. They also regularly violate labor contracts by delaying wage payments; and although often this is a matter of necessity, there are also large elements of arbitrariness, calculation, and corruption in management's treatment of workers. There are documented cases, for example, of managers paying themselves huge salaries while pleading poverty to their workers, and evidence that wages are withheld disproportionately from low-paid workers.[14] Even where unions want to confront managers on such issues, they have been closed out of access to information about enterprise finances, and confront huge problems of nontransparency and obfuscation. In the post-privatization economy, enterprise-level unions have often been marginalized and sometimes forced out.

The FNPR has also suffered from political vulnerability because of its Communist origins and weak legitimacy. Earlier in the reform period there were fears that the FNPR might be banned along with the Communist Party, or dispossessed of its property, as happened with other state unions in some postcommunist polities. Though neither of these possibilities seems likely,[15] the government has proven able to weaken or exclude FNPR unions arbitrarily. In the fall of 1993, for example, when the union leadership sided with the parliament in its conflict with Yeltsin, the president responded by issuing a decree that transferred management of the critical social insurance funds (SIF) from the unions to an independent, off-budget fund. Though such a move had been under discussion, the government's ability to accomplish it unilaterally and punitively illustrates the union's vulnerability and the absence of any legal basis for its prerogatives. The government also excluded the FNPR from meetings of the Tripartite Commission for a time—a move of largely symbolic significance, which illustrated the unions' dependence on government for recognition and status.

One additional dimension of the FNPR-manager-state relationship should be discussed. The Russian government has, at least sporadically, sought to create "market rules" that will push managers toward more efficient and profit-oriented behavior while eliminating some of workers' traditional protections. A series of presidential decrees, for example, has commanded managers either to transfer their enterprises' social infrastructure to municipal governments or to privatize them. A draft revision of the labor code revision would eliminate severance pay and other protections for dismissed workers, in order to make the labor force more flexible and to facilitate layoffs. In a market economy, most business elites would support such changes, which reduce their costs and release them from social obligations. In Russia, managers seem less interested in changing the rules than in evading them selectively, according to their own survival strategies. For example, although they have cut back, most managers have kept more social infrastructure than the government would like or real markets would allow. They may be partly motivated by a residual paternalism, but other calculations dominate: It is cheaper to keep workers by allowing them access to sunk-cost infrastructure than it is to actually pay them; and regional governments usually defend large enterprises that provide social services, and in some cases bail them out financially.[16] It is also clear that some wages (an indeterminate amount) are paid "off the books" to avoid the high social security contributions (equal to 38 percent of the wage bill) required of enterprises.[17] Unions and workers get some relief from such behavior. So although they fight with the government over the rule changes, unions generally collude in these survival strategies for whatever short-term advantage they can derive. In a letter to Chairman Shmakov, for example, Deputy Minister of Labor and Social Development Aleksandr Orlov condemned such collusion, charging that the Federation was "abandoning the struggle against criminalization of the economy.... [You] do not protest the disproportionate remuneration of labor and ... often [make] deals with criminal managers."[18]

Besides the FNPR, there are independent unions in Russia that either broke away from FNPR or developed from the grass roots. Most were founded in 1991 or 1992, during the initial burst of democracy, and looked much more like their

Western counterparts: Members joined voluntarily; leaders had authority; and managers were excluded from membership, and were viewed as the bargaining partner and adversary of labor. The independents established themselves in a limited number of sectors, mainly mining, which spawned the well-known Independent Miners' Union (NPG), and transport, along with one interbranch union, Sotsprof. They took a generally pro-market, pro-reform, and pro-Yeltsin position. The independents, however, managed to organize at best several hundred thousand members. They suffered from several liabilities: Their pro-reform and pro-Yeltsin positions became an increasingly hard sell with workers as the economy worsened; they had to compete with the comparatively resource-rich FNPR; and they suffered from inexperienced leadership, corruption, unenforceable rights, and the weakness of Russian civil society. The strongest of the independents nevertheless exercised a democratizing pressure, forcing FNPR unions to become more responsive to members; and at least in the coal mining sector, the two now cooperate. At the same time, continued hardship has taken its toll, and many of the most militant workers view both unions with contempt. At least among the miners, there is talk of new challenges from below and a "third wave" of leadership.[19]

Given the multiple weaknesses of Russian unions, then, does it matter what they demand, or whose side they are on? I argue that it does matter, for several reasons. First, union cooperation with management was necessary for "insider privatization," the basis of Russia's current industrial ownership structure. The Russian government's initial privatization plan would have given majority ownership to outsiders, but a coalition of managers, unions, and others pressed for the "insider" option. Managers could not have taken control of their enterprises openly; they needed the "labor collective" as a front, and the unions provided it. Whereas privatization made workers into substantial shareholders at their enterprises, the unions' failure to give them any independent voice on boards of directors has facilitated managers' lack of accountability and responsibility.[20] Unions' general inability or unwillingness to confront managers over their performance, arbitrary treatment of workers, or corruption does the same. In sum, unions' cooperation at the enterprise level has strengthened managers and minimized the pressures on them "from below," in exchange for diminishing levels of employment security and social service provision.

Unions in National Politics

From the outset of reform the FNPR leadership has made its strongest alliances with managerial organizations in national politics (see Table 6.3). In 1992 it joined the then-powerful Russian Union of Industrialists and Entrepreneurs, and became affiliated with the Civic Union, in a broad alliance that helped bring down the neoliberal government headed by Prime Minister Yegor Gaidar (who resigned in December 1992). In the December 1993 Duma elections the FNPR

TABLE 6.3   Union-Management Alliances in Russian Party Politics

Year	Unions	Managerial organizations, parties
1992	FNPR	Russian Unified Industrialists' Party
		Civic Union
1993	agroindustrial unions	Agrarians
	forestry, construction, material unions	Civic Union
1995	FNPR leadership	Russian Unified Industrialists' Party
	agroindustry, timber, communications unions	Agrarians
	regional unions	Congress of Russian Communities

SOURCE: OECD Economic Surveys: Russian Federation, 1997 (Paris: OECD, 1997)

leadership, chastened by the government's accusations that it had acted as a political organization rather than a labor union during the October events, lay low and made no endorsements. Several constituent unions did, however, ally with or endorse parties, in each case management-affiliated or advocating a version of the "managerial agenda." Trade unions of the agroindustrial complex, the largest in the FNPR, supported the Agrarian Party, with the FNPR's former chairman, Klochkov, running as a candidate on the Agrarian's election list. The party's key platforms included subsidies and protectionist policies for agriculture and related food-processing and manufacturing sectors. Forestry and construction unions supported the Civic Union, which favored subsidies and cheap credit for industry. Some local unions supported the Communists, although the leadership ignored Zyuganov's overtures to an alliance. Both Agrarians and Communists gained support in this election, whereas Civic Union got less than 2 percent of the vote, indicating that managers had virtually no voting constituency.

The independents, after failing in an effort to create their own bloc, divided their support among candidates who were more or less pro-reform. The NPG endorsed Gaidar's party, Russia's Choice. The air traffic controllers' union supported the liberal Democratic Russia. Sotsprof supported Shakhrai's Party of Russian Unity and Accord, which championed regional rights.[21] All of these unions were too small to provide significant electoral support, even if they could bring along their whole memberships. Still, their political leanings show that the independents had made a clear break with old managerial interests and, at this stage, favored the reformist and liberal agenda.

In the December 1995 Duma elections the FNPR leadership played a more prominent role, making a series of alliances and tactical moves in the months before the vote. In May it formed an electoral block with the Russian Unified Industrialists' Party (ROPP). In the summer it agreed to join Ivan Rybkin's left-of-center bloc but could not bring regional affiliates to support this party, which many saw as too pro-government and pro-Yeltsin. In the end FNPR unions divided among several parties, almost all of whom again endorsed versions of the "managerial agenda." The FNPR's national leadership, ignoring the Civic Union's implosion in 1993, joined with Volskii and Shcherbakov's ROPP to form the electoral bloc Trade Unions and Industrialists of Russia–Labor Alliance. The bloc's program had six main planks:

- give more credits to large enterprises;
- protect domestic industry from "unfair" competition from imported goods;
- give governmental support to high-tech industries that could become the engine for a future economic boom;
- slow privatization;
- pay wage and pension arrears; and
- develop protections against unemployment.[22]

Its strategy was to mobilize those working in large enterprises through its network of regional branches. The bloc received about 1 million votes, or 1.5 percent of the popular vote, and no seats—demonstrating that a coalition of labor and industrialists has no popular support, nor the support of much of the FNPR leadership at regional levels. Even the union's central leadership may have preferred Rybkin and a more liberal agenda. Regional and branch unions defected from Volskii, but many supported other parties that endorsed versions of the "managerial agenda." The agroindustrial, timber, and communications unions supported the Agrarians. Some regional unions supported the Congress of Russian Communities, which included in its leadership Yurii Skokov, who chairs the Congress of Commodity Producers. Its economic platform was based on the Commodity Producers' calls for more protected markets and greater state support for industry.[23] Some regional unions again supported the Communists, who go beyond the managers in seeking a greater state role in the economy and who have alliances among some regional managerial elites. The independents, by this time split into two confederations, also divided their support among several liberal and pro-government parties. Having expended large amounts of energy in the 1995 Duma elections, the FNPR proceeded to make no endorsement in the most critical postcommunist race, that between Yeltsin and Gennadii Zyuganov, for Russia's powerful presidency. The independents generally preferred Yeltsin, but their support for him had weakened to such an extent that they did not manage a collective endorsement. Neither the future offered by Yeltsin nor the partial return to the past proffered by Zyuganov held any attraction for the unions.

What is the significance of unions' role in national politics? Election outcomes make clear that the central leadership commands few votes, and in the limited available survey evidence, workers report that unions have minimal influence on their electoral choices.[24] The question is more complicated at the branch and regional levels, where, for example, it seems quite likely that the agroindustrial unions have pushed votes toward the Agrarians. A full analysis would be very complicated and is beyond the scope of this chapter; but there are two points worth making in this context. The first is that FNPR unions have used whatever influence they do have to strengthen the weight in the Duma of antireform parties that favor more statist economic policies. The second and more important point is that both central and regional union leaders look for political leadership to parties that are strongly tied to managerial organizations. Socialist and social-democratic political elites, who articulate a separate working-class interest, have tried since 1992 to make alliances with FNPR unions, but except for the Moscow Regional Federation, they have had little success. Since 1997, though, the FNPR's leadership has shown an interest in this direction, with Shmakov calling for a strong social-democratic movement and Andrei Isaev, the dynamic chair of the Union of Labor (the union-based party created for the 1995 election) working to activate a labor party. The two have also threatened to direct more protests against managers.[25] These developments indicate strains in the union-manager alliance; but divisions within the FNPR and the legacy of unions' historical subordination to management militate against a social-democratic turn in Russia's labor politics.[26]

The Tripartite Commission

Representatives of Russian labor, management, and government also meet regularly in the Tripartite Commission for the Regulation of Social and Labor Relations. Here the FNPR holds most of labor's seats, with Sotsprof and the Labor Confederation of Russia (KTR), a confederation of independents, also participating. As elsewhere, the typical pattern is for unions to side with management representatives in pressuring the government. Every year since 1992 the Commission has negotiated a General Agreement on a range of issues, including wage levels, unemployment insurance, and safety-net policies, as well as the "managerial agenda." The 1998–1999 General Agreement, for example, called for an active state industrial and investment policy, state support for the agroindustrial complex, protection for domestic goods producers, lower taxes on production, and regulation of prices and tariffs charged by natural monopolies.[27]

From the beginning these Agreements have carried little weight. The commitments are vague and have no legal status, and the government largely ignores

TABLE 6.4   Budgetary Subsidies and Budget Investment Grants (as percent of GDP)

	1992	1993	1994	1995
Budget subsidies	10.4	3.0	1.8	1.3
Budget investment grants	2.3	1.2	0.7	n.a.

SOURCE: *Transition report 1997: Enterprise Performance and Growth* (London: EBRD, 1997), p. 83; *Russian Federation: Toward Medium-Term Viability* (Washington, D.C.: World Bank, 1996), p. 54.

them. Organizations representing management lack a mandate from the majority of directors, and as I pointed out earlier, the unions are internally divided.[28] The Tripartite Commission does accomplish three things: It gives the FNPR the position of national-level bargaining partner for most of Russia's workers; it gives the government a show of democratic negotiation with the unions; and it provides one more forum in which the "managerial agenda" is promoted.

The Labor-Management Alliance: Success or Failure?

How successful has the management-labor alliance been in pressing its agenda for subsidies and soft credits, state investment, protectionism, tax cuts, cheap energy, and other forms of state support for a "revival of production"? At first cut, we would have to say that it has largely failed. Early in the reform period, government spending on subsidies was very high, Viktor Gerashchenko's Central Bank was liberal in its lending, and joint labor-management pressure for subsidies and soft credits made a great deal of sense. But as can be seen from Table 6.4, since 1992 overall budgetary subsidies to enterprises as well as budget investment have been slashed.

Payments to the still subsidy-dependent agricultural and mining sectors were cut drastically, as were state orders for military factories, and direct subsidies to other sectors have been largely eliminated. The Central Bank ceased extending soft credits in 1995, and interest rates have remained high and credit prohibitively expensive. Of course, enterprises can still lobby for exceptions and exemptions. As a World Bank assessment concluded: "The remaining system of government financial transfers to enterprises is very complex and opaque. There are a multitude of channels."[29] But the overall pool of potential benefits is far smaller.

In the area of protectionism also, the "managerial agenda" has fared poorly. Imports have risen steadily, expanding by 25 percent in 1995, 11 percent in 1996, and according to the State Customs Committee, an additional 17 percent in 1997,[30] whereas domestic producers continued to lose market share (see Table 6.5). Quotas have been discussed or put into place for some goods, and there are exemptions and more evasion, but the average import tariff has changed only slightly.

A 1997 OECD study concluded: "On the whole a fairly liberal trade policy was maintained ... consistent with Russia's stated desire to be treated as a market

TABLE 6.5   Russian Imports of Goods and Services (millions U.S. dollars)

1994	1995	1996
63,311	79,516	85,999

SOURCE: *OECD Economic Surveys: Russian Federation, 1997* (Paris: OECD [Organization for Economic Cooperation and Development], 1997), p. 225.

economy and join the World Trade Organization, and despite the intensification of protectionist pressures."[31] Even the alliance's demands for reduced taxes on production, which have support from pro-reform groups, were not met, as tax reform remained tied up in political controversy.

A closer look, however, suggests a more qualified answer to our question. Although most direct subsidies to enterprises have ended, implicit subsidies in the forms of free or cheap energy and de facto or de jure tax exemptions, as well as tolerance of large-scale enterprise debt, are rampant. Beginning in 1995, enterprises and institutions ceased on a large scale to pay their energy bills. By the middle of 1996, for example, Gazprom was being paid for only 23 percent of the gas it supplied. In a kind of implicit deal, the government then compensated the energy sector. Shleifer and Treisman described the deal in these words: "Insolvent farms, enterprises, and state installations that demanded inflationary credits were to some extent appeased with free or cheap energy; the energy sector was repaid in tax breaks, perks, and export privileges. This constituted an implicit fuel subsidy [amounting to almost 35 trillion rubles from mid-1994 to mid-1996] to many insolvent enterprises and budget sector organizations."[32] Such energy subsidies were provided especially to the agricultural and defense sectors. Electricity prices were also frozen temporarily in mid-1995, and gas and railroad transport prices (a particular demand of Rosugol's), in the fall.[33] Enterprises' nonpayment of the high production taxes is also epidemic, as Shmakov himself acknowledged at the FNPR's Third Congress.[34] Though the government has made sporadic and rather arbitrary efforts to penalize or close down tax debtors, it has seldom followed through. And even though bankruptcy legislation is in place, enterprises are allowed to function in deep debt and long-term legal insolvency. In sum, although the alliance has so far largely failed in its pressures for direct subsidies, state investment, and protectionism, it has arguably contributed to effective demands for indirect subsidies and enterprise tax and debt relief. These policies can promote survival if not revival, and they show that the labor-management alliance at the national level has gained important albeit diminishing returns.

Protests and Strikes

There are two major types of labor activism in Russia: semiannual national days of protest that are sponsored and coordinated by the FNPR, and strikes that begin at the enterprise or sectoral level with or without the support of unions. The over-riding issue for both is the crisis in wage arrears, which grew from about 2 trillion rubles in June of 1995 to almost 6 trillion rubles in June 1997, reaching 138 percent of the average monthly wage bill before declining some in the latter part of that year.[35] Arrears were cited as the main cause of protests by 98 percent of all affected enterprises in 1997.[36] Demands for relief were directed mainly at governmental actors—first and foremost, the federal government. Only about 20 percent of wage arrears were in fact owed by government agencies at various levels, but protesters saw the federal government's responsibility as much broader. This fact points to four central causes of unpaid wages:

1. budget nonpayments—where the federal government has failed to transfer funds to regional or local governments which prevents them from paying public sector workers;

2. debts for state orders—where the government has failed to pay for materials delivered by defense contractors, energy consumed by public users, and other materials and services it ordered;

3. consumer debt and mutual nonpayments within industry—where wage arrears, overtaxing of production, and/or an insufficient supply of money make it impossible for industrial and individual consumers to pay debts;

4. the government's failure to enforce labor contracts and payment discipline.

The governor of Amur oblast summarized this situation well. Criticizing the center's efforts to blame leaders of regions and enterprises for the months of delayed wages, he said: "The state is the chief defaulter; it bears responsibility for its ill-conceived economic policy."[37] Workers often demand meetings with government ministers, even deputy prime ministers, in order to settle strikes. Regional and local governments are also targeted. In sum, the dynamic of conflict has not shifted primarily to labor-management relations, though there is more conflict here than in the past. Government is still generally seen as responsible for economic problems, and as disposing of the resources to address them.

The reasons for this are complicated. First, workers tend to be most active and strike-prone in those sectors—education, health care, and mining—where the state bears direct financial responsibility and is the adversary (see Table 6.6). Secondly, the FNPR's largest unions are concentrated in the public sector, where wages are low and declining and arrears are widespread (though the latter are not greater as a proportion of the wage bill than in the privatized sectors). All but four of Russia's 89 regions were in debt to their teachers, doctors, and cultural workers

TABLE 6.6   Strikes By Industry in 1996 and January–June, 1997* (in thousands)

	No. of Strikes		No. of Working Days Lost	
	1996	*J–J 1997*	*1996*	*J–J 1997*
Industry	527	202	2,231	1,058
Coal mining	445	n.a.	1,853	n.a.
Education	7,396	13,803	1,488	2,809
Health care	229	653	163	320
Total	8,278	14,970	4,009	4,395

*1997 data are for number of enterprises and organizations and strikes of more than one day.

SOURCE: *Russian Economic Trends*, 1997, no. 1, p. 131; 1997, no. 3, p. 99.

in 1997; wage arrears typically extended six months or longer; and virtually all of that debt was owed by government (see Table 6.7).[38]

Moreover, in politically chaotic regions such as Primorye, public-sector workers suffered disproportionately and strike levels were particularly high. In protests over wage arrears, teachers and doctors picketed regional administration buildings, staged hunger strikes, and in the end often settled for a portion of back wages. The situation with the miners, the other heavily strike-prone group, is more complicated. (See Chapter 5 in this volume.) First, although some mines have been privatized, most are still state-owned. Second, the Russian government, in cooperation with the World Bank, has developed a restructuring program that is intended to close half of all mines and has already closed about 60. The restructuring program is to be aided by a $1.2 billion loan from the World Bank, including funds for retraining, resettlement, and social needs of displaced miners.[39] But miners and their unions have failed to receive much of the promised aid. According to one report, mine closures have left several thousand miners "in suspension": "Very few of the closed-down mines can boast that all of the liquidation measures—moving, finding jobs, paying allowances, wages, pensions—are carried out, and this is a major source of tensions."[40] Nor have unions received much of the aid guaranteed for monitoring and for legal and social support.[41] Miners' grievances stem from a combination of wage arrears, apprehension about the future, and the conviction that the government is cheating them of promised international aid. Strikes are also common in the defense sector, where unions and managers demand both that the government pay overdue debts for state orders and that it send out commissions to resolve the future of their enterprises in the absence of new state orders.[42] Generally, strikes are much less frequent in the privatized sectors of the economy.

It is also true that very often, in practice, the management-government distinction breaks down for Russian protesters. It is common for strikes to begin with workers occupying the office of the enterprise director, who pleads nonpayment

TABLE 6.7 Budget Arrears As Percent of Total Arrears (1997, second quarter)

Total	Industry	Construction	Agriculture	Health	Education
20.5	4.8	5.6	1.6	80.9	98.7

SOURCE: *Russian Economic Trends*, 1998, no. 1, p. 46.

and overtaxation, and then to move on to that of the mayor.[43] What ensues is often a game of mutual blaming, in which the local government blames federal arrears and the federal government claims either that the money was sent and has been misused or stolen or that it has been used to offset regional tax arrears, until in the end workers tire of "talk about which budget owes them, federal or local."[44] In fact, such obfuscation has itself become a major source of grievance. Leonid Gordon, a longtime observer of the Russian labor scene, has concluded that the arbitrariness and powerlessness miners have experienced around wage issues has become a deeper sense of grievance than their actual economic losses: Ninety percent of workers surveyed by VTsIOM in spring 1997 reported participating in protests less because of wage arrears per se than because of discontentment and the sense that they are being deceived.[45]

There is one other significant dimension of Russian labor protests: They often function as a kind of regional lobbying or demand-making on the center.[46] The FNPR's national protests are commonly supported by regional authorities, who help coordinate, provide security, and sometimes direct their personnel to participate—all in hopes of getting more payments from the center.[47] Enterprise-based protests may also be taken up by regional authorities in order to press for resources, protest policies, lobby for exceptions, or simply to redirect discontent to the center.

The potential complexity of strikes—the way in which they might involve workers and managers, regional lobbying and central politics—is well illustrated by a strike at the Polet Aerospace Association in Omsk in fall 1996. Yeltsin had recently created the Temporary Extraordinary Commission for the Strengthening of Tax and Payment Discipline and had issued presidential decree no. 1212, which ordered budget debtors to close all accounts except for paying the treasury. Polet, like so many Russian enterprises a tax debtor, was scheduled to restart after a temporary shutdown, and its workers rallied to protest the edict, which would have kept their factory closed. The governor supported their demands as being in the region's interest; and the regional newspaper published a joint appeal of local authorities, trade unions, and managers against decree no. 1212, or for an exemption. Regional authorities next proposed that Polet's debt be covered by a mutual offsetting agreement against the federal government's debts to the region for teachers', doctors', and military personnel's salaries. Then the region demanded that the "tax persecution of labor collectives" be halted, the edict repealed, and a temporary procedure be established for the use of financial resources by enterprises in debt to the budget, allowing them to first pay wages.[48] Here we see clearly the regional coalition of workers, managers, and political authorities against the center, and the structure of interests that underlies it. (In the event, Polet survived but remained in crisis, with its workers striking again and blocking a road in spring 1997 to protest months of wage arrears.)[49]

National Protests

The FNPR's national days of protest represent the union's major effort to mobilize its members and pressure the government. Though the numbers participating are always in dispute, these are broad, interregional and intersectoral protests bringing out teachers, doctors, coal miners, power and timber industry workers, and others. The largest such demonstration, in March 1997, involved at least 1.2 million people.[50] The demands were multiple, including the clearing of wage and social benefit arrears; an end to the growth of unemployment; fulfillment of the Tripartite Agreement; and elements of the managerial agenda, such as lower taxes on production, and state regulation of prices charged by natural monopolies.[51] The protest included "regional lobbying," with many governors and city and *raion* administration heads taking part, working with the unions to organize the protest, and putting forth their own, more specific programs.[52] In the final analysis, though, this protest (like all the others sponsored by the FNPR) was anemic. The majority of participants simply demonstrated during the designated day; and although Shmakov claimed that 16,000 enterprises held strikes, some of these lasted less than 24 hours. The outcomes of these protests are also disappointingly similar: They are mainly intended to pressure the government for transfers of funds to the regions, with which to pay public sector wages.

In response to the protest, the prime minister sat down with Shmakov to draw up a schedule for repayment of the state's wage debt as well as to draft some largely meaningless agreements on union control over wage payments. The government then used its usual "fire brigade" budgetary methods to pay off some back wages, producing, as Table 6.8 shows, a substantial decline in arrears in the health and education sectors by the end of 1997. As the table also shows, the effect on arrears in the largely privatized industrial and construction sectors was minimal. Moreover, there is no evidence that the union intended to hold out for any of its other demands: Shmakov stated clearly that the sole criterion for the protest's success was a decline in wage arrears.[53] And even this was quite temporary. Within several months, wage arrears again had accumulated, as the government had turned to other priorities, and the cycle of protest was repeated. The union's tactics are impressively self-limited, perhaps because it fears the government's retaliation against more aggressive protests, and because its leadership doubts that the rank-and-file would turn out. And while the FNPR does back political demands, it typically drops them at the first sign of concessions.

TABLE 6.8   Wage Arrears As Percent of Wage Bill (first and fourth quarters, 1997)

	Total	Industry	Construction	Agriculture	Health	Education/Culture
1997 Q1	138	156	108	260	116	133
1997 Q4	105	141	83	233	27	31

SOURCE: *Russian Economic Trends*, 1998, no. 1, p. 45.

Private Sector Strikes

The role of managers in Russian strikes is unclear. For the most part, managers do not lead strikes. Sometimes they are the initial targets of strikes; sometimes they encourage workers' demands; and most of the time, they are, in the words of one expert, "happy that they are not the target."[54] There are some strikes directed exclusively against enterprise managers, and most observers agree that the numbers of these are increasing, mainly because the economic state of enterprises continues to worsen while many managers are obviously prospering. Such strikes tend to be of two types: either triggered by cases of gross managerial corruption or mismanagement, or directed against managements that undeniably have resources. In an example of the first type, the trade unions commission at the Progress Russian Aircraft Factory was convinced that their former director had made improper use of 2 billion rubles, and they timed their strike to coincide with the report of the audit chamber investigating him. In another case, at the Vorgashorskaya mine in Vorkuta, which owed its workers billions of rubles in wage arrears because of customer nonpayments, trade union activists blamed the former director for concluding supply contracts that placed unilateral liability on the mine.[55] In cases of the second type, a trade union at a Gazprom subsidiary in Tyumen oblast struck to demand back wages, claiming that "the workers hear Gazprom is investing money ... [and that] the upper echelon lives in luxury."[56] Similarly, in 1997, the FNPR led a series of successful strikes, mainly against foreign-owned firms such as the Procter & Gamble plant in Tula, where the regional administration supported the protest against layoffs. Thousands of court cases have also been brought against managers for nonpayment of wages, without much success.[57] But in general, workers strike little in the privatized sector, because they believe that these enterprises have no resources; because they fear the loss of jobs that provide at least some benefits (there are reports of punitive dismissals against strikers); and because their unions do not encourage such strikes.

There is no clear evidence that the scale of labor protest in Russia is increasing (e.g., the 1998 national protests were smaller than those in spring 1997), but both the politicization and the desperation of strikers clearly are. Demands for the government's resignation, kidnappings of managers, hunger strikes, regional strikes involving workers from numerous sectors, and the blocking of major roads and railway lines by workers, though not new, have escalated. Although the FNPR and independent unions often go along with these tactics, they do not initiate them, and the potential for more radical leadership from below, or for wildcat actions, is very real. The most militant workers have despaired of bargaining with the federal government. Polls in the latter Yeltsin years indicated that a majority of the population (even in prosperous Moscow) endorsed strikers' blocking of major transportation lines and their demands for the Yeltsin government's resignation.[58] Talk of strikes leading to an "Albanian scenario," though no doubt exaggerated, reflect widespread apprehension among Russians. Whatever side the unions are on, many workers feel increasingly isolated.

Conclusion

In sum, Russia's major unions have sided with management throughout the reform period. In 1992, the FNPR allied with Civic Union against Gaidar, and helped managers pressure Chubais to amend his privatization program. In politics, the FNPR's national leadership has made alliances with the successive political fronts of Volskii's RSPP; and although it has not managed to bring along many branch and regional union organizations, these have gravitated toward a range of other management-affiliated parties and movements, including the Agrarians and the Congress of Russian Communities. Some regional organizations support the Communists. Unions and management, particularly in the old industrial branches, share a perspective that the government's policies are to blame for the collapse of industry, and have a common view of the solution, reflected in the "managerial agenda." Unions at all levels have endorsed positions and platforms from this agenda: state investment and industrial policies, subsidies and cheap credit, protectionism, and state price regulation of natural monopolies. They have not succeeded in forwarding much of this agenda, but they have sustained pressure in the Russian polity for the implicit subsidies and financial laxity that allow most enterprises to survive.

Unions have not gained the support of their rank and file for the alliance with management at the electoral level; but at the enterprise level, they have helped convince workers to cooperate with the privatization program. Yet they have also reinforced workers' powerlessness and managers' lack of accountability by failing to translate workers' privatization share ownership into influence. They have also encouraged workers to collaborate in the various "survival strategies" adopted by managers, and have discouraged labor-management conflict by directing popular discontent toward the state. The union's public statements and demands promote the perception that the government and its policies are to blame for economic problems and that high taxes and state payment arrears prevent the profitable operation of most enterprises. Though 80 percent of wage arrears are in the private sector, the FNPR uses its periodic national protests mainly to pressure the government over public sector arrears.

Another pattern overlays the state-management-union triad: Unions, managers, and local and regional authorities combine to press the central government for money, exceptions, and policy changes. Such "regional lobbying" has been apparent in many local strikes and in the FNPR's national protests, which first and foremost have accomplished a transfer of funds from the central government to the regions. Labor protests that do emerge are often directed into this pattern, which both undercuts direct labor-management conflict, and typically confronts both unions and workers with a morass of conflicting claims about who in fact owes the funds from which their wages should be paid. Ultimately, unions cooperate both with managers and with regional political authorities in an effort to maximize claims on the federal government. At the same time, the unions' capacity to voice or channel workers' grievances seems to be diminishing as protest tactics become more extreme.

The union-management alliance has brought some gains, but overall it has paid diminishing returns. Managers have decreasing need for unions' cooperation in the post-privatization economy and provide less for them to distribute to members; and the state commits fewer and fewer resources in response to the alliance's claims.

Notes

For research assistance on this paper I would like to thank Matthew Crosston of Brown University, and for comments, Mark Kramer.

1. Peter Rutland, "Business lobbies in contemporary Russia," *International Spectator*, vol. 32, no. 1 (January–March 1997), pp. 23–37. The list of what business elites want from the government is on p. 31; I have slightly modified it here.

2. See, for example, the appeal of the RSPP's Eighth Congress to the Russian government in *Rossiiskaya gazeta* (hereafter, *Rosgaz*), 10 December 1996; the demands of Rosugol's chief in *Rosgaz*, 21 March 1997; and the program for "extrication from crisis" by a conference of leaders of machine-building industry enterprises in *Rabochaya tribuna* (hereafter, *Rabtrib*), 11 June 1997, trans. in *Foreign Broadcast Information Service: SOV* (hereafter, *FBIS:SOV*), 11 June 1997. Although these managerial organizations are weak in comparative terms, they constitute the most articulate collective voice of Russian managers, and the same can be said for the FNPR and Russian labor.

3. See the text of Shmakov's speech in "III S"ezd Federatsii nezavisimykh profsoiuzov Rossii," *Profsoiuzy,* no. 1, 1997, pp. 1–4.

4. See, for example, *Trud,* 8 April 1997.

5. Among the things enterprise unionists have to lose are their access to offices, cars, and other perquisites, and this leads many to minimize their conflicts with managers (interview with Greg Schulze, Director of Organizing, Free Trade Union Institute, 19 June 1996, Washington, D.C.). New unions that take a more adversarial attitude toward management have emerged, but they remain very small.

6. See Richard Rose, *New Russian Barometer V: Between Two Elections*, occasional paper (Glasgow, U.K.: University of Strathclyde, Centre for the Study of Public Policy, 1996), pp. 44–45.

7. Interview with Renfrey Clarke, Moscow correspondent for the Australian *Green Leaf Weekly*, Moscow, 22 June 1998; Clarke was citing an estimate by Boris Kagarlitsky, who has worked closely with the FNPR.

8. Richard Rose, *New Russian Barometer IV: Survey Results* (Center for the Study of Public Policy, University of Strathclyde, 1995), p. 17. Unions were ranked lowest in influence among nine named actors; "Ordinary workers" were seen as having considerably more influence.

9. "III S"ezd," p. 2; T. Chertvernina, P. Smirnov, and N. Dunaeva, "Mesto profsoiuza na predpriyatii," *Voprosy ekonomiki*, no. 6 (June 1995), pp. 83–84.

10. Interview with Yurii Levada, director of VTsIOM, Moscow, 23 June 1998.

11. Interview with Clarke.

12. *Trud*, 10 December 1996.

13. The quote is from Joseph Blasi, Maya Kroumova, and Douglas Kruse, *Kremlin Capitalism* (Ithaca, N.Y.: Cornell University Press, 1997), p. 107. The few cases reported elsewhere in which unions did attempt to exercise influence on the boards only confirm their weakness.

14. See Padma Desai and Todd Idson, "Wage Arrears in Russia" (unpublished paper, January 1998).

15. Stephen Crowley argues that the FNPR's concern for its property makes it fearful of antagonizing the government; but Irene Stevenson makes the convincing point that legal ownership of this property is by now too complicated and obfuscated to allow for renationalization (interview with Irene Stevenson, Director, American Center for International Labor Solidarity, Moscow, 23 June 1998).

16. *OECD Economic Surveys, Russian Federation, 1997* (Paris: OECD, 1997), p. 17. *Sunk-cost infrastructure* refers to existing infrastructure, in which the investment has already been made.

17. *Russian Federation: Toward Medium-Term Viability* (Washington, D.C.: World Bank, 1996), p. 23.

18. Quoted in *Trud*, 4 March 1997, pp. 1–2, trans. in *FBIS:SOV*, 5 March 1997.

19. Interview with Leonid Gordon, Director, Department of Social and Labor Studies, Institute of World Economy and International Relations (IMEMO), Moscow, 24 June 1998.

20. Blasi, Kroumova, and Kruse estimated that rank-and-file employees were majority owners in about 30 percent of private-sector Russian companies in 1996 (*Kremlin Capitalism*, p. 193).

21. Linda J. Cook, *Labor and Liberalization: Trade Unions in the New Russia* (New York: Twentieth Century Fund, 1997), pp. 61–64.

22. For the coalition's platform, see *Rabtrib*, 4 November 1995.

23. See *Kemerovo, Kuzbass*, 20 September 1995, trans. in *FBIS:SOV*, 20 September, 1995.

24. Timothy J. Colton, "The Russian Voter in 1993: Some Patterns in the National Survey Data," memorandum for the Russian Election Conference, Harvard University, 9 April 1994, pp. 12, 32.

25. *Trud,* 15 October 1997; interview with Pavel Kudyukin, member of the Presidium of the Russian Social Democratic Union and senior research fellow, Institute for Comparative Political Studies, Russian Academy of Sciences, Moscow, 25 June 1998.

26. Analysts have pointed to several other factors that undermine the potential for social democracy in Russia, including the overall weakness of unions, a lack of social differentiation and consciousness, and the discrediting of the "socialist" concept or its wedding to a retrograde nationalism in the contemporary Communist movement.

27. For the text of the agreement, see *Profsoiuzy i ekonomiki,* no. 2, 1998, pp. 90–95; see also *Trud,* 9 April 1997.

28. On the Tripartite Commission, see *Trud,* 10 December 1996; Walter D. Connor, *Tattered Banners: Labor, Conflict, and Corporatism in Postcommunist Russia* (Boulder: Westview, 1996).

29. *Russian Federation: Toward Medium-Term Viability,* p. 53. Rutland ("Business Lobbies") stresses such particularistic lobbying as the main form for managers.

30. For the 1997 figure, see *Russian Economic Trends* (London: Whurr), 1998, no. 1, p. 52.

31. Quoted from *OECD Economic Surveys, Russian Federation, 1997,* p. 67.

32. Andrei Shleifer and Daniel Treisman, *The Economics and Politics of Transition to an Open Market Economy: Russia* (Paris: OECD, 1998), p. 53.

33. Ibid., p. 51.

34. See "III S"ezd," p. 3.

35. *OECD Economic Surveys, Russian Federation, 1997,* p. 50; *Russian Economic Trends,* 1998, no. 1, pp. 44–45.

36. *Russian Economic Trends,* 1997, no. 3, p. 98.

37. See *Sovetskaya Rossiya,* 25 March 1997, p. 1, trans. in *FBIS:SOV,* 25 March 1997.

38. See *Rossiiskie vesti,* 26 November 1997, pp. 1–2; the four exceptions were Moscow and St. Petersburg regions, the Yamalo-Nenets autonomous territory, and the Jewish Autonomous Oblast.

39. Stephen Crowley, cited from Johnson's Russian List, 22 July 1998.

40. See *Rossiiskie vesti,* 25 March 1997.

41. Interview with Stevenson.

42. However, more defense enterprises now are finding foreign buyers than before—a trend that led to a marked increase in Russian arms exports in 1997.

43. Interview with Stevenson, as well as many press accounts of actual strikes.

44. See *Trud,* 4 December 1996, p. 1.

45. Interviews with Stevenson, Levada.

46. This pattern was brought to my attention by Kaku Kimura, a graduate student at Harvard University in spring 1998. Paul Christensen also refers to this pattern, calling it "a type of local and regional corporatism." See Christensen, "Why Russia lacks a labor movement," *Transitions,* vol. 4, no. 7 (December 1997), p. 48.

47. For example, in the spring 1997 "day of protest" in Altai, heads of administrations in cities and oblasts were instructed by the territorial administration to participate in the protests.

48. See the report in *Trud,* 21 November 1996.

49. ITAR-TASS, 5 March 1997, cited in *FBIS:SOV,* 5 March 1997.

50. The government estimated between 1.2 million and 1.8 million; the FNPR claimed more than 5 million.

51. See *Trud,* 8 April 1997.

52. See *Trud,* 29 March 1997.

53. *Moskovskii komsomolets,* 25 March 1997, cited in *FBIS:SOV,* 25 March 1997.

54. Interview with Boris Kagarlitsky, Moscow, 23 June 1998.

55. These strikes were reported, respectively, in *FBIS:SOV,* 4 November 1997, citing Moscow's NTV, 4 November 1997; and *FBIS:SOV,* 27 January 1997, citing Moscow Radio Rossii, 27 January 1997.

56. *Obshchaya gazeta,* 6–12 February 1997, trans. in *FBIS:SOV,* 12 February 1997.

57. See *Rosgaz,* 21 March 1997; Stevenson interview. Workers cannot make claims against the personal property of managers.

58. Interview with Levada.

CHAPTER 7

The August 1998 Crash: Causes and Consequences

Peter Rutland

In 1997 the Western specialists who had been advising the Russian government since 1991 were still full of optimism. Less than a decade after the collapse of Soviet socialism, the rudiments of a capitalist economy were in place in Russia. During the calendar year 1997 Moscow was the most rapidly growing stock exchange in the world, rising by 85 percent in dollar terms. President Boris Yeltsin's election victory in 1996 seemed to show that the political coalition for reform was firmly in the saddle, and it was hoped that the newly privatized enterprises would finally start to invest and grow. In spring 1997, Yeltsin appointed a new reformist team under Prime Minister Viktor Chernomyrdin, in a bid to restart the reform momentum that had been lost in 1996 due to Yeltsin's electioneering in the first half of the year and his ill health in the second. Yeltsin appointed former privatization chief Anatolii Chubais and Boris Nemtsov, the youthful governor of Nizhnii Novgorod, as first deputy prime ministers, and they proceeded to launch a "second liberal revolution," tackling the yawning state budget deficit. They planned to crack down on corruption, to boost tax collection, and to cut subsidies to energy users. They also wanted to break up the monopolies that still controlled the gas and electricity industries.

Alas, the liberals' spring offensive in 1997 was fought off by the barons who controlled the energy industries, while the financial oligarchs began feuding among themselves over the division of the remaining spoils in the state sector. They fought for posts in the government, and they fought over the privatization of the Svyazinvest telecommunication company and the remaining state oil companies. Apart from conservative state bureaucrats and self-interested oligarchs, the reformers also had to deal with the Communist-controlled State Duma. Rule by decree had worked in 1992–1994, when the task was to remove controls and give away state assets. Building a lasting infrastructure for a market economy, however, could only proceed on the basis of laws—a point repeatedly made by foreign investors, but one that seemed to fall on deaf Russian ears. Laws are clear and transparent for all to see, and can only be altered by a lengthy procedure. Decrees, in contrast, were often kept secret, and were issued (and countermanded) at the stroke of a presidential pen. Only the parliament could pass the new laws needed to move forward with market reform: laws to revise the tax system; to introduce a new civil code; to allow the buying and selling of land; and to create a list of sites open to foreigners under production sharing (which was permitted under a law passed in 1995).

The political roller-coaster continued in fits and starts, on a timetable driven by Yeltsin's shuttling between Kremlin and sanatorium. When Yeltsin was physically fit, he would bang his fist on the table, and raise hopes that the reformers would be able to persuade the president to push through the needed reforms. Once again, liberal hopes were raised in March 1998, when Yeltsin peremptorily fired Viktor Chernomyrdin, the grandfather of Gazprom, who had loyally served Yeltsin as premier since December 1992. Yeltsin seemed fearful that Chernomyrdin was becoming too independent and was developing a yearning to replace Yeltsin as president when the time came for him to step down, in 2000— or sooner, if his health deteriorated. Yeltsin replaced Chernomyrdin with Sergei Kirienko, a 35-year-old banker and political unknown who had come to Moscow from Nizhnii Novgorod with Boris Nemtsov.

Kirienko's appointment provided the opportunity for a renewed surge of Western optimism that another perceived political barrier to reform (Chernomyrdin) had finally been removed. Before Kirienko had time to find his way around the corridors of the Kremlin, however, he found himself having to deal with the delayed aftereffects of the Southeast Asian financial meltdown that began in fall 1997—and with a domestic financial crisis of Russia's own making.

A Hot August

The August 1998 financial crash in Russia caught the world by surprise, and caused observers to call into question the character and viability of the Russian political and economic system. The August crisis punctured the general mood of cautious optimism about the Russian economic transition that had prevailed in Western capitals. The Russian government's abrupt announcement of a ruble devaluation and suspension of foreign debt payments on August 17 was unexpected. Only the month before, the IMF had assembled a US$22 billion aid package that it assumed would protect the ruble against speculative attack. The ministers of the Russian government were so convinced that they had patched together a fiscal package to keep the wolves from the door that in the second week of August they dispersed for their vacations in exotic corners of Europe. Things started to unravel on Thursday, August 13, with a letter from George Soros to the *Financial Times* predicting that Russia would have to devalue the ruble. Chubais, who had been handling negotiations with the IMF, cut short his vacation in Ireland and chartered a plane to return to Moscow.

Over the next week, the shaky edifice of market reform that had been assembled in Russia over the preceding seven years came crashing down. On Monday, August 17, payments on most categories of Russian international and domestic government debt were suspended, and the government announced a widening of the corridor within which the ruble was pegged to the dollar. Panicked individuals and companies in Russia tried to change all their rubles for dollars, and the financial system froze up. Imports plunged and domestic prices surged by 60 percent. By September 7, the value of the ruble had fallen by more than two-thirds (from 6 to 21 rubles to the dollar).

The reformist government of Sergei Kirienko, hailed by U.S. officials after Kirienko's appointment in March 1998 as talented and committed to reform, was forced to resign. The State Duma twice rejected Yeltsin's initial nominee to replace Kirienko—Chernomyrdin—and it looked as if a major political crisis was in the offing. On September 11, Yeltsin accepted a suggestion that he appoint Foreign Minister Yevgenii Primakov as prime minister. Primakov, a former intelligence agency chief, was a conservative figure acceptable to the Communists, and his appointment was quickly and enthusiastically approved by the Duma. Primakov brought back into the government former Communist apparatchiki such as Central Bank head Viktor Gerashchenko and former central planning chief Yurii Maslyukov—the latter, as first deputy prime minister. Suddenly, there was concern that Russia's domestic and foreign policies might take a giant step backward.

Why had observers been caught off guard by the August crisis? Their complacency stemmed from the core assumption that Russia's stability could be ensured, provided that Yeltsin, a tried and tested friend of the West, was at the helm of state. It was assumed that given Russia's military and political importance, the vast resources of the international economic community would always be made available to prevent some sort of economic meltdown in Russia. Because Russia was considered "too big and too nuclear" to be allowed to fail, the financial resources of the West presumably would always be there to ensure the stability of the Russian government—a government that was pursuing, at least halfheartedly, a policy of economic liberalization. The key moment of vulnerability had been the June 1996 presidential election. When Yeltsin (narrowly) passed that test, the West breathed a huge sigh of relief, and Western experts confidently argued that democracy had been consolidated in Russia.

The Roots of the August Crash

The causes of the August crisis can be divided into two categories. First, there were a number of deep-seated structural problems with the Russian economy signaling that the ambitious reform program had run ahead of the actual adaptive capacity of the Russian economy. These problems included a militarized and geographically irrational industrial structure; lack of rule of law; absence of state capacity for running a market economy (such as tax collection and a regulatory framework); and corrupt elites. These chronic problems weakened the health of the Russian economic system and increased its vulnerability to opportunistic infections such as the price shifts and loss of confidence that emanated from the 1997 Asian crisis.

Second, there were a series of policy errors by the Russian government that can be seen to have led directly to the crisis. Chief among these were two decisions connected to the stabilization program adopted at the urging of the IMF in 1995: the decision to fix the ruble exchange rate at too high a level, and the government's resolve to finance the yawning budget deficit through international borrowing.

In 1995 the Russian government committed itself to maintaining a predictable exchange rate for the ruble. A stable exchange rate would signal its commitment to conquering inflation and would reassure foreign investors that the latter would be able to repatriate their investment and profits without exchange rate losses. Hence in July 1995 the Central Bank announced a "corridor" within which the exchange rate would be maintained (the upper and lower limits were initially fixed at 4,300/4,900 rubles to the dollar). Unfortunately they were slow to tighten the money supply, and domestic inflation ran at 130 percent throughout 1995. This caused the ruble to appreciate in real terms against the dollar—to the tune of about 30 percent by December 1995. The Central Bank switched to a more flexible "inclined corridor" (akin to a crawling peg) in July 1996. In 1996 annual inflation came down to a respectable 22 percent, and the ruble more or less held a constant value against the dollar. This success was in part thanks to a tight monetary policy and in part due to a $10.1 billion, three-year loan approved by the IMF in March 1996—not coincidentally, in the lead-up to the presidential election, when Yeltsin was fighting for his political life. In the course of 1997, inflation fell to 11 percent, although the ruble appreciated in real terms by about 5 percent against the dollar.

The initial exchange rate had arguably been set at a level (about 50 percent of the dollar purchasing power parity) that was rather high compared to that of other economies at the same level of development (having less than $5,000 per capita annual income).[1] The main practical benefit of a highly priced ruble, apart from the psychological satisfaction of having a "strong" currency, was that it boosted the ability of Russian consumers (especially those with money) to buy more imported goods. Imports fueled the emergence of a middle class in Moscow and elsewhere, which was an important part of Yeltsin's 1996 electoral victory. The IMF thought that the exchange rate was defensible, given Russia's current account trade surpluses. Russia was running a surplus of about $15 billion each year, thanks to its oil and gas earnings. The usual indicators of vulnerability to an international payments crisis looked to be in good shape. The ratios of external debt to GDP and of annual repayments to export earnings (each around 15–25 percent) were manageable and well below what was considered crisis level by international standards. However, the IMF did not allow for the fact that over the previous seven years most of those export earnings had disappeared abroad in capital flight and were not actually flowing back into the Russian economy (neither into investment nor into tax revenues).

Also, the continuing domestic inflation since the introduction of the currency corridor (especially during its first six months) had pushed up the value of the ruble to 65 percent of purchasing power parity (PPP) by the end of 1995, and to 70 percent by 1998. This had the effect of pricing Russian manufactures out of export markets and exposing them to fierce import competition. Russia was not competitive in finished goods (e.g., autos) at any price. But Russian manufacturers of semifinished industrial products such as steel, paper, and chemicals, were potentially competitive and were hit by the real appreciation of the ruble. For a counter-example, take the case of China, whose economic miracle is in large part due to the fact that the government has maintained currency controls (the yuan is not freely convertible into other currencies) and has held the exchange rate down to about 20 percent of PPP. Russia was hardly the first government (and surely not the last) to lock itself into defending an increasingly vulnerable exchange rate. Political pride, and the belief that the international community was watching the stability of the exchange rate as the key indicator of the government's commitment to reform, trapped Russian leaders into this policy.

Defenders of Russia's exchange rate policy argue that the appreciation of the ruble was a natural and largely unavoidable consequence of the country's hydrocarbon wealth. The consequent trade surpluses would naturally push up its exchange rate and drive up the price of domestic capital (the "Dutch disease"). However, there are several reasons why it was not a good idea for the government to allow Russia to turn itself into a "petro-state" entirely dependent on the wealth generated by its energy sector. First, this would entail the destruction of much of Russia's non-oil manufacturing industry, with considerable social and political costs. Second, with the liberalization of capital flows and the weakening of the Russian state's capacity to collect taxes, much of the oil and gas wealth was flowing abroad. (Capital flight was estimated at $20–25 billion a year in the early 1990s, and at $10–15 billion by the end of the decade.) Third, such a policy increased Russia's exposure to cyclical fluctuations in the global economy and vulnerability to a downturn in world commodity prices—of the sort that occurred in 1997–1998.

Fourth, the haphazard privatization of the oil and gas industries starved the sector of much-needed investment. The exclusion of foreign investors and the continuing uncertainties and ambiguities about the property rights of the new Russian owners meant that little investment was taking place in the development of new fields or in the extraction rates from existing fields. Production of natural gas remained roughly static during the 1990s, and oil output slumped by an alarming 40 percent. Oil exports could be maintained at a stable level only by diverting supplies from consumers inside Russia and the newly independent states, who were unable to pay world market prices. This situation could not last indefinitely. It was hoped that once the dust had settled from the privatization scandals, the new owners would be able to start investing. A most encouraging piece of news came in November 1997, with the announcement that British

Petroleum was buying a 10 percent stake in Sidanko, Russia's fifth-largest oil producer, for $570 million. This was the first major entry to the Russian market by a Western oil company. Sidanko had been sold to Vladimir Potanin's Oneksimbank under the 1995 loans-for-shares scheme. Alas, before BP could start to restructure the company, Sidanko was plunged into bankruptcy by the August 1998 financial crash.

Neither a Borrower Nor a Lender Be

The second error that lay behind the August crash was the government's decision to finance the deficit through borrowing—something urged on it by the IMF, which extolled the virtues of "noninflationary deficit financing."[2]

Russia's apparent success in achieving monetary stabilization in 1995–1997 was not accompanied by similar stabilization on the fiscal front. Fiscal balance remained elusive. Government spending was slashed, but revenues eroded even faster. By 1997 the federal government was collecting a mere 10 percent of GDP in taxes but still making spending commitments of around 18 percent of GDP. Regional and local governments raised and spent another 12–14 percent of GDP, usually without running up a deficit (because of finance ministry controls). The fiscal gap (equal to 6–10 percent of GDP) was plugged by borrowing, mainly from overseas investors. Unfortunately, the "successes" of economic reform were directly connected to the deteriorating performance in fiscal policy. The tight money policy had driven much of industry into reliance on barter transactions, which proved hard to tax. Liberalization had slashed government revenue from export and import tariffs and made it easier for firms to hide earnings from the tax men—especially export earnings. Likewise, privatization had taken most firms out of state ownership and had also made it more difficult to tax them. Also, the whole political economy of reform had developed on the basis of special deals for insiders—concessions here to forestall opposition from Soviet-era industrialists, concessions there to win the political support of the new financial oligarchs. The Achilles heel of Russia's "crony capitalism" was tax collection. Freed from the controls of the central planners, these new owners were able to evade taxes on a massive scale. As a result, even after monetary stabilization was achieved, fiscal balance remained elusive.

The government came under huge pressure from the IMF to keep the fiscal deficit below 2–3 percent of GDP. To do this, spending had to be slashed. The "fat" had already been cut from the budget—procurement of weapons and equipment for the military had dropped to almost zero after 1992, for example. (One politically important exception was that funds were allotted for the testing of a new intercontinental nuclear missile, the SS-10.) Savings would have to come out of federally funded wages and social benefits. This was politically risky, since the recipients had the right to vote, and potentially, the capacity to demonstrate (e.g., by lying down on railroad tracks and blocking industrial transport) if things became intolerable. By the end of 1995 about one-quarter of all workers had arrears in their wage payments, with an average of one month. The concentration of arrears was highest among public servants such as teachers and health workers, where arrears of more than three months were the norm. Pensions were also being paid from one to three months in arrears. Hence considerable efforts were made in spring 1996, as part of Yeltsin's election campaign, to clear the backlog of pension and public sector wage arrears.

Even in 1997–1998 the federal deficit remained obstinately high, at around 5–6 percent of GDP. The deficit was financed through the sale of treasury bills (in Russian, "short-term state obligations," or GKOs). This financial instrument, which had been introduced in 1995, was considered far preferable to the alternative—which was to cover federal spending by printing more rubles, surely triggering inflation. The IMF hoped that the resort to GKOs would be a stopgap measure. Within a few months, it was hoped, the federal government would improve its tax collection capabilities. Also it was assumed that once the recession ended, tax revenues would start to pick up. Most of the bonds were 90-day (some were only 30-day), and for such a short-term exposure the rate of return was attractive. Foreigners were keen to enter the GKO market but were subject to a 25 percent cap on their rate of return and to quotas limiting the amount of the market they could command. GKO nominal rates averaged 63 percent in 1996, but fell to a low of 26 percent in 1997 (when inflation was 11 percent).

By 1997 there was growing concern about the mounting pile of GKO debt—with new bond issues being used to raise cash to pay off the previous bonds. But given that the Russian government had entered the debt business late in the game, the total stock of national debt was still only around 50 percent of GDP—low, by international standards. However, the maturity of the national debt was precarious, with almost none beyond 90 days. Pessimists started warning that the government was constructing a debt pyramid, a giant, state-sponsored Ponzi scheme, which could come crashing down if subject to some exogenous shocks. Unfortunately for Moscow, storm clouds were gathering that were capable of delivering such shocks.

The Crisis Breaks

The first sign of impending trouble came before the Asian crisis broke. In the first half of 1997, Russia's export earnings leveled off, whereas its imports continued to grow. In July 1997, for the first time in a decade, Russia's current account slipped into deficit. This set alarm bells ringing, since Russia's financial balancing act hinged on the maintenance of that trade surplus. Increasingly strident calls surfaced—from maverick economist Andrei Illarionov to financier Boris Berezovskii—for a devaluation of the ruble.

Then came the Asian financial meltdown. Its effects on Russia were twofold. First, as Asian stock markets started to fold in October 1997, there was a headlong flight from emerging markets by international investors. Partly this was due to a psychological shift, a flight from risk in all emerging markets. Partly it was driven by the practical desire to cash out gains in the Russian market in order to compensate for losses in Southeast Asia. Second, over the next several months the world recession that resulted from the Asian crisis caused a slump in the world price of all major commodities—including Russian export staples such as oil and steel. The oil price fell from an average of $18 a barrel in December 1997 to a mere $11 a barrel by the end of 1998. (Most of Russia's natural gas is sold at fixed prices under 20-year, take-or-pay contracts, so gas earnings were not seriously affected by the global recession.) The slump in oil prices was a severe blow to Russia, which relied on oil for 35–40 percent of its export earnings. It was estimated that each $1 per barrel fall in the price of oil cost the Russian government $1 billion in lost revenue (with annual federal revenue then running at $30 billion a year).

With Russia's external balances eroding fast, the pressure massively increased on its treasury bill market, the main instrument for preserving financial stabilization. GKO interest rates started to rise again in 1998, amid growing nervousness among investors about exposure to the Russian market. By June the total stock of GKOs (which were denominated in rubles) was about $40 billion, of which about half were held by foreigners or by Russian banks that had borrowed from foreigners to buy the bonds. (The extent to which Russian banks had borrowed dollars to buy GKOs was not apparent until after the crisis.) Interest payments were accounting for some 30 percent of federal expenditures, increasing the pressure to cut other forms of spending. By June the government was finding it hard to find buyers for GKOs, even at annual rates in excess of 100 percent. In July 1998, to reduce exposure to a possible ruble devaluation, the government converted $6.4 billion of GKOs into Eurobonds at 15 percent interest, denominated in dollars. However, that still left $11 billion of GKOs that would fall due by the end of September.

Into the breech stepped the IMF. The IMF was fearful that a precipitate ruble devaluation would cause panic in international markets and produce precisely the crisis that it was designed to stave off. So, after heated discussion, the IMF came through with a $22.6 billion aid package (approved by the IMF board on July 20), including $4.8 billion in ready cash, which it was confident would protect the ruble against speculative attack. In return for its bailout, the IMF insisted on an emergency package of spending cuts and tax increases to bring the fiscal deficit below 3 percent of GDP. Meeting on July 15, the State Duma accepted twelve of the government's proposed bills and only rejected two regarding tax increases; Yeltsin announced his intention to enforce by decree the bills the Duma had rejected.

However, even the IMF's $4.8 billion was insufficient to close the yawning gap between the Russian government's borrowing needs and investors' skittishness about the GKO pyramid. The IMF bailout provided just enough cash for most of the major Western lenders to liquidate their GKO holdings during the final weeks of July. Then came George Soros's fateful letter of August 13 to the *Financial Times*, and panic ensued.

After August

Alarmists predicted a complete economic collapse—hyperinflation, the breakdown of food supplies, and the introduction of rationing—which might trigger anything from a fascist coup to the resurrection of communism. Even sober observers foresaw efforts to reintroduce elements of central planning, such as price controls, the suspension of ruble convertibility, and the renationalization of enterprises that had been corruptly privatized.

In the event, none of these dire scenarios played out. True, the initial impact of the crash was dramatic. The ruble slipped from 6.2 to the dollar on August 16, to 22 to a dollar at year's end, where it stabilized. The crisis primarily affected the monetized side of the economy (retailing, banking, and services). Agriculture and industry, which were conducting from 40–70 percent of their business in barter or other nonmonetary instruments, were relatively insulated from the effects of the crisis. The financial freeze (a temporary inability to complete banking transactions) caused a sudden drop in imports and exports and the effective collapse of the commercial banking sector. Russian banks (ironically, led by the state-owned Sberbank) held $27 billion in GKOs prior to the August crash. Even worse, they had borrowed about $10 billion from foreign banks to finance these speculative purchases. The collapse caused them to lose more than half their assets, plunging them into insolvency. The government forced some banks to merge but kept most of them afloat by releasing Central Bank credits. Menatep Bank lost control over Yukos, the second-largest Russian oil company, when it defaulted on a loan of $236 million that it had backed with Yukos shares. As a result, Germany's state-owned Westdeutsche Landesbank acquired a 15 percent stake in Yukos, and Daiwa Bank, a 14 percent stake.[3] Alfa Bank, which had reduced its exposure to GKOs in the weeks before the crisis, emerged strengthened and was able to buy up assets from other banks.

Imports fell by about half in the four months following August. For 1998 as a whole, imports compared to 1997 fell by 25 percent to $58 billion; exports fell 17 percent, to $75 billion. (The fall in exports was largely due to the decline in world oil prices.) The fall in imports was partly offset by a revival in domestic production as consumers switched to Russian products; industrial production rose 10 percent in the fourth quarter.[4] Exports were expected to rise after the deep devaluation of the ruble. After falling 0.5 percent in the first quarter of 1998, GDP dropped about 8 percent in the second and third quarters, leaving an officially reported GDP decline of 4.6 percent for the year as a whole. Average inflation in the first seven months of 1998 was 7 percent. Prices then rose 38 percent in September, 4.5 percent in October, 5.7 percent in November, and 11.6 percent in December—showing that Primakov's government did not resort to the printing presses. Inflation for the entire year of 1998 was 85 percent—high, but not cata-strophically so. In January 1999, inflation eased to 8.5 percent, and 3.8 percent in February. The stock exchange (RTS) plunged 85 percent in dollar terms in 1998, but rebounded 27 percent in the first two months of 1999 and 85 percent by year's end, reversing the loss of the previous year.

One year after the crisis, in September 1999, industrial production had recov-ered from the post-August slump and had risen 18 percent above the September 1998 trough (and 7 percent above the same month in 1997).[5] In the first seven months of 1999, Russia ran a foreign trade surplus of $15.6 billion, compared to a mere $400 million in the same period of 1998. GDP growth for 1999 was 1.8 percent, the best since the collapse of the Soviet Union. Through careful manage-ment of its meager resources, the Primakov government made some progress in reducing the backlog of wages owed to workers on regional government payrolls, which fell from 13 billion rubles (or an average delay of 2.1 months) in January to 8.3 billion (1.3 months) in April.[6]

The crisis also altered the relationship between Moscow and the international financial community—strengthening the former at the expense of the latter. This was ironic, since one might have expected such a crisis to increase the leverage of international lenders. The reverse happened in the Russian case, be-cause the devaluation and default punctured the illusion that the IMF's previous policies had been working. In the wake of the August crash the Russian govern-ment felt emboldened to ignore IMF advice, and it reintroduced export tariffs on oil (15 euros per metric ton), which it had reluctantly abolished at the IMF's behest in 1996.

The debt default (technically, a 90-day moratorium) bought time and increased Russia's bargaining leverage. Russia had US$17 billion in interest and principal falling due on its international loans in 1999: a sum it was in no position to pay. There were three main sets of debtors to worry about: the international institu-tions, which had lent more than $25 billion to Russia since 1991; the banks and governments holding the $80 billion debt left over from the Soviet Union; and Western banks holding GKOs. (The government managed to keep up payments on certain other categories of debt, such as Eurobonds.)

One of the first signs that it was business as usual with Moscow was the World Bank's decision in February 1999 to lend it $400 million for the coal industry and $400 million for road building. Russia was indeed "too big and too nuclear" for the international institutions to walk away from. In order to avoid the embar-rassment of a formal default on sovereign debt, the IMF agreed to a new $4.5 billion loan facility in June 1999 (which would be used solely to meet the pay-ments on IMF loans falling due in 1999). As a condition of this loan, the IMF had to affirm that it saw positive trends in Russia's monetary and fiscal policies. Moscow's rescheduling talks with the holders of Soviet-era debt, the London and Paris creditors' clubs, also continued. These lenders had agreed to resched-ule the Soviet debts in 1995 and 1996 on fairly generous terms, over a 25-year period. The banks themselves had mostly wiped these assets from their balance sheets long before (in late 1995, these debts were trading on secondary markets at 5 cents on the dollar).

Negotiations with the Western banks holding GKOs frozen on August 17 dragged on for months. Some American banks lost as much as $500 million each in the August crash, but they had little expectation of recouping their losses. Some banks settled for the meager terms that Moscow was offering—a package of long-term securities, equivalent in cash to less than 5 cents on the dollar. These banks agreed in the hope that by showing goodwill they would be the first to gain access to the lucrative Russian market in the future.

One important exogenous factor helping Russia's recovery was the rebound in world oil prices, which doubled in the course of 1999. The new Russian oil export tariff raised $1.5 billion (6 percent of federal revenues) in the first half of 1999, enabling the federal government to run a primary budget surplus of 3 percent of GDP by summer 1999. This was a radical turnaround from the fiscal crisis of the previous summer.

The overall effects of the August shock were a long-overdue correction in the ruble exchange rate; a deflation in the power of the bank oligarchs; and more business steered in the direction of Russian manufacturers. By late 1999, in most respects Russia's economy looked pretty much the same as it had in mid-1997. The August 1998 events were the worst economic crisis Russia had experienced since 1991, but its overall effect on the country's economic development was quite modest.

Political Fallout Muted

The political impact of the crisis, once the panic had subsided, was surprisingly muted. There was no significant political backlash against market reform or international integration from the Russian opposition or society at large. On the contrary, a January 1999 poll indicated, "As a result of the crisis [Russia's] political regime, strange as it may be, not only did not grow weaker but even grew stronger."[7] Although 49 percent of the poll respondents reported a "very significant" fall in living standards, very few reported taking part in any political activity, and a majority still supported the idea of transition to a market economy (47 percent, juxtaposed with 39 percent who did not).

The immediate effect of the crisis was the collapse of the government of Sergei Kirienko and its replacement by a government headed by former spy-chief Yevgenii Primakov. Initial fears of a radical transformation in the political system, with social upheaval and perhaps even an attempted return to communism, proved unfounded. In fact, the overall impact of the crisis was to reinforce rather than undermine the basic political institutions of Russia. Some individual careers were damaged or boosted by the crisis, and some financial circles rose while others fell. But the crisis did not open the political system to any significant new political actors.

There was no outbreak of social unrest in the wake of the crisis. Although individuals stormed banks in a fruitless effort to recover their savings during the days and weeks following the August devaluation, there was no substantial, organized social protest movement. In fact, political mobilization had been more pronounced in the months leading up to the crisis than in its wake: May and June had seen strikes and the blockage of railway lines by striking coal miners (who succeeded in winning modest financial subsidies from the government).

The main immediate consequence of the August crisis was, paradoxically perhaps, a reinforcement of constitutional procedures and a slight alteration in the lopsided balance of powers between legislative and executive branches. The crisis weakened President Yeltsin vis-à-vis the parliament, but it did not lead to any radical or systemic change in the political system. The Communists were not able to exploit the crisis to dislodge Yeltsin from power. At first it appeared that the new government might try to reverse the economic reforms introduced since 1992. But in fact there was no radical change of course in economic policy.

The crisis shifted the balance of power within the executive branch, weakening the financial oligarchs and strengthening the "power ministries" (the army, the interior ministry, and the Federal Security Service—the main successor organization to the KGB). This seems to have been the most lasting political consequence of the August crisis. Not only was the new premier, Primakov, the former head of the Foreign Intelligence Service, but both of his successors as premier were also drawn from the security organs. Yeltsin unceremoniously fired Primakov in April 1999, fearing that the wily ex-diplomat was becoming too popular and developing presidential aspirations. More to the point, Yeltsin feared that Primakov might launch anticorruption investigations that would not spare the members of Yeltsin's inner circle (including his family).[8] Yeltsin replaced Primakov as prime minister with former interior minister Sergei Stepashin, one of the triumvirate of ministers who had launched the Chechen war back in December 1994. Stepashin lasted only till August 1999, when he too was fired for being too weak in the face of parliamentary efforts to nail some of Yeltsin's cronies (including Boris Berezovskii) on corruption charges, and for failing to stop Chechen attacks on Dagestan. As a replacement for Stepashin, Yeltsin chose the 47-year-old Vladimir Putin, then head of the Federal Security Service—a fifteen-year KGB veteran who had never been elected to public office. Putin, untainted by any whiff of personal corruption, was enthusiastically confirmed as prime minister by the Duma.

It is not clear exactly what long-term significance can be attached to the succession of prime ministerial appointments from the ranks of the security apparatus in the twelve months after the August crisis. These prime ministers did not reverse the course of economic policy pursued by their predecessors. In foreign policy they have been more inclined to espouse tough rhetoric toward the United States, but this has much more to do with Russian dislike for NATO's May 1999 air war against Yugoslavia than with the 1998 financial crisis. Another possible consequence of the resurgence of the security apparatus may have been the relaunching of offensive operations against the rebel province of Chechnya in August 1999. However, the immediate cause of the Russian assault was the attacks by Chechen militants on neighboring Dagestan. Thus it is hard to trace the causal chain behind the rise of the security elite back to the August crisis.

Since 1996, a shift has occurred in the balance of power between federal and regional leaders, to the benefit of the latter. Such a trend had been gathering pace already before the August crisis, especially after regional governors started to be directly elected (from 1996 on). Summer 1997 saw a major confrontation, with Yeltsin trying to dismiss the eccentric governor of Primorskii krai in the Russian Far East, Yevgenii Nazdratenko. The Federation Council, the upper house of the Russian parliament (composed of the heads of the executive and legislative branches in each of Russia's 89 provinces), refused to allow Nazdratenko's dismissal. Another important victory for regional interests came in April 1998, when the Duma and Federation Council passed—over Yeltsin's veto—a law transferring 33 percent of the stock in the state's electricity monopoly EES to regional governments. This gave them extra leverage in their continuous pleading for cancellation of their energy debts.

The August crisis seemed to reinforce this decentralization of political power. At first many governors tried to use the crisis as an excuse to reintroduce price controls and even restrictions on the export of goods from their region. However, within a few weeks such efforts proved unwise (because they merely interfered with the market) and unnecessary (since supplies started flowing again). The new Primakov government made more effort to reach out to regional leaders than its predecessor: Eight governors were even invited to attend meetings of the national cabinet. The new budget for 1999 gave regions the option to levy a regional sales tax of up to 5 percent (which was quickly instituted in some 40 regions).[9]

Regional bosses also used the financial crisis as an opportunity to try to regain control over some enterprises located in their territories, on grounds of insolvency. Others persuaded the federal government to transfer ownership of some firms to regional authorities in exchange for their forgiveness of federal debts to their regions. But these changes were incremental rather than revolutionary, and the trend predated the August crisis.

Conclusion

By late 1999 a broad consensus had emerged on the roots of the August 1998 crisis, although experts were still divided over whether the crisis was inevitable or could have avoided with better foresight. In contrast to the consensus on the causes of the crisis, there was still great uncertainty as to its consequences and long-term significance.

The August crisis exposed the deep institutional flaws of Yeltsin's Russia: its unnerving combination of disrespect for rule of law alongside the continued presence of a powerful security apparatus. It challenged naïve assumptions that opening the doors to free trade and competitive pricing would automatically create the conditions necessary for the spontaneous emergence of a market economy. However, the crisis did not usher in any radical structural changes in Russia's political economy. It forced a severe but overdue devaluation of the ruble, which helped to revive domestic manufacturing. It weaned the government from its previous overreliance on domestic and international borrowing to plug gaps in the national budget. But it did not shift policy in the direction of protectionism. It caused the government to fall, and strengthened the influence of the security ministries. Whereas some of the financial oligarchs saw their empires implode, others grew in influence, and the overall character of relations between business elites and the political system underwent no radical change. The August crisis did not dislodge Yeltsin from the Kremlin, nor did it lead to any fundamental shift in the presidential system of government that he had fashioned. It is an open question whether the system of oligarchic capitalism created by Yeltsin will survive the departure of its architect and founder from the Kremlin—whether Yeltsinism will outlive Yeltsin.

Notes

1. Vladimir Popov, "Will Russia achieve fast economic growth?" *Communist Economies and Economic Transformation,* vol. 10, no. 4, 1998, pp. 421–449.

2. Daniel S. Treisman, "Fighting inflation in a transitional regime: Russia's anomalous stabilization," *World Politics,* vol. 50, no. 2, 1998.

3. *Wall Street Journal,* 31 May 1999.

4. *Wall Street Journal,* 8 March 1999.

5. *Russian Economic Trends,* October 1999. Unless otherwise stated, data on economic performance are taken from the quarterly and monthly reports of *Russian Economic Trends,* published by the Working Center for Economic Reform, in Moscow.

6. ITAR-TASS, 25 May 1999.

7. Leontii Byzov and Vladimir Petukhov, "August shook pockets but not heads," *Obshchaya gazeta,* no. 7, 18–24 February 1999. Based on a poll by the Russian Independent Institute of Social and National Problems.

8. Yeltsin's son-in-law is a director of Aeroflot, and according to press reports was implicated in the laundering of the airline's foreign earnings through Swiss bank accounts.

9. Radoslav Petkov and Natan Shklyar, "Regional responses to the August crisis," *Transitions* (Prague), March 1999.

Index

About the Contributors

Laura Belin is pursuing a doctorate at the University of Oxford. She previously covered Russian political affairs and media issues for the Prague-based Open Media Research Institute and for Radio Free Europe/Radio Liberty. She is coauthor, with Robert Orttung, of *The Battle for the Duma: The Russian Parliamentary Elections of 1995* (1997).

Linda J. Cook is associate professor of political science at Brown University. She is the author of *Labor and Liberalization: Trade Unions in the New Russia* (1997) and coeditor, with Mitchell Orenstein and Marilyn Rueschemeyer, of *Left Parties and Social Policy in Postcommunist Europe* (Westview, 1999).

Virginie Coulloudon has a Ph.D. in history and is an associate at the Davis Center for Russian Studies, Harvard University, where she heads the research project "The Elite and Patronage in Russia."

Stephen Crowley is associate professor of political science at Oberlin College and author of *Hot Coal, Cold Steel: Russian and Ukrainian Workers From the End of the Soviet Union to the Post-Communist Transformations* (1997).

Floriana Fossato is a correspondent for Radio Free Europe/Radio Liberty in Moscow.

Donald N. Jensen is associate director of broadcasting at Radio Free Europe/Radio Liberty in Prague. He was formerly second secretary at the U.S. embassy in Moscow.

Anna Kachkaeva is the media expert for Radio Free Europe/Radio Liberty's Russian Service.

David Lane is a fellow of Emmanuel College and reader in sociology at Cambridge University. He is the author of *The Rise and Fall of State Socialism* (1998) and coauthor, with Cameron Ross, of *The Transition from Communism to Capitalism* (1998).

Peter Rutland is professor of government at Wesleyan University. He is the author of *The Politics of Economic Stagnation in the Soviet Union* (1992) and editor of *Holding the Course: 1998 EWI Annual Survey of Eastern Europe and the Former Soviet Union* (1999).